*THE FREEDOM OF
FRENCH CLASSICISM*

PRINCETON PUBLICATION IN

MODERN LANGUAGES

No. 9

SECVRVM CARCER FACIT

Sa prifon l'affeure.

E L V Y *qui le premier m'ofta la liberté,*
Me mit en feureté :
De fa grace ie fuis hors de prife & de crain-
te.
Pieges , appas , filets , font pour moy fuperflus;
Pour moy la fraude eft vaine , inutile eft la feinte,
Vn prifonnier ne fe prent plus.

O

A *devise morale* from the Jesuit Lemoyne's *Devises héroïques et morales*, published in Paris by Courbé in 1649.

THE FREEDOM OF FRENCH CLASSICISM

BY E. B. O. BORGERHOFF

PRINCETON, NEW JERSEY
PRINCETON UNIVERSITY PRESS
1950

❖

*The publication of this book has been aided
by the Princeton University Research Fund*

62982

Printed in the United States of America by Princeton
University Press at Princeton, New Jersey

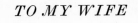

TO MY WIFE

"Notre affaire, en beaucoup de choses, avait l'air de n'être pas publique, quoiqu'elle ne fût pas cachée. Cela paraît galimatias; mais il est de ceux que la pratique fait connaître quelquefois et que la spéculation ne fait jamais entendre. J'en ai remarqué de cette sorte en tout genre d'affaires." (Retz, *Mémoires, Oeuvres*, G.E.F. ed., Paris, Hachette 1870-1929, vol. I, p. 241.)

❖

Nescire quaedam magna pars sapientiae.
. . . . .

"Mais il faut remarquer, qu'il y a des choses qui sont incompréhensibles dans leur manière, et qui sont certaines dans leur existence; on ne peut concevoir comment elles peuvent être, et il est certain néanmoins qu'elles sont." (*La Logique de Port-Royal*, Paris 1668, p. 385.)

❖

"Il y a de certaines choses qu'on n'entend jamais quand on ne les entend pas d'abord." (Mme de Sévigné, *Lettres*, 14 May 1686.)

Introduction

O VER a quarter of a century ago C. H. C. Wright said
that the average university student's understanding of the nature of French Classicism was limited to
something vague about the three unities.* The students
who created this impression in Mr. Wright's mind were
not altogether to blame; they were the victims of a tradition which centered the theory of Classicism in formal
distinctions and which based the history of its development in France upon the establishment of rules for
literary composition.

There is probably less danger of this particular kind
of oversimplification today, and yet it is surprising how
doggedly the tradition lingers on in textbooks and in
much teaching and criticism.† French Classicism remains
for the general reader a dogmatic, academic, absolutist
organization of literature and art created out of a growing devotion to reason, to "la belle nature" and to the
rules, which progressively relegated the rationally un-
demonstrable and unanalyzable to a distinctly minor or
off-center position in the Seventeenth Century's scale of
aesthetic values. This is the conception formed by such
critics as Saintsbury, Brunetière, and even to some extent Spingarn.** Along with it goes the conclusion that
the French Seventeenth Century had in fact two literatures: a pre-classic, or sub-classic one (sometimes called
Baroque),‡ and a classic one, with the year 1660 marking
roughly the definitive victory of the latter over the former. Such a view was given final authority by Bray's
capital work *La Formation de la doctrine classique en*

* *French Classicism*, Harvard University Press, Cambridge,
1920.
† See for instance the treatment accorded Boileau by Mr.
Allen Tate in his article on Longinus in the *Hudson Review* for
1948, vol. I, no. 3.
** See bibliography.
‡ For a good summary of the Baroque question, and an excellent bibliography of studies on it, see the *Journal of Aesthetics
and Art Criticism* for December, 1946.

*France.** This was unfortunate, for the book appeared just at a time when a revision seemed imminent, and with its thorough documentation and well presented evidence it very nearly put a seal for all time on the traditional interpretation.

Fortunately, however, opinion cannot exist without controversy, and in recent years, as I have suggested, the French Seventeenth Century, or the Age of Louis XIV, or Classicism itself have in one way or another been freshly scrutinized, revaluated, and revised in the works of a number of scholars and critics.† This activity, though for the most part analytical and fragmentary rather than synthetic, testifies to the enduring vitality of the period and indicates that French Classicism, whatever it may be supposed to represent, has lost the remote pompousness and embalmed imperturbability for which it was so long and so unfairly praised or blamed.

But it is not only the century's vitality which has been revealed; it is also its complexity, and with this the complexity of the dominating literary spirit of the times, be it called Baroque or Classic. This complexity becomes especially noticeable when it is understood, as it must be, that no one wishes to abandon completely every tenet of the traditionalist view of Classicism. There is no reason for doing so. It is rather a question of ordering the elements of tradition and the elements of revaluation into some sort of harmonic structure where each reinforces the other, and where even contradictions will emerge as meaningful and characteristic. It may be that the principle of contradiction itself plays a leading role in the creation and maintenance of that vital complexity which

* Paris, 1927 (2nd ed. 1931). While the present study was in preparation there appeared Bray's interesting *La Préciosité et les précieux* (Paris, Michel, 1948), in which the view of the Seventeenth Century (if not of its Classicism) is more balanced and more in accord with recent opinion.

† Among others: Wilmotte, Spingarn (*Essays*), Lombard, Fidao-Justiniani, Gaiffe, Mélèse, Baldensperger, Naves, Maulnier, Mornet, Peyre, Reynold, Pintard, Chinard, Bénichou, Busson, Bray, Mongrédien. This list (chronological) is by no means complete. See bibliography.

we have come to recognize in French Classicism. It is along such lines as these, I think, that something remains to be done.

I did not originally approach the study of Classicism from precisely this standpoint. Rather I arrived at it in the process of trying to discover the real significance to the century of a relatively innocent term, the "je ne sais quoi," which seems to have become fairly widely used at that time.* It was not long before I concluded that beneath this little phrase there lay a way of thinking which was essential to the complex of Classicism and which unified it to a marked degree. And I concluded further that if we could understand this way of thinking we should be well on our way to understanding the complex. I therefore began to read with an eye to discovering other evidence of such thinking, and it soon appeared that not only the "je ne sais quoi" but other ways of expressing and embracing the indefinable and the inexplicable were so inseparable from any discussion of literature as to make some critics and writers of the century seem guilty of a kind of partnership in secrecy, a kind of conspiracy to protect the ineffable.

It seemed to me significant that this should have taken place in the century of Classicism. Why, at a time when so much was being defined and explained, should the indefinable be allowed such autonomy? One could perhaps say that after everything else had been neatly packaged, anything remaining would, of course, be gathered together and conveniently put into a category labeled "indefinable," something like the "miscellaneous and unidentified" file, and thus be at least attainable and mentionable. Nothing would be more natural, but I am sure that there is more to the affair than this sort of expedient dismissal, because, for those who concerned themselves with it, the concept of the indefinable was a real and effective element in human affairs, and what is most interesting, they were glad to admit its existence and effective-

* See below, Chapter v, section 2 on Bouhours.

ness. Moreover those who took it seriously were not, as one might suppose, the anti-classics of the time, but were among the most prominent representatives of the preparation and flowering of the Age of Louis XIV.

It is the presence of this notion of the indefinable in literary theory and practice which interests me principally, but the implications thereof are not to be forgotten, and one may see in the literary criticism as well as in the works of literature themselves the reflection of a density which is based on the sense of, or the desire for, or perhaps even the fear of a reality whose dimensions are impenetrable and limitless. To examine the meaning of this sense as it applies to the Seventeenth Century in France from all existential points of view would of course entail a labor of far greater scope than any I have attempted in the pages to follow. Indeed even in the domain which I have selected my presentation remains deliberately incomplete because, as I have tried to explain, the rationalist aspect of Classic literary sensibility surely needs no demonstration, and furthermore I am not attempting to exploit the possibilities of what might be countless other aspects. The literary equivalent of Bremond's great work* remains to be written. The present study would at best be only a partial introduction to such a work.

I should add also that to one who is thoroughly familiar with the facts of the century, this study, not being a history, will present mostly a point of view. I have chosen, in some cases quite arbitrarily, certain Seventeenth Century figures and I have completely neglected others. Out of these last, I suppose, a whole second book could be made. Nothing is said, except in passing, of the gentlemen of Port-Royal, of Saint-Evremond, Mme de Sévigné, La Mesnardière, d'Aubignac, Sorel, Le Bossu, Perrault, Huet and others. The reasons for these omissions are various; I hope they will be understood as existing. The reasons for my choices will I think be obvious.

It will be noticed that quotations of critical remarks

* See bibliography.

are very frequent. This will, I fear, annoy some readers, but for others it may make the sole virtue of the work.

I have tried to envisage the reader as having some knowledge of French Classicism, but of a general rather than a special nature. I would have him consider first the theme—the reality of the indefinable—and next the figures as illuminating variations on that theme, and finally the relation of these to the complexity and to the vitality of French Seventeenth Century Classicism in literature.

I have been helped in the preparation of this book by many kind people. I should like here to thank my father J. L. Borgerhoff, professor emeritus of Western Reserve University, for many useful suggestions and for help in reading the manuscript and the proof. I wish also to thank my colleagues in Princeton University for their forbearance, and in particular Professors Gilbert Chinard, Américo Castro, and Ira Wade for numerous valuable indications with respect not only to the subject matter but also to the manner of presentation. I am also grateful to Mrs. J. S. Finch of Princeton, New Jersey, for a helpful reading of the manuscript.

E.B.O.B.

Contents

Contents

THE FREEDOM OF
FRENCH CLASSICISM

I: The New Dogmatism

THE QUARREL OF RONSARD AND THE QUARREL OF THE CID

THE first years of the Seventeenth Century in France may be safely described as a time in which, for a number of reasons, a spirit of restraint, of regulation and of planning was beginning to oppose effectively the spirit of scepticism, individualism, and strife characteristic of the Renaissance. The reasons for this change of atmosphere, if we could disentangle them from the complicated web of disorder which makes up the world of Rabelais, Ronsard, and Montaigne, would tell us a great deal about the period, but they need not occupy us here, for it is enough to know, as we do, that this growing dogmatism is reflected in matters of literature.

The period can be said to terminate around 1637 with the Quarrel of the *Cid*. The official view of this argument over Corneille's play sees it as the first major victory for dogmatic criticism, and considers that from this moment on it was but the matter of a few years before a whole absolutist pattern was set for the century once and for all. Though I do not share this now obsolescent view, I certainly see the Quarrel as a crystallization of ideas which at least set a fundamental problem for the century.

Of the pre-*Cid* era one can say this much: literary trends are discernible, and from whatever point of view we wish to observe it, certain characteristics stand out. There were two parties: a liberal party, which was really reactionary and traditionalist; and a dogmatic party, which was revolutionary. The paradox, if it is one, seems less strange in our day than it might have seemed a century ago. But it is typical, and the same sort of thing will later be true of the Quarrel of the Ancients and Moderns,

3

when the Ancients were the liberals and the dogmatists were the Moderns.

The opposition of the two parties emerges in the discussion of abstract problems having to do with general standards as well as in the arguments over the concrete issue of the heritage of Ronsard. Ronsard had been the giant of Poetry, and he was either to be worshipped or to be hewn down. He was a symbol.

As is well known, the great opponent of Ronsard was Malherbe, the theoretician and example of the new school. Foreshadowings of this quarrel had been discernible however in the years before 1600 in the works of men like Du Vair and Laudun. The role of Malherbe in the actual creation of a new style is not important to us for the moment. What is important is that he represented a conception of poetry which was technical and restrictive, while the defenders of the old style and of Ronsard held a position which was free, inspirational, and extensive. The best known of this second group are Régnier, Théophile, and Mlle de Gournay.

The argument, begun in 1606 with Malherbe's *Commentaire sur Desportes*, continued on through the century but ceased to be vital around 1630. In this year the last edition of Ronsard until 1781 was published, and the first complete edition of Malherbe appeared. The school of Malherbe had won its battle. But the century was to regret it, or at least it was to know the price it had paid for its famous order and clarity. But what is of peculiar interest here is that critics and writers were made especially conscious of the conflict, perhaps eternal and insoluble, between inspiration and technique, between poetry felt and poetry to be communicated, between artistic freedom and perfectionist constraint. I do not think that the century ever lost the consciousness of that conflict. Perhaps in some respects it solved it, but it did not for that reason forget it. Agrippa d'Aubigné, looking back to the Pléiade, had challenged the new school, saying, "Je demande seulement à ces législateurs que pour avoir autorité sur le siècle que les grands Maîtres de ce temps-là ont prise, et qu'ils puissent être allégués comme ceux-là *exemplo*, que nous voyions de leurs mains des Poèmes épiques, héroïques ou quelque chose qui se puisse appeler oeuvre."* When honest critics, later surveying the field of lyric or heroic poetry, asked themselves if the challenge had ever really been met, the answer was not easy. Yet the very fact that the Seventeenth Century put the discipline of hard-wrought, communicable and at the same time musical verse upon itself even while knowing the cost and the danger of such discipline may have served in some ways to deepen its poetic consciousness.

In the theater an analogous condition prevailed in the years before the *Cid*. The problem was stated differently of course, for the immediate issues were not the same. Here it was less a question of language and inspiration and more a question of believability and fitness. Moreover the formal tradition of drama was pretty well established so that there was less of the revolutionary aspect to the critical program of the new drama. Fundamentally however the issue was again one of freedom and individuality (as expressed for instance in Ogier's preface to Schelandre's *Tyr et Sidon* in 1628, and in many of Corneille's prefaces) *versus* the imposition of restrictive formulae agreed upon by playwright, critic, and public. But there had to be applied a special criterion because of this particular way of having to face the problem. This special criterion was the pleasure of a massed audience. Drama is an art for which the public as a body exists. It is perhaps because responses are immediate, crystallized and publicized that the theater has so often been the battleground of criticism. For the average dramatist successful composition, rightly or wrongly, is not merely the satis-

* See on this period in detail W. F. Patterson, *Three Centuries of French Poetic Theory, (1328-1630)*, University of Michigan Press, Ann Arbor, 2 vols., 1935, vol. I, pp. 752ff. The quotation from d'Aubigné is to be found in the *Oeuvres*, ed. Réaume, de Caussade et Legouez, Paris, Lemerre, 1873-1892, I, 462, *Lettres do poincts de science*, XI, and not in the preface to *Les Tragiques*, as it might seem from Mr. Patterson's reference to it.

5

faction of internal requirements.* Has any serious lyric
poet, I wonder, ever based his theory of poetry on his
experience with the public? This is what Corneille did,
and Racine fought hard with the critics who, he thought,
misrepresented the audience. The history of criticism is
marked with "querelles" over plays. A play could become
an issue more easily than a sonnet (though, in the Seventeenth Century this could and did happen too) and
widespread discussion could quickly result, with consequent and proportionate attention to principles of literary
composition. Conversely also, because of this involvement with the public as a critical body, the stream of
drama seems on the whole to have run its course more
smoothly than that of lyric poetry. Once the type has been
accepted it is harder to alter it. It is possible to say, I
think, that since 1630 or so we have had really only two
kinds of drama: the serious-poetic and the comic-prosaic-
social. I am speaking of literary drama of course. From
Ibsen on we have been trying to develop a third kind
which seeks to express a poetic and tragic conception of
the ordinary man through the medium of a surfacely pro-
saic-comic tradition.

I suggest this probably oversimplified idea of the
drama in order to bring out the fact that once the standard of serious drama was accepted by the Seventeenth
Century it was to remain in force for two centuries. Could
the same be said for lyric poetry, if there was any? A
revolution in dramatic taste seems more deep-rooted
when it does occur, and it is more easily made to sym-
bolize an age. If it is objected that the Romantic drama
was short-lived, the answer is that it was not a real revolution.

I have dwelt on the above to explain why I feel that
the Quarrel of the *Cid* is more significant than the Quarrel of Ronsard, although the two are certainly related. In
the case of the former the alteration in taste was more

* See, in connection with the relation of *genres* to public presentation, André Gide in his *Interviews imaginaires*, New York,
Editions Jacques Schiffrin, 1943, pp. 102ff.

6

positive and moved up to the work of a great dramatist, while in the case of the latter the motion was away from the work of a great poet toward the work of a lesser one. The *Cid* therefore represents a point reached, and held, with all the tensions involved in the imposition of not only a new style, but perhaps even a new form, and with a relatively large segment of the general public implicated. Bray said that the Quarrel of the *Cid* involved a whole poetic.* I prefer to say that it involved a whole aesthetic. Granted that all the problems are interrelated, the difference seems to be about this: that the discussion over Ronsard brought into question the personality of the artist, his manner of composition, his role in society, and his responsibility to an ideal of art. But in the Quarrel of the *Cid*, while all of this was inherent, there was added the whole question of attractiveness and along with it the question of taste and the question of believability in relation to an established technical code and an established moral code. In other words the Quarrel of the *Cid* deepens the ontological and epistemological aspects of the problem of art. Far from settling any questions by the adoption of "les règles," the extent to which absolute standards were respected only made the problem more acute. If *goût* came to be talked about more and more as the century wore on it was precisely for this reason. I have said already what the problem of lyric poetry and the problem of drama had in common: the independence of the artist and the application of general standards to his work. The Quarrel of the *Cid* brought into question the independence of art itself.

Now if this period of which I have been speaking saw the development of a new dogmatism and the decline of an old individualism, it was inevitable, human nature being what it is, that there should emerge with a certain sharpness an attitude which, while not in outright opposition to the dogmatism, resisted it as much as it supported it. We can call this attitude the new liberalism.

* *Op. cit.*

7

Three of its most prominent representatives were Guez de Balzac, Jean Chapelain and Pierre Corneille. The first of these was perhaps the most truly representative, the second being somewhat to the right of center, and the third being to the left of center. Balzac is therefore the first figure whom we shall examine.

II: The New Liberalism

·◁═══════▷·

1. THE *AGRÉMENT INEXPLICABLE*: BALZAC

JEAN-LOUIS GUEZ DE BALZAC stands in accepted literary history as a builder of the Classic doctrine and a shaper of the Classic spirit. Already in 1665, in the essay which served as introduction to his collected works, he was considered to have been particularly effective in developing a strong, expressive prose style, and to have been thus the counterpart of Malherbe. But this style was developed against the background of a definite aesthetic, and in this he built quite as much, though he generally receives insufficient credit for this part of his labors. His opinions, we shall find, carried throughout the century. I ought probably to say "the opinions which he held," because I shall not claim any special originality for one who was accused of wide borrowings* and who himself was quick to ward off the accusation by referring to his own "lieux communs." But much of what he says will appear again in Pascal, Méré, Rapin, Boileau, La Bruyère and Fénelon, and he must be given credit at least for propagating these notions, echoes though they may be of Cicero, Montaigne, and others.

Perhaps Balzac's best known critical utterance is the letter to Scudéry about the latter's observations on the *Cid*.[1] It seems as good a document as any to begin an acquaintance with his way of looking at literature. Scudéry had claimed that Corneille by some magic succeeded in dazzling the greater part of the Parisian audience into thinking that the play was much better than it really was. What more could one ask?, says Balzac, "Avoir satisfait

---

* Particularly in the *Conformité de l'éloquence de M. de Balzac avec celle des plus grands hommes du temps passé et du présent*, by André de Saint Denis of the Pères Feuillants, circulated probably before 1628, but published in that year along with a defense of Balzac by Ogier. See below, p. 24.

tout un Royaume, est quelque-chose de plus grand et de meilleur que d'avoir fait une pièce régulière . . . il y a des beautés parfaites qui sont effacées par d'autres beautés qui ont plus d'agrément et moins de perfection. Et parce que l'acquis n'est pas si noble que le naturel, ni le travail des hommes si estimable que les dons du Ciel, on vous pourrait encore dire que *savoir l'art de plaire* ne vaut pas tant que *savoir plaire sans art*."[2]

The problem thus is stated in one of its phases very simply. These same terms and the same problem are going to be discussed again and again during the century. The conclusion of the letter runs as follows: "Vous savez qu'on apporte souvent du tempérament aux Lois, et que l'Equité conserve ce que la Justice pourrait ruiner. N'insistez point sur cette exacte et rigoureuse justice. Ne vous attachez point avec tant de scrupule à la souveraine raison. Qui voudrait la contenter, et suivre ses desseins et sa régularité, serait obligé de lui bâtir un plus beau Monde que celui-ci."[3]

This attempt to find a course between equity and justice, this tempering of the law, will be a distinguishing characteristic of Balzac in his own work and in his judgment of others. It supposes a superiority to the merely man-made and to the mere man. It is the manifestation of an aspiration to a higher degree of humanity, measured, it is likely, by an idea of divinity. And we shall see that no matter what the topic, Balzac will seldom allow himself to forget his Christianity.

But this humanity could, at one level at least, be expressed in nonreligious and even pagan terms. For one of the best examples of it was the famous Roman *urbanité*. Here is how Balzac describes it in the second of his *Discours*, which were published in the *Oeuvres diverses* in 1644, the topic being the conversation of the Romans: It can be, "un certain air du grand Monde et une couleur et teinture de la Cour, qui ne marque pas seulement les paroles et les opinions, mais aussi le ton de la voix et les mouvements du corps." Or it is "une impression encore moins perceptible, qui n'est reconnaissable que par ha-

sard, qui n'a rien qui ne soit noble et relevé, et rien qui
paraisse étudié ou appris, qui se sent et ne se voit pas, et
inspire un génie secret que l'on perd en le cherchant." Or,
in a more extended sense, it may be "la Science de la Conversation et le don de plaire dans les bonnes compagnies."
Finally, more narrowly, it is "une adresse à toucher l'esprit par je ne sais quoi de piquant, mais dont la piqûre
est agréable à celui qui la reçoit parce qu'elle chatouille
et n'entame pas, parce qu'elle laisse un aiguillon sans
douleur et réveille la partie que la médisance blesse."[4]

This quality then is hard to define and so are its effects.
It has to do with ease, naturalness, and the security which
comes with independence, a certain negligence, and a
certain contempt for the book of etiquette: "Il n'y a point
de doute que, dans leur plus familier entretien, il n'y eût
des Grâces négligées et des Ornements sans art, que les
Docteurs ne connaissent point, et qui sont au dessus des
Règles et des Préceptes."[5]

For Balzac one of the greatest examples of this way of
being as reflected in a personality was Maecenas, who
was so eminently persuasive, "même avec la négligence
de l'entretien le plus familier."[6] But of course the notion
of the value of negligence as opposed to the rules in the
composition of works of literature is what interests us
here. Balzac had said in the second *Discours*, from which
I have quoted, that the Roman orators undoubtedly assumed this urbanity after divesting themselves of their
oratorical trappings, as it were, appearing then in a more
human guise. This suggests a sort of natural opposition of
the easy negligent manner to the needs of eloquence.
Balzac realized this, though he was not to make that opposition one of principle. He concluded for instance a
letter to Monsieur de Rampalle in 1640 with these words:
"Vous voyez par la négligence de cette lettre que je me
suis défait de mon Etat de Déclamateur: J'ai renoncé
absolument au genre démonstratif, et ne me mêle plus
d'Eloquence: Mais je fais grande profession de vérité, et
vous me devez croire, vous protestant que je suis, Monsieur," etc.[7] Precisely what *genre démonstratif* meant to

11

him might be understood if I may quote from another letter to le P. Vital Théron, written in 1643: "Mon Révérend Père, Vous faites des plaintes de votre vieillesse, et je suis résolu d'en faire l'Eloge. Je veux louer publiquement et dans le genre Démonstratif, cette vieillesse privilégiée et chérie du Ciel; libre et exempte de tous les mauvais tributs que les autres paient à la Nature; proposée en exemple par nos Déesses, à l'ambition et au courage de nos jeunes gens. Les Hivers de Naples me la représentent; ces Hivers tous pleins de lumière et tous couronnés de roses; Celle de Massinisse a été moins verte et moins vigoureuse, et l'enfant qu'il fit à quatre-vingts ans, n'était point une production comparable au Poème que vous avez fait à soivante-quinze. C'est-à-dire que le feu qui descend du Ciel," etc.[8]

It is to be supposed that Balzac considered the passage just quoted to be serious eloquence. But one is never sure of the amount of play that went into such compositions. It would surely be wise to imagine a good deal of the virtuoso's objectivity in everything that he wrote. Be that as it may, within the limits of the *genre démonstratif* itself the criterion of ease and negligence should continue to operate. Balzac believed this, and through his statements of this belief we are led to another opposition, already hinted at in the passage on urbanity, between the natural and the obviously arranged, between the simple and the scrupulously contrived. In the fifth *Discours* which is called "Paraphrase ou de la Grande Eloquence" there is an extended discussion of this opposition. In one passage the reader will be tempted to foresee Pascal's "beauté de village":

"L'Eclat ne présuppose pas toujours la solidité; et les paroles qui brillent le plus, sont souvent celles qui pèsent le moins. Il y a une Faiseuse de bouquets, et une Tourneuse de périodes, je ne l'ose nommer Eloquence, qui est toute peinte et toute dorée; qui semble toujours sortir d'une boîte; qui n'a soin que de s'ajuster, et ne songe qu'à faire la belle: qui par conséquent est plus propre pour les Fêtes que pour les Combats, et plaît davantage qu'elle ne

sert; quoique néanmoins il y ait des Fêtes, dont elle dés-
honorerait la solennité; et des personnes, à qui elle ne
donnerait point de plaisir."[9]

Now this "Eloquence de montre et de vanité" can
please momentarily but it is very different from "la vraie
Eloquence" which is dynamic and robust, though "la
Négligence même a du mérite sur elle, et ne fait point de
tort à sa Dignité," but it avoids "des fredons efféminés,
et une mollesse compassée, semblable à cette nouveauté
vicieuse, dont les premiers sages se sont plaints, qui cor-
rompit la vigueur de la Musique, et préféra la délicatesse à la gravité. Ayant reçu de la seule grâce de la Nature la justesse des nombres, et des mesures, elle n'a que
faire de compter scrupuleusement les syllabes, ni de se
mettre en peine de placer les dactyles et les spondées,
pour trouver le Secret de l'Harmonie. Un pareil secret ne
s'acquiert point; Il faut qu'il vienne au monde avec celui
que nous nommons Eloquent: Les préceptes lui sont inutiles en cette occasion; et n'en déplaise aux Maîtres de
l'Art, qui se veulent mêler de tout, il ne doit qu'au Ciel
la bonté de ses oreilles, et la parfaite disposition de leurs
ressorts."[10] Before Aristotle can be of any use then, "il
faut qu'un grand esprit naisse, et un grand jugement
avec lui."[11]

So there is in Balzac a large emphasis on natural genius.
This is nothing new in criticism, yet the emphasis is distinctive of Balzac not only in degree and frequency, but
in the extent to which his whole approach to literature is
affected by it. With him it is more than lip service to an
unavoidable authority. Rather, he will oppose it again
and again to the authority of the *doctes*, of the professors,
not only when it is a question of eloquence itself, but
also when it is a matter of the capacity for judging eloquence. Here is a passage from a letter to Méré which
Balzac wrote in 1646: "Le témoignage d'un seul qui voit
clair, doit être préféré au soupçon et à l'ouir dire de tout
un peuple d'Aveugles: Et vous avez bien plus de droit
de juger des ouvrages de l'esprit, vous qui avez de l'esprit
et du jugement, que ces Docteurs remarquables par le

défaut de l'une et de l'autre pièce, qui se servent de la Science contre la raison, et accusent Aristote de toutes leur mauvaises opinions."[12]

It is interesting to note that the opposition is stated in terms of *seeing*. What Balzac is talking about is *insight*. Pascal will state the case similarly. Another way of stating it is of course in terms of *taste*, and indeed this is the century of what Spingarn has called the "school of taste." Though we generally associate the discussion of *goût* with the second half of the century, still Balzac wrote to the abbé Talon in 1645, "Puisque vous goûtez mes derniers Ecrits, et que vous avez le goût extrêmement bon. . . ." Méré will carry this on, if ungratefully.[13]

Urbanity, ease of motion (intellectual as well as physical), insight and taste, then, all have to do with simplicity and naturalness. But there is another way in which these qualities are centrally operative in literature. This is in the actual imitation of nature. But we shall see that even here the terms in which the problem is stated are already familiar. In the sixth *Discours*, addressed to Chapelain, apropos of Ariosto's *I suppositi*, Balzac discussed the character and instructive power of comedy. He began by saying that to judge a certain kind of comedy it was necessary to "prendre l'esprit de Bourgeois et quitter celui de Courtisan."[14] And here another opposition is going to be set up, between the simply natural and the affected and courtly. This opposition will lead to interesting consequences. There is a place for both perhaps, but, "Parmi nous jusqu'ici on a confondu les deux caractères, et l'Imitation de la vie privée a été plus loin que son objet. On a demandé des portraits qui embellissent et non pas qui ressemblassent. Quand la matière a été rustique, et qu'elle a désiré le Naturel et le sauvage, on a voulu le Poli et le Cultivé. . . . N'avons-nous pas vu chez les Poètes Courtisans des Villageoises coquettes et affectées, des Bergères chargées de pierreries et de toile d'or, peintes et fardées de tout le blanc et le rouge de nos voisins?"[15]

14

Here is certainly Pascal's "beauté de village," and here too is Molière. But Balzac further anticipates Pascal by carrying his discussion through the question of naturalness and simplicity over to outright naïveté and finally into religion.

"Nos Muses, Monsieur, sont toujours filles de Jupiter; Mais elles ne chantent pas toujours la victoire de leur Père contre les Titans, et ne sont pas toujours en festin et en cérémonie avec lui. Elles veulent être toujours belles: la beauté ne déplaît et n'ennuie jamais; Mais elles ne sont pas toujours ajustées, le soin est souvent suspect à ceux qui le voient et incommode celles qui le prennent. Elles ont des Robes de parade et des Habillements à tous les jours; et si Ronsard et du Bellay revenaient au Monde, ils vous jureraient qu'ils les ont vues en juppe et en leur déshabillé danser dans les bois aux rais de la Lune."[16]

Balzac was not content to dismiss the naive as merely an additional aspect of art but was rather inclined to give it dominance. The inevitable complications involved in such a procedure immediately appear. That the Graces are represented as nude meant for him that negligence (which might perhaps be thought of here as lack of ornament) had charms to touch the heart unmoved by studied dress, a fact which I think no one would deny. But there is more to it than that: "certains défauts bien ménagés" can be turned to advantage and "la crasse, les haillons, la tristesse, l'indifférence, les froideurs mêmes et les dédains, donnent de l'amour."[17] This passage from simplicity to outright lack of normal or conventional attractiveness led him to consider the significance of primitive art. In certain simple ceremonies of past times "Il y eut des images de quelques Dieux, qui semblaient plutôt venir de la main d'un Charpentier que de celle d'un Sculpteur, tant elles étaient grossières et mal polies; Mais on les faisait ainsi tout exprès," and there Balzac was in the position of all admirers of primitive art, of art which does not abide by the conventionally accepted standards of beauty; "on les faisait ainsi tout exprès, et cette rudesse était de l'essence de la Religion comme ici elle est de l'essence de l'Art."[18] The link here with Biblical style is obvious. Thus before him Longinus, thus after him Boileau.

However, the particular point he was trying to make was that, emotional persuasion being in direct proportion to the hiddenness of the means, instruction in comedy to be effective must be felt rather than seen. And so he objected, of course, to direct moralizing in comedy. There were examples actually of the discussion of theology and of Aristotle in some foreign plays. The French were perhaps just as extravagant, but they were so in a less lofty way: "Ils discourent seulement, au lieu de parler, c'est-à-dire ils parlent en Beaux esprits, et ne parlent pas en honnêtes gens."[19] They fail to distinguish between natural eloquence and the eloquence of the school. "Et par conséquent les jeunes filles, les Soldats et les nourrices, représentées par ces beaux esprits, sont d'une espèce qui ne se trouve point parmi nous; sont des personnes inconnues, étranges, extraordinaires; sont d'un autre Monde que le nôtre, ou il faut dire, . . . qu'ils ont changé tout-à-fait le nôtre."[20]

Now we have the opposition of the *honnêtes gens* to the *bel esprit* in the interests of realism. The *bel esprit* and the *Docteur* and Aristotle and the rules are on one side; urbanity, simplicity, naturalness, and *honnêteté* are on the other. And an essential empiricism is seen to emerge, quite consistent with the quality of liberalism which I have supposed for Balzac. This is brought out strongly in the passage continuing from this same discussion. I should like to quote it by way of rounding out this phase of Balzac's thought. He had said that these bad comedies had utterly misrepresented the world. He went on, "Ils en ont gâté l'essentiel et le propre, pour en vouloir purifier le matériel et le terrestre. Ils ont perdu le corps, pour en vouloir extraire l'esprit. Ils ont ôté aux choses leur visage naturel, leur première et véritable forme, les marques et les signes par lesquels elles se reconnaissent. Ils ont effacé la vie en la polissant."[21]

The empiricism of which I speak naturally implies, or can imply, a distrust of reason. Without going into the details of Balzac's real philosophical position we can say at least that he had a strong distaste for the rationally explained and the rationally organized. His letter to Scudéry has already indicated this. He disliked the pat answer and the fine distinction. In the third discourse of the *Aristippe*, published in 1658 but written much earlier, he complained of what he called the "Spéculatifs" in politics, the "tireurs d'essence" who see everywhere a hidden design, a concealed motive. And he asked of Augustus, is it possible that he made love only "par maxime d'Etat, et ne voyait les Dames de Rome que pour apprendre les secrets de leurs Maris? Y a-t-il de l'apparence que son âme ne se remuât que par règle et par compas, que toutes ses actions fussent si guindées et tous ses vices si étudiés? A mon avis, c'est faire le Monde plus fin qu'il n'est. C'est interpréter les Princes commes quelques Grammairiens expliquent Homère: Ils y trouvent ce qui n'y est pas, et l'accusent d'être Philosophe et Médecin en des endroits où il n'est que faiseur de contes et de chansons. Contentons-nous quelquefois du sens littéral."[22]

The Grammarian here takes his place beside the *bel esprit*, if there is any distinction between them.* Overinterpretation on the part of the critic (or the politician) is the counterpart of overscrupulousness on the part of the artist. A letter to Perrot d'Ablancourt in 1635 praised the modern polish and the civilized tone of a certain writer. The hitherto savage inhabitants of the banks of the Seine were learning to speak "plus humainement," said Balzac, and were becoming "amoureux discrets" as well as "personnages raisonnables." But, he thought, this particular writer had been overzealous: "Cettui-ci ne s'attache même que trop à la raison, et aux préceptes de l'art. Il a si grand peur de faillir, et de se méprendre, que quelquefois il écrit plutôt en Grammairien qu'en Orateur: Et parce qu'il passe de la licence au scrupule, peut-être que sa régularité si exquise ne vous semblera pas bien naturelle."[23]

*For the extreme of Balzac's anti-pedantic attitude, one should read the exaggerated satirical prose portrait, *Le Barbon*, first published in 1648.

17

But it is in the *Socrate Chrétien* (1652) that the deep opposition of regularity to nature and to real beauty is most fully expressed. In the avant-propos, which is dedicated to Abel Servien, Balzac wrote that he was glad if his manner of instructing without dogmatizing had met with approval, though there was nothing new, he insisted, in this way of skillfully penetrating the soul "sans y donner l'alarme par des Arguments en forme," since the ancients had practiced it. And he defended a "gaieté" in style which would be as far from "bouffonnerie" as it would be from "tristesse." He even defended certain excesses and passions, and the wisdom of folly. "O beaux Esprits, qui faites des Livres et qui jugez des Livres qu'on fait, que vous connaissez peu le mérite de cette façon d'écrire!"[24]

He was feeling strongly because he had just had to read the Italian panegyrists whose words were nothing but silk and thornless flowers and rare perfume. "Quoi davantage? l'Art observé jusqu'à la superstition, ne souffrait pas à l'Esprit le moindre mouvement de liberté. Une clarté au reste, une nétteté incomparable, ou certes qui ne peut être comparée qu'à la sérénité de ces beaux jours, quand il n'y a pas un nuage dans le Ciel, ni une haleine de vent sur la Terre. Le Calme pourtant qui languissait dans tous les endroits du gros Volume me faisait languir avec lui, et me tenait en cet état incommode où l'on ne peut veiller ni dormir, où l'on ne fait que s'étendre et que bailler. . . . Une si continuelle Bonace me sembla plus importune que la Tempête."[25]

Balzac saw a particularly irritating example of this sort of self-consciousness in some recent renderings of the Psalms, where the ornamentation and decoration hid the original simple beauty of the Biblical verse. The seventh of the discourses in the *Socrate chrétien* contains a spirited criticism of such treatment: "Le Prophète qu'on m'a fait voir dans la Paraphrase qu'on m'a montrée m'a fait compassion dans l'état où je l'ai vu. J'ai eu pitié de l'extravagance de son équipage, de sa ridicule galanterie, de son air de Cour, et, tout ensemble, de ses marques de

Collège. Les fleurs de Rhétorique, la broderie du stile figuré, l'ostentation et la pompe de l'Ecole, pourraient être bien en un autre lieu, mais ici elles ne sont pas en leur place. Celui que j'ai vu est un chercheur de pointes et un faiseur d'antithèses. C'est un Sophiste, c'est un Déclamateur, c'est tout autre chose qu'un Prophète. . . . cela s'appelle en la langue de la Raison friser et parfumer les Prophètes."[26]

These pieces, he says, resemble the portrait of Theseus by Parrhasius wherein the subject seems to have been fed on roses instead of good red meat. "Ce sont de belles images, mais elles n'ont pas été tirées après le naturel, mais elles n'ont pas été faites pour ressembler, mais ce qu'elles représentent n'y est pas reconnaissable. Pareilles pièces sentent Paris, la Cour et l'Académie: Mais elles n'ont rien de Jérusalem et de Sion, rien du Tabernacle et du Sanctuaire." The prophets have but little use for this kind of dressing up: "Ces ornements les déshonorent, ces faveurs les désobligent. Vous pensez les parer pour la Cour et pour les jours de Cérémonie, et vous les cachez comme des Mariées de Village sous vos affiquets et sous vos bijoux."[27] And Balzac quotes Cardinal du Perron who had said that two things separated everywhere else are joined in the Scriptures: simplicity and majesty. But in the paraphrase all this is lost: "Ce n'est plus l'ouvrage de la Nature, ce sont les inventions et les changements de l'Art."[28]

The excesses of both the Schools and the Court combined then to make an unnatural, untrue representation of the original. But this sort of thing seemed to Balzac not only against nature, but really against religion. He felt this particularly in the case of the Spanish neo-scholastics. And in this once more he foreshadows the Pascal of the *Provinciales*. The fifth discourse of the *Socrate Chrétien* was called "De la trop grande subtilité dans les choses de la religion." In it Balzac wrote "Ces Montagnes d'écritures accablent les têtes et n'édifient point les esprits. Ces volumes se forment d'un débordement d'humeurs corrompues, se grossissent des superfluités et des excréments de l'esprit humain. Les Monosyllabes des Sages valent bien mieux que tant de Chapitres et de Paragraphes, que tant de Distinction, tant de Divisions et de Subdivisions."[29] And he compared them to the wilderness of the north where one travels for days without sight of human habitation. He attacked the presumptuousness of the enterprise. "Nous devons du respect à cette Majesté qui se cache, de ne vouloir pas la découvrir, de ne la chercher pas avec tant de diligence et d'empressement. Arrêtons-nous à ses Dehors et à ses Remparts, sans la poursuivre jusque dans son Fort et dans ses retranchements. Adorons les voiles et les nuages qui sont entre nous et elle."[30]

So this presumptuousness is in a deep sense anti-poetic. And this is what we need badly to know about the spirit of the Seventeenth Century: that it saw the forces of anti-poetry gathering and that it tried to stop them as much as it tried to help them. Balzac, in speaking of his own style of religious writing, had said in a letter to D'Argenson in 1645, "N'attendez rien pourtant, s'il vous plaît, de régulier, ni de dogmatique. Je n'ai point d'argumentation en forme: Je n'ai point coupé ma matière par divisions et subdivisions. J'ai choisi le style des anciens Prophètes, plutôt que celui des Docteurs modernes, et si je ne suis Théologien comme Bécan, je voudrais bien l'être comme Orphée, si c'est trop de dire comme David."[31]

So he set up the magnificence of Biblical poetry, whose language is above rules and regularity, against the polished restricted style of those who would paraphrase it. Returning to the seventh discourse of the *Socrate Chrétien* we read: "Il n'y a rien de commun entre la musique et le Tonnerre. Ce n'est pas dans ce bruit épouvantable qu'on marque des accords et des mesures: Ce n'est pas aussi dans une âme agitée de Dieu qu'il faut chercher de l'art et de la méthode. Cet ordre et cette suite si scrupuleuse sont peu dignes de la liberté de l'esprit de Dieu, sont des marques de contrainte et de servitude, sont des chaînes et des fers que brise et met en pièces du premier coup cet Esprit dominant et Souverain." Whosoever would put order and regularity into the Psalms could not possibly reproduce the simplicity and majesty of Biblical language: "Qu'ils aillent porter ailleurs leur délicatesse et leur douceur, leur proportion et leur régularité."[32]

But Balzac, it must be remembered, was not complaining *simply* about regularity. It was rather the self-consciousness and overelaboration that went along with a certain kind of mannerism which provoked him. If it distorted nature and killed poetry it was not because nature is less ordered but because she is more simple. He said of Ariosto for instance (in connection with his discussion of Heinsius' *Herodes infanticida*) "Quoique souvent le désordre soit divertissant dans ses écrits, et que sa confusion délecte plus qu'elle n'embarrasse, c'est toujours désordre et confusion."[33] He was after all an admirer of Malherbe, and had as early as 1624 included him in what he called "le Triumvirat de notre éloquence" (the others being Coëffeteau and du Vair).[34] And in the Malherbe-Ronsard argument he was unquestionably on the side of the former. Some of his strongest language was used to say what he thought of Ronsard's shortcomings. The thirty-first *Entretien** is devoted to this question. He made out that he was reluctant to say what he thought of Ronsard because that poet had so many admirers in official circles "encore aujourd'hui." It is interesting to note his estimate that three-quarters of the Parlement de Paris and generally the other Parlements, along with the University and the Jesuits, were still taking Ronsard's part against the Court and the Academy.[35] Nevertheless Balzac made of Ronsard the sad example of a whole way of writing which he heartily condemned. He said, "Ce Poète, si célèbre et si admiré, a ses défauts et ceux de son Temps, comme j'ai dit autrefois d'un grand Personnage. Ce n'est pas un Poète bien entier, c'est le commencement et la matière d'un Poète. . . . C'est une grande source, il le faut avouer, mais c'est une source trouble et boueuse. . . . Du naturel, de l'imagination, de la facilité tant qu'on

* The *Entretiens* appeared in 1657.

veut, mais peu d'ordre, peu d'économie, point de choix,
soit pour les paroles, soit pour les choses; une audace insupportable à changer et à innover; une licence prodigieuse à former de mauvais mots et de mauvaises locu-
tions, à employer indifféremment tout ce qui se présentait
à lui, fût-il condamné par l'usage, trainât-il par les rues,
fût-il plus obscur que la plus noire nuit de l'hiver,
fût-ce de la rouille et du fer gâté."[36]

As for the vaunted philosophy and learning of Ronsard
and the other poets of the "vieille Cour," this is ridiculous. Philosophy, Mathematics, Greek and Latin were by
them all misplaced and travestied. "A proprement parler,
ces bonnes gens étaient des Frippiers et des Ravaudeurs.
Ils traduisaient mal au lieu de bien imiter. J'oserais dire
davantage, ils barbouillaient, ils défiguraient, ils déchirai-
ent, dans leurs Poèmes, les Anciens Poètes qu'ils avaient
lus; et n'y voit-on pas encore maintenant Pindare et Ana-
créon écorchés tout vifs, qui crient miséricorde aux cha-
ritables Lecteurs, qui font pitié à ceux qui les reconnaissent en cet état-là."[37]

But Malherbe, when it came to imitating, was the
equal or the superior of his models, even though French
is inferior to Latin as a language for poetry. Balzac
thought that French required special care. He had written in 1624 to Boisrobert, "Il est certain . . . qu'il n'y a
point de Muses si sévères que les Françaises, ni de langue
qui souffre moins le fard, et l'apparence du bien que la
nôtre: De façon que toutes sortes d'ornements ne lui sont
pas propres, et sa pureté est si ennemie de la licence des
autres, qu'il se fait souvent un vice Français d'une vertu
étrangère. Mais en cela il faut se conseiller avec le jugement, et les oreilles. . . ."[38]

And of a sonnet by Malherbe he said in the thirty-sec-
ond *Entretien*, "Il ne se peut rien voir de plus pur, de
plus harmonieux, ni de plus Français que ce sonnet."[39]

So his ideal was one of purity and of craftsmanship, all
of which was perfectly consistent with his insistence upon
simplicity and naturalness. His ninth *Entretien*, addressed to Chapelain, was entitled "Qu'il n'est pas pos-

sible d'écrire beaucoup et de bien écrire." In it he praised
the spare volume of the Italian poet Giovanni Della Casa
saying, "Cet excellent homme jouissait d'une santé assez
vigoureuse, il vivait dans le loisir tantôt de Rome et tantôt de Venise: Et néanmoins il n'a laissé en toute sa vie,
qu'un Livre de l'épaisseur de deux Almanachs. Ce n'est
pas qu'il eût l'esprit stérile, et qu'il cultivât une terre
ingrate: car jamais homme n'apporta au monde de plus
grands avantages naturels, ni plus de disposition à l'Eloquence. Mais c'était l'Eloquence Attique qu'il cherchait,
et non pas l'Eloquence Asiatique. Il aimait mieux une
petite pièce de terre, où il n'y eût que de belles fleurs,
des simples exquis et des plantes rares, que de grandes
campagnes de blé noir; que de pays tous entiers, où il ne
recuellît que de l'avoine et du gland."[40]

"L'éloquence Attique" was Balzac's quest too. But if
this implied a restrictive sense, it was not to be applied
too rigidly to subject matter. He was not, he said, of the
opinion of Malherbe, who wished that all metals were
gold and all flowers roses. "Je n'ei garde d'approuver la
suppression de tant de belles peintures et de tant de
bonnes odeurs."[41] Indeed language, and especially poetic
language, exists precisely to make all subjects agreeable.
"Il n'est point de matière qui ne soit capable d'ornement,
et qu'un bon ouvrier ne puisse embellir. Les épines les
plus sèches des Sciences reverdissent, et jettent des fleurs,
quand on les sait planter dans le champ des Muses. Y a-t-
il rien de si vilain que le mal de Naples, et rien de si beau
que le Poème que Fracastor en a fait?"[42] I include this
last statement to show how far Balzac was willing to go.

This is why, though with some reservations, he was
willing to keep at least some of the *genre burlesque*,
which the increasing sense of dignity and *bienséance* in
the century was trying to suppress. There were some
works of Marot and Scarron which he would miss.[43]

On the question of *bienséance* his position was very
clear: "La bienséance exige que nous voilions la défor-
mité des choses de l'honnêteté des paroles; mais il n'est

jamais permis de corrompre les verités écrites par un scrupule de Rhétorique."[44]

It was natural for more reasons than one that his preference for the Attic style should involve imitation of the Ancients. But because this style meant for him a certain vigor as well as purity, he was careful to distinguish between the spirit and the outer semblance, and this meant that whatever the artist does must first come from his own energy if he is to achieve the ideal combination of strength and delicacy. He wrote in 1646 to Lavaux Saint James, "Il vaut mieux ressembler aux Anciens par le coeur et par l'esprit, que par la mine et par la façon des habillements, Les Anciens mêmes ont dit que ce n'est pas tant de la bouche, que de l'estomac que procède le bien dire. La douceur et la pureté méritent d'être louées: Mais la force et la grandeur sont au-dessus de toute louange, et si on voit couler les ruisseaux avec plaisir, on regarde avec admiration les tempêtes de la Mer. . . ."[45]

He had said much earlier in the letter to Boisrobert from which I have already quoted,* that he did not consider himself a slave of the Ancients, nor bound by their laws. The whole of this letter incidentally amounts to a proclamation of Balzac's sense of independence. It is the one in which he describes himself as a being on whom "ses jarretières et ses aiguillettes pèsent." Descartes in 1638 made use of that same phrase in a letter to Huygens[46] to describe Balzac as an "amateur de la liberté." Tallemant[47] mentions Balzac's sartorial peculiarities, so the statement was probably sincere, although the frère André Saint Denis[48] suggested that the phrase was borrowed from Francis Bacon! But, to return to the question of the Ancients, the tones and the moods to be learned from them could also be learned singly or in combination from such an artist as the Della Casa whom he so much admired, and who, he said in the fourth *Entretien,* is "aujourd'hui . . . proposé pour exemple à ceux qui cherchent la pompe et la dignité du style, et qui veulent ajouter la force et l'éclat à la douceur et la clarté."[49]

* See above, p. 9 note.

Force and *éclat, douceur* and *clarté*. Vague words perhaps, but words which live in the vocabulary of criticism
throughout the century and which express the aspiration
of the Baroque. The combination of these, which is the
ideal, cannot be had, it is felt, without a great amount of
work and care. In the tenth discourse of the *Socrate
Chrétien* Balzac was complaining about the lack of literary training in so many writers on religious matters. He
insisted that knowledge of doctrine was not enough, for
when doctrine is badly expressed it is lost. He thought
that overloading of argument blocked understanding.
The arguments got in each other's way too frequently,
and the writer should clear much of this away before considering his work accomplished. But this takes time, and
Balzac thought it should. "CET HOMME, disait-on à Paris
lorsque j'y étais, A FAIT UN GRAND LIVRE PARCE QU'IL N'A
PAS EU LE LOISIR D'EN FAIRE UN PETIT."[50]*

But above all of these considerations of simplicity and
naturalness and purity as aims for the careful craftsman,
there is a higher eloquence, a higher sublimity which perhaps has nothing to do with craftsmanship at all, and
which certainly has nothing to do with Aristotle. This is
the eloquence of the heart, which proceeds from Christian humility. It is easy to see that this kind of eloquence
will be closer to the sort of thing that Balzac wanted than
the eloquence of the Schools. Christian humility was unknown to Aristotle: ". . . comme il n'a presque rien ignoré
des choses inférieures, il n'a presque rien su de celles du
Ciel. Pour aller là, il était trop régulier et trop méthodique."[51] This was said in the eleventh discourse of the
Socrate Chrétien. In the sixth of these discourses Balzac
had said in answer to the objection that Church Latin is
bad, "Je vous déclare de la part de Dieu qu'il ne demande
point de Harangues étudiées, qu'il se contente de l'Eloquence de nos coeurs et de nos soupirs, que les Barbar-
ismes des gens de bien le persuadent mieux que les Figures des Hypocrites."[52] And further on in the same discourse, "C'est donc le Monde visible que Dieu a aban-

* Cf. Pascal, end of sixteenth *Provinciale*.

donné aux arguments et aux disputes des Philosophes et
non pas le Monde caché: C'est la face extérieure de la
Nature et non pas les Secrets de la Religion. La connaissance de ses Secrets n'a point été exposée à la curiosité
de beaux Esprits."[53]

So that the example of the real, the final eloquence is
the divine simplicity of something like the *ego sum* of
Jesus. Whatever might be the virtues of "l'Eloquence Attique, de l'Asiatique, de la Rhodienne," Balzac advises
his listener in the second of the *Socrate* discourses, "réser-
vez toute votre admiration pour le laconisme de Jésus-
Christ."[54]

Now it seems to me that whatever might be Balzac's
capacity for rhetoric and however we might therefore
question his sincerity, there is no doubt that his thoughts
are to some extent, and I believe to a considerable extent,
the thought of the century. So I should like to pursue
this notion of Christian humility a little further, keeping
in mind however that our theme is literary and not religious or philosophical.

The first of the *Socrate* discourses was called "De Jésus-
Christ et de sa Doctrine." In it we may read the following: "Le seul Jésus-Christ a pouvoir de conclure et de
prononcer, et sa seule Doctrine nous peut mettre l'esprit
en repos. Elle définit, elle décide, elle juge souveraine-
ment. Elle tranche les difficultés. Elle coupe les noeuds,
et ne s'amuse pas à les démêler. Elle nous assure en
termes formels QUE LES CHOSES VISIBLES ONT COMMENCÉ,
ET QUE LES SUBSTANCES SPIRITUELLES NE FINIRONT POINT.
Depuis la publication de cette Doctrine, nous disons
hautement et affirmativement que le Monde ne s'est pas
bâti soi-même, mais qu'il y a je ne sais quoi de plus vieux
et de plus ancien, qui a travaillé à une si admirable Architecture."[55]

This passage which seems so innocent had to be defended, because the term *je ne sais quoi* was misunderstood. It was assumed by some that Socrate doubted the
existence of anything at all which created the world.
Balzac answered this objection in an *Extrait d'Une Dis-*

sertation, addressed to the Reverend Père Don André de Saint-Denis, of the Pères Feuillants. Certain expressions, Balzac said, are permitted as oratorical "manner of speaking": "Et lorsque Socrate dit au même Discours *que je ne sais quoi de plus Ancien que le Monde a bâti le Monde,* ce je ne sais quoi est encore une de ces paroles figurées qu'il ne faut pas prendre à la lettre, et qui reçoivent une interprétation favorable. Ce n'est pas un terme d'irrésolution par lequel Socrate doute si c'est Dieu qui a bâti le Monde: C'est un terme d'humilité, c'est un aveu d'ignorance, par lequel il confesse que Dieu est une chose inconnue à l'Homme, et qui ne se peut ni bien définir ni bien nommer."[56]

It is this humility or the desire to achieve it, or if you will, to simulate it, which keeps Balzac consciously undogmatic in matters of literature as well as in matters of religion and politics. The suspicion of an ultimate unanswerability can fortify, or is fortified by empiricism. At the political level for instance, we have seen Balzac refusing to suppose that Augustus' every decision could be explained rationally. Here is an expansion of this notion from the *Aristippe:* "Les Grands événements ne sont pas toujours produits par les grandes causes. Les ressorts sont cachés et les machines paraissent: et quand on vient à découvrir ces ressorts, on s'étonne de les voir si faibles et si petits. . . . Une jalousie d'amour [n'est] rien en apparence; et par ce Rien commencent les Tragédies dans lesquelles on versera tant de sang et on verra sauter tant de têtes. Ce n'est qu'un nuage qui passe et une tache en un coin de l'air qui s'y perd plutôt qu'elle ne s'y arrête. Et néanmoins c'est cette légère vapeur, c'est cette nuée presque imperceptible, qui excitera les fatales tempêtes que les Etats sentiront, et qui ébranlera le Monde jusqu'aux fondements."[57]

This is Cleopatra's nose and Pascal will call it a "je ne sais quoi." A *lieu commun* to be sure, but a deep laid one and with many implications.

At the religious level, there is in the tenth discourse of the *Socrate* a whole passage on tolerance. Balzac approved the idea of speaking about the Protestants as "les gens de l'autre opinion," or "ceux de la nouvelle opinion." It seemed to him worthy of Greek civility and reflected commerce with books.[58] This was obviously not to approve the new opinion. Christian humility was not to be carried that far, nor ignorance to become doubt.

But at the human level Balzac in this same discourse could confess himself greatly puzzled. He was discussing certain outstanding cases of unregenerate impiety: Vanini and Cosimo Ruggieri, and especially another foreign prince who, when asked by his regular pastor (a protestant minister) to make his final profession of faith, answered "JE CROIS QUE DEUX ET DEUX FONT QUATRE ET QUE QUATRE ET QUATRE FONT HUIT." But this original of Molière's *Dom Juan* was in all other respects a model of good conduct. "C'est ce qui m'oblige à avouer, à la honte de la Nature humaine, que l'Homme est un animal bien divers et bien bigarré, que les Centaures et les Chimères ne l'étaient pas davantage; que non seulement il est composé de pièces différentes, mais quelquefois aussi de pièces contraires."[59]

This whole tenth discourse had to do with the matter and expression of certain sermons which Balzac was examining, so that the final humility he had to manifest was directed at his own work and at the whole business of making and criticizing phrases. Because "Ce que nous allons faire dans la Chapelle vaut bien mieux que ce que nous venons de faire dans le Cabinet." Then follows the famous passage which begins, "Vous vous souvenez du vieux Pédagogue de la Cour," and which ends, "La Mort l'attrappa sur l'arrondissement d'une Période, et l'an climatérique l'avait surpris délibérant si *Erreur* et *Doute* étaient masculins ou féminins. Avec quelle attention voulait-il qu'on l'écoutât quand il dogmatisait de l'usage et de la vertu des Particules? . . . La Propriété, la régularité, la beauté même du langage ne doit pas être la fin de l'homme. Il ne faut pas songer aux roses et aux violettes quand la saison de la récolte est venue."[60]

And this applies not only to the business of the language, but the ideas thereby expressed have to be considered in the same light. Balzac wrote in the thirteenth *Entretien* which was addressed to Chapelain, "Avouons la vérité; Nous pourrions avoir part, mes compagnons et moi, parmi les Saints de Jésus-Christ, si nous avions apporté autant d'étude à la correction de notre vie qu'à celle de notre language. . . . Dans nos Académies nous parlons sans cesse de l'Idée du Bon et du Beau: nous courons après une certaine perfection, que nous pensons avoir vue je ne sais où. C'est perdre ses paroles et ses pas, que de parler et de courir de la sorte. Cherchons le Bon en sa source, et le Beau dans la première Beauté. Cherchons la perfection; mais cherchons-la plutôt en nos actions qu'en nos paroles: faisons cas de celle qui nous peut rendre éternellement heureux, plutôt que de celle qui nous est entièrement inutile."[61]

This sense of the ultimate questionability of criticism, of the intellectual, is reinforced by the conviction that, as Balzac said in the sixteenth *Entretien*, "N'en déplaise à l'Université, il y a une Logique naturelle et des Sages ignorants."

Balzac seems to have had a faith in the reality of the individual naive experience which limited, though it did not destroy, his enthusiasm for the eloquence which was his life. This faith strengthened his support of the simple and the natural, of the *honnête* in all its senses. And it made him distrust system and theory divorced from experience. At the basis of this attitude was a religious consciousness which, if it was at all artificial on his part, was still designed to appeal to those for whom he wrote. By way of illustrating conclusively this empiricism and this religiosity, I should like to end this chapter with two quotations which seem to me significant and decisive. The first is from the twenty-sixth *Entretien*. The subject is "De l'utilité de l'histoire aux gens de Cour." Balzac is discussing for the benefit of a certain nobleman the books which he considers useful to the growing courtier: "Dans les Livres que les Anciens ont écrits de la Prudence civile, il faut avouer qu'il y a bien du galimatias de l'Ecole et de déserts! que de lieux incultes et sauvages éloignés de l'usage et du commun des hommes! La République de Platon, les Politiques d'Aristote, tant qu'il vous plaira: mais surtout je recommande l'Histoire à vos jeunes gens. Sans l'Histoire, la Politique n'est qu'un Spectre creux et plein de vide, qu'on remue par je ne sais quelles petites distinctions et divisions de l'Ecole pour jouer et amuser les Enfants. Cette Belle Politique étant separée de l'Action et de l'Exemple, ne s'entend pas elle-même."[62]

The second of these quotations is, once again, from the *Socrate*, in the fifth discourse. Balzac is telling the story of an argument between a certain Gentilhomme de Saintonge and a certain clergyman, "fameux et redoubtable Dialecticien" over a matter of fact which the Gentilhomme declared he had witnessed and which the clergyman maintained could not be so for four indisputable reasons, arguing that the eyes deceive, the senses lie, "que l'Homme extérieur est sujet aux illusions; que la Nouvelle dont il s'agit implique contradiction morale, et peut-être contradiction physique etc." Balzac concluded, "Après cet exemple, fions-nous à la souveraine Raison; Faisons conscience de douter de l'infaillibilité d'un Maître ès Arts; Ne Faisons point de différence entre les visions de nos Docteurs et les oracles de notre Doctrine; Recevons les Nouvelles du Monde à venir sur la parole de ces gens-là qui jugent si bien des Nouvelles du Monde présent. Bon Dieu, qu'Aristote et que sa Dialectique ont gâté de têtes! Qu'il y a dans le Monde de Fous sérieux; de Fous qui se fondent en raison; de Fous qui sont déguisés en Sages! O mon Dieu, que le silence du Sanctuaire est bien meilleur que le babil des Académies, et qu'il vaut mieux marcher dans la simplicité de vos voies que de s'égarer dans les labyrinthes d'Aristote."[63]

I said at the beginning of this chapter that Balzac's contribution to the development of French prose was made against the background of a definite aesthetic. By now it should appear that this aesthetic is neither very complex, nor wholly consistent, nor what we should call complete.

But it suggests a real understanding of literature, and it is vigorous and free. This is because in its turn it was maintained against a background of religious consciousness which could absorb many inconsistencies and much inconclusiveness without destroying judgment and sense. I believe that this was true of the Seventeenth Century as a whole.

CHAPELAIN

Jean Chapelain, regent of letters during a great part of the century, presents a somewhat different and more complicated case from that of his good friend and correspondent Balzac. Much more the professional critic than Balzac, his problems were proportionately more difficult because his judgments could hurt. He shouldered all the responsibility which Balzac shook off when he retired to the banks of the Charente. His position became official with the *Sentiments de l'Académie* on the *Cid*, and this position was consecrated when he became Colbert's adviser. That he recognized his power is evident in his correspondence, which shows that in many respects he envied Balzac his solitude and independence. It is one thing to discuss in private what interests you on the basis of broad principles, or to discuss the principles themselves, and it is another to have to pass on the worth of specific works. In such a case it is certainly easier to praise than to condemn, especially when, like Chapelain, you possess a highly developed social sense. For these reasons, if Richelieu called Chapelain *l'élogiste général*, and if Voiture called him *l'excuseur de toutes les fautes*, these shortcomings must be looked upon with indulgence. For, though he is irritating at times, he was, I believe, an honest man, and a fair-minded one. He was inconsistent perhaps, and sometimes confused, but all in all his record is not so bad. He encouraged La Fontaine, he protected the young Racine. He really approved of Corneille, as we shall see. He thought the *Astrée* the best of the romances. He appreciated Pascal and Molière. Granted that there was little danger in these judgments, they must still be put on the credit side of the ledger.

But even in the case of more doubtful personalities, it is evident that Chapelain was systematically equitable. Several examples will illustrate this. Of Marino's *Adone* he said "c'est une mer qui n'a ni fond ni rive et que jamais personne que Saint-Amand n'a pu courir entièrement, mais le détail en est riant et les descriptions délicieuses."[1] Saint-Amand himself, he thought, had power as a descriptive poet but lacked the ability to write convincing dialogue, or to describe "les moeurs et les passions, qui me semble, avec nos anciens, la principale vertu de la poésie et celle qui touche, qui émeut, qui persuade et qui ravit. . . ."[2] But an outstanding example of this attempt at fairness was his final judgment on La Mesnardière's *Poétique.** When he heard that it was to appear he wrote to Balzac (who, he always insisted was his confidant) "L'auteur de cette nouvelle Poétique est . . . excellent naturaliste, et qui a fait un petit traité des esprits servant aux sens. Mais il a quitté ce qu'il savait bien faire pour gâter le *Panégyrique* de Pline par des additions et pour faire une comédie du *Promenoir de Montaigne*, de la *Pucelle*† que vous connaissez, le tout sans doute plutôt mal que bien. Nous verrons les imaginations de ce nouveau législateur et je suis trompé si nous les suivons, car, à ce que j'entends, il ne veut pas suivre *il maestro di color che sanno*: il le prétend devancer et, pour ce faire, prendre d'autres routes. C'est un homme que je caresse et que je fuis, suivant ma méthode d'agir avec ses têtes de vif argent."[3] But when the *Poétique* appeared, and he had had a chance to examine it, though he knew that what he thought was good in it had come mostly from Scaliger and Heinsius, still he stated that it had been *agréablement* and *solidement* done, that it would be useful and that it had filled a bad lacuna in French letters.[4] To be sure the complete lack of originality of the work

* Cf. Helen Reese Reese, *La Mesnardière's Poétique*, Johns Hopkins, Baltimore, 1937.
† Mlle. de Gournay.

had reassured Chapelain, but as other letters show, he thought this naturalist turned man of letters personally a rather ridiculous figure and his qualified approval remains generous.

Fidao-Justiniani thought that this spirit of equity reflected an ideal of *préciosité*,[5] and it is true that Chapelain was an habitué of the salon of Mme de Rambouillet, that he praised the conversation there for its lack of pedantry, and that he conceived of that ideal in worthy terms. This is revealed by a description of a mutual acquaintance, written in a letter to Balzac. He appreciated this person's "agréable mélange . . . de solidité et de galanterie, de philosophie et de gaieté," and said, "En effet je lui trouve ce don d'urbanité que Cicéron affectait et qui est d'autant plus difficile à acquérir qu'il fait le caractère le plus essentiel et la partie principale qui constitue l'honnête homme."[6] Chapelain was conscious of this spirit, and he protested frequently that his only aim was to arrive at the truth, yet that his opinions were given only as his own, and that he held it the part of honor to treat even those who had offended him with civility.

In short, he tried hard not to be an extremist. Even the fortitude which he boasted was tempered. He wrote, again to Balzac, on the occasion of the death of a friend. "Vous savez bien que mon stoïcisme est mitigé et que je me suis permis des exceptions, pour mon usage, à la sûreté des préceptes de ces âmes ferrées. Vous savez bien que je me suis toujours reservé la liberté des larmes* pour la perte de mes amis et des vertus éminentes, et que je tiens ce faible si beau et si digne de l'humaine société que je l'ai par élection toujours préféré à cette fermeté diamantine dont ces M\ts font une ambitieuse profession."[7]

He prided himself too on his spirit of independence. At one moment he thought that Balzac had expressed him-

---

* Cf. Descartes in a letter of condolence to Pollot in 1641, when he wrote "Je ne suis pas de ceux qui estiment que les larmes et la tristesse n'appartiennent qu'aux femmes et que pour paraître homme de coeur on se doive contraindre à montrer toujours un visage tranquille." (*Correspondence, ed. cit.*, III, 278)

self as completely in agreement with the Stoics. Upon receiving a negative answer to his query, with an explanation, he declared himself relieved, and happy to know that his friend maintained a "manière libre de philosopher." He further stated that the category in which Balzac had thus placed himself was "sans doute la plus naturelle de toutes et celle dont tout le monde peut être, sans pourtant convenir d'aucun autre principe que de celui de n'être assujetti à aucun et de se garder la liberté de condamner ses propres maîtres. Notre raison ne peut être soumise qu'à la raison et il n'y a rien qui la cabre davantage que l'autorité lorsqu'on la veut faire passer pour indubitable. Je me moque des *autos eute* (sic?)* et de cette déférence aveugle aux sentiments d'un homme qui en cette qualité, quelque parfait qu'il soit, ne peut manquer d'être sujet à errer. Des maximes que posent les philosophants, je n'admets que celles qui s'ajustent à ma conception, et qui sont universellement reçues par les personnes de bon sens. Ce que l'autorité fait au plus dans mon esprit, c'est de me donner la curiosité d'examiner s'il a lieu de l'admettre pour règle, et si la réputation du Docteur est un effet de son mérite ou de la faiblesse de ses écoliers."[8]

Balzac replied to this, "Vive donc cette belle liberté." But even Chapelain's independence was tempered, for Balzac commended his assertion that only religion had the right to impose authority.[9]

Whatever may be the sincerity of Chapelain's presentation of himself (he also admitted a morbid presentiment of trouble), however much his independence was theoretical and his equitableness prudent, these qualities represent nonetheless an ideal which he held, a conception of the critic and man of letters which he would at least wish to embody.

I have thought this character of Chapelain worth dwelling upon since it provides a background for some of the more important judgments which he made, and which should now be examined.

* Should probably be *autos eipe*, i.e. *ipse dixit*.

If there is an accusation leveled at Chapelain more frequently than the one of compromise, it is the one of dogmatism. How these two charges can be made simultaneously is at first glance hard to see. But his connection with officialdom naturally makes him the representative of academic standardization and this naturally implies doctrinaire decisions. Besides, he was unquestionably devoted to Aristotle and to the notion of rules. But here again his attitude was tempered.

His first major critical attempt was the justification of Marino's *Adone* in 1623, and there is no doubt that it is a perfect example of rationalistic and dogmatic judicial criticism. Yet this very attitude was being taken in the defense of an "irregular" form—an epic of love. Chapelain declared, we know, that he had done it at the request of Marino, who too late had discovered that heroic narrative poems were supposed to satisfy certain formal requirements and who feared that the Italian critics, then stricter than the French, would demolish his work.[10] The preface may therefore be looked upon more as a *tour de force* (if we are to believe Chapelain, who had no illusions about the regularity of the *Adone*) than as a piece of serious criticism.

On the side of the highly dogmatic and rationalistic must also be put the famous *Lettre à Godeau* in support of the unity of time. But the statement on which Chapelain's reputation generally rests is of course the *Sentiments de l'Académie*, the analysis of Corneille's *Cid*.

Now about this much discussed treatise two things must right away be said. In the first place, Chapelain really liked the *Cid*—with qualifications. He wrote to Balzac in 1637, "J'apprends aussi avec plaisir que le *Cid* ait fait en vous l'effet qu'en tout notre monde. La matière, les beaux sentiments que l'Espagnol lui avait donnés, et les ornements qu'a ajoutés notre poète français, ont mérité l'applaudissment du peuple et de la Cour qui n'étaient point encore accoutumés à de telles délicatesses. Il est bien vrai, entre nous, que le *Cid* se peut dire heureux d'avoir été traité par un Français et en France, où la finesse de la poésie du théâtre n'est point encore connue. En Italie, il eût passé pour barbare. . . ."[11]

In the second place he was most reluctant to judge it officially and publicly. In another letter to Balzac we read, "Ce qui m'embarrasse, et avec beaucoup de fondement, est d'avoir à choquer et la Cour et la Ville, les grands et les petits, l'une et l'autre des parties contestantes, et en un mot tout le monde, en me choquant moi-même sur un sujet qui ne devait point être traité par nous; et, croyez-moi, Monsieur, qu'il n'y a rien de si odieux, et qu'un honnête homme doive éviter davantage, que de reprendre publiquement un ouvrage que la réputation de son auteur ou la bonne fortune de la Pièce a fait approuver de chacun. . . ."[12]

The reluctance, I grant, is probably more prudent than benevolent, but in any case Chapelain did not warm to the task. A letter to Boisrobert, Richelieu's secretary, does him less credit. The judgment we remember was to be made by the Academy to settle the Quarrel over the merits of the play and principally to decide between the claims of Scudéry and those of Corneille. Chapelain wished Boisrobert to explain to His Eminence that he and his colleagues would agree with the partisans of Corneille on non-essentials, though they considered the play "défectueuse en ses plus essentielles parties," on the theory that if they gave it some credit they would have a better chance of winning over those who had been "taken in" by it.[13]

Yet even if this calculation is borne in mind, it must not be forgotten that Richelieu had to be placated as much as the Court, the public, and the playwrights concerned. It is consequently hard to determine just where the sincerity—or insincerity—lay. The result however was that the *Sentiments* can be regarded as an admission of the limitations of the rules almost as much as they can be considered an application of those rules. The truth probably lies in accepting both of these views.

One ought to remember too that the *Sentiments* were, like Balzac's letter, a criticism of Scudéry's criticism and so in many instances a defense of the *Cid*, and that further, the main line of the criticism concerned *bien-séance* and the related *vraisemblance* rather than the more formal precepts. This is so true that Chapelain at one point complained that Corneille in trying too hard to follow the rules of composition fell afoul of the rules of nature.[14] And finally it should be noted that Chapelain in defending the play against those who wished to condemn it completely, asked the indulgence of the *savants*, saying that, "ils doivent se représenter que l'abus étant si général dans la plupart de nos poèmes dramatiques, soit pour l'élection des sujets, soit pour leur économie, il y aurait quelque espèce de rigueur à demander à un homme de ces temps toutes les conditions qui y sont requises par Aristote."[15]

Chapelain said to Balzac, when the treatise had been published and it was known that he was the author of most of it, ". . . si vous me demandez ce qui m'en semble, je vous confesserai que j'en tiens le biais de l'introduction adroit, ayant à choquer le jugement de la Cour et du Peuple, que j'en crois la doctrine solide, et qu'à mon avis la modération et l'équité y règnent partout. Avec tout cela je vous protesterai que j'aimerais mieux avoir fait la lettre que vous avez faite sur cela que notre volume, continuant à vous dire que c'est un des ouvrages plus accompli qu'on ait vu, dans ces derniers temps."[16]

And, perhaps partly because he knew that Balzac had defended it, Chapelain continued to think well enough of the *Cid* to use it as a basis of comparison for his estimates of other plays. Desmaret's *Scipion*, he reported, had had only a mediocre success, "bien au-dessous du *Cid*."[17] Scudéry's *Amour tyrannique* was a success and the enemy of Corneille "s'est surpassé soi-même. Mais, pour cela, il n'a pas surpassé *le Cid* quelque défectueux que nous l'ayons trouvé."[18]

Finally, when Corneille came to see him, although he seemed to Chapelain to have been silenced by the judgment of the Academy (to which he would have replied, he said, with great effect, had he not been afraid to "choquer les puissances"), Chapelain did not regard this as a victory, but instead encouraged Corneille to come back at Scudéry "en faisant quelque nouveau *Cid* qui attire encore les suffrages de tout le monde et qui montre que l'art n'est pas ce qui fait la beauté."[19]

One may insist, then, upon Chapelain's ability to understand the point of view of the admirers of the *Cid* and to see many worthy qualities in the play. His admission in the *Sentiments* that, whatever might be its faults, it contained an *agrément inexplicable*[20] was not at all a grudging one. Nor, if we do him the justice of reading more widely in him, do we find it to be of an isolated kind.

His opinions of Malherbe and Ronsard and of French poetry in general reveal this understanding. They seem, incidentally to have changed but little throughout his career.

In 1632 he wrote to Mlle de Gournay, who had made him out to be a disciple of Malherbe, "Quant à l'homme que vous appelez mon prototype, il a valu beaucoup en son temps, mais non pas assez pour me rendre son imitateur, comme vous le supposez. . . . L' idée de l'art est mon seul exemplaire, sur lequel je me règle uniquement, et qui seul me ferait espérer ne marcher pas indignement après ces grandes lumières [Homer and Virgil] si j'avais autant d'ardeur pour cette belle poésie qu'il le faudrait et que vous le croyez. . . . Je reviens à ce moderne dont vous me faites l'écolier avec si peu de fondement, et vous dis qu'il était parfait en ce métier de la sorte que le commun en imagine la perfection. Je vous dis qu'il tournait mieux les vers ni que moi ni que vous-même. Mais je vous dis aussi qu'il ignorait la poésie, de la sorte que tous les maîtres des bons âges l'ont connue, et qu'il l'ignorait beaucoup plus que vous ni que moi-même, c'est-à-dire extrêmement."[21]

The expression here is very strong, as is the distinction between technical perfection and poetic genius. Malherbe the perfect versifier is condemned as a poet. But worse, French poetry after him suffered from the emi-

nence which he had attained, in that this ignorance of
poetry was perpetuated in his successors, and fortified by
continued imposition of restrictions for which he was
originally responsible. So Chapelain complained to Balzac in 1640: "uant au jugement de M. de Malherbe, je
l'estime peu pour la haute Poésie et les choses qu'il y fait
principalement considérer. Il l'arguait* et voulait que
cette ignorance fût une vertu dont il a longtemps infecté
son siècle. C'était un borgne dans un royaume d'aveugles,
et, comme il avait ses lumières fort bornées, je crois qu'un
homme de lettres doit se garder de le prendre pour guide
dans les opinions qu'il doit suivre, s'il ne veut broncher
bien lourdement. Ce qu'il a d'excellent et d'incomparable,
c'est l'élocution et le tour du vers et quelques élévations
nettes et pompeuses dans le détail qu'on pourra bien
imiter, mais jamais égaler. Ces parties toutefois ne sont
guères plus poétiques qu'oratoires, et ceux-là ne lui ont
guères fait de tort qui ont dit de lui que ses vers étaient
de fort belle prose rimée."[22]

In 1662 in a letter to Grentemesnil Chapelain made
the same complaint about the restrictions placed on
French poetry. But he judged that it was not for him to
deliver French poets from their chains "et ce serait s'opposer en vain au torrent."[23] History might have allowed
him a better name if he had attempted the task which he
so stoically rejected, but then we expect to find no revo-
lutionaries here.

Even if one did not agree with Chapelain's estimate of
Malherbe, one could scarcely disagree with the view of
poetry which underlies it. This view is brought out more
clearly still in his defense of Ronsard. This defense turns
the picture upside down so to speak, without altering the
values.

For this we must return to that exchange of opinions
with Balzac which occurred in 1640 and from which I
quoted above. In answer to Balzac's query as to whether

* Or "ignorait." The MS. reading is difficult. See *Opuscules
critiques, ed. cit.*, p. 423, note 1.

the epithet *great* had been applied by Chapelain to Ronsard seriously or ironically (it is revealing that Balzac should have to have this explained to him), Chapelain wrote: "Vous me demandiez par l'une de vos précédentes si l'épithète de *Grand* que j'avais donné à Ronsard était sérieux* ou ironique, et vouliez mon sentiment là-dessus. Ronsard sans doute était né poète autant ou plus que pas un des modernes, je ne dis pas seulement français, mais encore espagnols et italiens. . . . Il n'a pas, à la vérité, les traits aigus de Lucain et de Stace, mais il a quelquechose que j'estime plus, qui est une certaine égalité nette et majestueuse qui fait le vrai corps des ouvrages poétiques, ces autres petits ornements étant plus du sophiste et du déclamateur que d'un esprit véritablement inspiré par les Muses."[24] Ronsard, continues Chapelain, is "dans le détail" like Virgil or more properly Homer, and this is more true of him than of any other poet known to him or to Balzac. If he had been born at a time when the language was more polished, he would have surpassed any poets writing in the Seventeenth Century or at any other time. Admittedly he was "sans art" having learned what he knew only from his reading of the Ancients, which resulted in an imitation which was "servile et désagréable" and in an anachronism which constituted a "défaut de jugement insupportable." These were Ronsard's two great defects, to have worked according to no previously laid out plan, and not to have written for his time. In this sense he was only a mason and not an architect, because he was not aware of true principles and therefore possessed no solid foundation. But, Chapelain concludes, "Avec tout cela, je ne le tiens nullement méprisable et je trouve chez lui, parmi cette affectation de paraître savant, toute une autre noblesse que dans les afféteries ignorantes de ceux qui l'ont suivi, et jusqu'ici, comme je donne à ces derniers l'avantage dans les ruelles de nos dames, je crois qu'on doit le donner à Ronsard dans les bibliothèques de ceux qui ont le bon goût de l'antiquité."[25]

* *épithète* was for some time masculine. Cf. Littré.

Balzac's answer to this letter was most courteous. He said he would have to reread his Ronsard. To this Chapelain replied (in the letter containing the Malherbe opinion which I quoted) that his own judgment might have been hasty and based on memories of youthful impressions. They agreed, he said, on Ronsard's defects "aussi bien que cette mauvaise manière d'imiter les anciens qu'il a prise plutôt en écolier qu'en homme de la Cour et selon le goût du collège que selon celui du cabinet." But, he went on, "je ne regarde pas dans la poésie les perfections opposées à ces defauts comme celles qui font le Poète principalement et qui lui acquièrent le nom de Grand. Selon moi, il y a deux parties qui constituent sa différence spécifique et qui doivent servir de règle pour reconnaître si le Poète est Poète légitime ou non, et ce sont le génie et le jugement. Qui a ces deux conditions est plus grand poète avec tous les défauts dont nous accusons Ronsard que ceux qui ont les qualités opposées, et à qui ces conditions manquent." If Ronsard had had judgment as well as genius there would be no question, and "c'est dommage comme vous dites que ce beau naturel et cette imagination féconde ne se sont rencontrés dans un temps comme celui-ci qui veut que l'on soit ajusté aussi bien que libre et dans lequel les Poètes sont réglés par le goût de la Cour plutôt que la Cour par le goût des Poètes."[26]

Much of the time, of course, Chapelain speaks as a poet almost more than as a critic, and I expect one of the keys to his character is his never fully satisfied desire to be recognized as a poet, even though he was quite aware of his shortcomings and of lacking just what he knew could not be supplied by the rules. In the first preface to *La Pucelle* he admitted (probably not too naively) having "que bien peu des qualités requises en un poète héroïque," and he has been charged with intending to compensate this lack by a perfect knowledge of the theory of the epic.[27] The charge is unfair. All he wished to do with his poem was to show that it was possible to write a respectable epic in his time and in French if one had a cer-

tain knowledge of the principles involved, even without
any too great "élévation d'esprit." I do not think he had
the slightest illusion of equaling, far less of bettering
Homer and thus of supplanting genius by the rules.[28] To
suggest that this was his aim is to put him about fifty
years ahead of his time, for such was the ambition of the
doctrinaires at the end of the century and at the beginning of the eighteenth.

Chapelain's conception of his work on the *Pucelle* was
very clearly set forth in a letter written in 1673 near the
end of his life to the Abbé Gayet, whose praises he ac-
knowledged with his never-failing modesty, saying however of the poem, "Ce n'est pas que je le méprise et que je
croie mal employé le grand temps que j'ai mis à le mettre
en l'état où vous l'avez vu en partie, parce que l'ayant
fort médité devant que de l'entreprendre, en ayant jeté
les fondements et levé le plan selon les règles que les bons
anciens nous ont prescrites, soit par leurs raisonnements,
soit pas leurs exemples, et essayé d'en élever la structure
avec les conditions requises à le faire, sinon brillant, du
moins sans ces irrégularités et difformités qui le déshon-
norent, j'aurais sujet d'espérer qu'il ne déplairait pas au
général des experts et de ceux qui, sans avoir intérêt à
mon louange, ni à mon blâme, en jugeraient sans passion
et avec connaissance de cause. . . ." The sentence, only
half finished, from here on pursues an invective against
malignant critics who do not even deserve to be shown
the right way.[29]

In other words Chapelain knew well that if he possessed the *jugement* required of the poet he did not
possess the genius. About thirty years earlier he had
written to Mlle de Gournay about his poem ". . . si, en
cela, j'avais à tirer vanité de quelque chose, ce serait
beaucoup plus de l'invention et de la disposition de
l'ouvrage que de la versification. Et je vous dirai, en pas-
sant, sans taxer la faiblesse du siècle, que j'estimerais
être le premier qui lui aurait fait connaître que les prin-
cipales vertus de la poésie ne sont pas dans les vers,
lequel, au jugement des premiers hommes de l'antiquité,

a été tenu même non nécessaire pour constituer l'essence
du poème."[30]

In this he was at least consistent. Malherbe the great
manipulator of verse could be his example. He knew the
dangers of playing with words. Perhaps this is why in his
letters he always affected a familiar and, for the times,
almost brusque style. He explained this manner of his in
a letter to Carrel de Sainte Garde, written in 1663. He
said of letters in general, "Comme j'estime fort les naïves,
il n'y a rien qui me déplaise davantage que les ambiti-
euses, et celles de ce dernier genre tenant du déclamateur
ne me dégoûtent pas moins chez quelques anciens que
chez quelques modernes, lorsque leur matière ne veut
que le style familier, duquel ces formes affectées cor-
rompent le caractère. Car pour les lettres de consolation,
de consultation, de relation, de justification, d'accusation,
je ne les réduis pas à ce style et je leur en assigne un entre
le sublime et le commun qui rejette les fortes figures et
qui n'exclut pas celles qui ne vont qu'à l'agrément. Vous
en avez de celles-ci dans Cicéron et dans le Caro qui
pourraient en servir de modèle. Nos Français ni vos
Espagnols ne les connaissent point, et les leurs sont toutes
ou du genre rampant ou de celui qui monte aux nues,
sans que pas un ait connaissance de cette médiocrité
dorée qui paraît si facile et dont le point est si malaisé
à attraper. Mais de combien d'autres natures d'écrits
ignorent-ils l'idée et l'usage, et combien peu s'en trouve-
t-il qui soupçonnent seulement qu'il y en ait d'autre à
suivre que celui qui règne chez les ignorants ou chez les
peu judicieux dont la société humaine est pour la plupart
composée? Ce n'est pas que je prétende réformer ces
abus, ce que je prétends c'est qu'encore que je puisse être
sujet à tomber dans le même désordre, du moins le re-
connais-je et vois-je que je ne suis pas estimable de m'y
laisser aller."[31]

And he takes credit in this matter of letter writing for
Balzac's shift to the familiar style. We read in a letter
to the Abbé Gayet in 1673 that he has always written
economically to his good friends and that this was the

manner used in his correspondence with Balzac. "Vous
le pouvez avoir vu dans le premier volume de lettres sur
lequel il a fini sa vie, dans le dessein de publier les autres
comme l'image de ses véritables pensées qu'il répandait
en sûreté dans mon sein et il voulait qu'on connût le vrai
état de son âme, ayant depuis notre connaissance renoncé à ce style ambitieux qui lui avait donné tant de
réputation, et qu'il avait enfin reconnu être plutôt de
déclamation que de véritable éloquence."[32]

Chapelain was loyal to judgment. This helped him to
see that elaborate style did not necessarily mean eloquence and that simplicity and naturalness could be attractive. But he was loyal to genius too and to the *agrément inexplicable* which seems at times to have nothing
to do with judgment.

He was not a reformer, but he was not a reactionary.
His concern was always to advance the cause of literature
and to improve it with advice and encouragement. The
pension list of writers which he drew up for Colbert is a
model of straightforward judgment which can scarcely
be criticized, considering the purpose for which it was
meant.

I believe that Chapelain's modesty was real because he
knew how complex and difficult the problem of literary
criticism is. His faith in rules is consistent with this
modesty.

Toward the end of his life he occupied himself more
and more with letters thought of in the larger sense of
erudition. He had always been interested in history, for
example, and had a very elevated conception of the responsibility, the integrity, the impartiality, and the morality of the historian. So much so in fact that he was
forced to tell Colbert that it would probably be impossible to find anyone worthy of writing the history of the
reign of Louis XIV.[33] One wonders what he would have
thought if he had lived to see Racine and, worst of all,
Boileau made royal historiographers!

Chapelain probably lacked a real artistic sense. It may
be that he even lacked that aspect of the critical sense

which was coming more and more to be called *goût*. But he knew about *goût* and used the term early in his writings, as for instance when he wrote to Balzac in 1638, "Un goût aussi exquis que le vôtre ne se repaît pas de choses triviales."[34] Later he said of himself to Heinsius, who had agreed with him about Balzac's *Aristippe*, "Je commence à croire que je n'ai pas le goût tout à fait mauvais en ces matières."[35] It seems to me that in some way he knew a great deal *about* literature, if he did not really *know* it.

Part of this knowing about literature was knowing about its mechanics and its architecture. But it was also knowing about its effect. He knew for instance what Tasso had done which he should not have done if his aim was to write a modern epic. But he also knew why Tasso could not have done otherwise. Tasso, he wrote to Isaac Gruterus in 1667, convinced Europe that it could have an epic genre and was not limited to the lyric or the medieval romance, "qui est un genre de poésie sans art et qui tient de l'ignorance et de la faiblesse des siècles barbares." Yet Tasso used love and magic. But he had to, because it was very much harder to please the public in his day by "la sévérite de l'héroïque" than by "l'aménité des inventions extravagantes et sans règle qui avaient accoutumé le monde à leur air, sans leur laisser voir les inconvénients qui résultaient de leur invérisimilitude et de leur irrégularité."[36]

And he wondered whether he ought not to have done like Tasso in the composition of his own work. But his desire to use his knowledge and his judgment was greater than his desire to please a still uncultivated public. Yet he knew the force of that public taste, and he respected it where others were concerned. And this respect he could feel, because part of his knowing about literature was knowing about the privilege of genius and about the *agrément inexplicable*.

The *agrément inexplicable* explains more than the success of the *Cid*, and allows the *Cid* to be more than a sport in an otherwise reasonably determined set of phenomena. It is, in short, that area of poetry untouched by mechanics, and Chapelain understood the meaning of its existence. It is necessary to remember that his rationalism, *a priori* judgments, and dogmatizing thereby escaped the absolutism with which he, like the century, is usually associated.*

2. THE LIBERALISM OF PIERRE CORNEILLE

ROBERT BRASILLACH in the introduction to his book on Corneille wrote in 1938 that while there were many different Racines, from Sainte-Beuve's to Thierry Maulnier's and the Abbé Bremond's, there was still only the same old Corneille, firmly frozen in the ice of honor and duty. While I do not believe that this is exactly fair to Lanson, Dorchain, Croce, Vedel,† and others who have lighted up this or that facet of Corneille's art, still Brasillach's observation was sufficiently true for him to write an original, suggestive, and sympathetic book which very effectively unfreezes Corneille. But it does not, I feel, explain why Corneille needed this thawing out, nor why the warmth of an affectionate bias was necessary to its accomplishment.

For I do not think the condition is entirely accidental. There are some artists who suggest the whole of themselves (though they may never reveal it finally) no matter from what side you take them; others seem to respond satisfactorily only if approached simply and consistently along a restricted line. Although the response of the second kind is naturally as limited as the approach, one is reluctant to attempt any other means of awakening it, for the moment this is done, the voice either fades away or else it multiplies itself into a confusing babble. They are full of contradictions, this second kind, but not as life is full of contradictions: they are split against themselves.

* Cf. Bray, *op.cit.*, and Collas, *Jean Chapelain*, Paris, 1911, but also Fidao-Justiniani, *op.cit.*, pp. 20-21 and 34.
† See bibliography for titles of these works.

They can be very good artists, but perhaps not of the greatest.

Let us see how this applies to Pierre Corneille, for I believe him to be one of the second kind. The more one scrutinizes him the more one is held by a feeling that there is in him somewhere a deep fissure, some kind of gap that never closed. If one looks for what might be called a central fact of Corneille, it is hard to find any that does not itself suggest this lack of fusion, or this lack of clarity. He was during his career a controversial and contradictory figure, and he remains so. For some he represents the surrender of French drama to the supposed absolutism of the classic system. For others he is a kind of Seventeenth Century romantic. We couple him with Racine, and we oppose him to Racine. We compare or contrast him with Shakespeare to raise or to lower him. Official France of 1660 called him the greatest dramatic poet in the world, although he was at that time already becoming outmoded, belonging really to a previous generation. For the Third Republic he was the founder of the French literary drama and the loftiest expression of the national character. But he was also, alas, as Brasillach remarked, a mainstay of the classroom, read because required, and actually produced only by the national theatre, a model of conventional oratory and morality. For some he signifies the French Seventeenth Century, for some he redeems it, and for others he merely clarifies it. Corneille has been made to represent what is most undying and what is most dead in French serious drama.

The reasons for this instability which remains somehow unproductive can be found, I believe, in Corneille's own conception of his work, as it is revealed by his critical writings as well as by his plays. He was one of the most thorough and most analytical critics of his century. This fact may in itself imply the presence of some kind of split in his artistic consciousness. Not that great poets cannot make excellent critics (Dryden, Coleridge, Baudelaire) but because Corneille based his theory and trained his analysis upon his own work almost exclusively.

As one attempts to consider the whole Corneille one is struck with pleasure first by the impression of a rather jovial but at the same time sensible air which runs through the critical works. Corneille speaks as a free man. Secondly one is impressed by the amount of fantasy which resides in the midst of his grandiose evocations of Roman history. I do not mean within the historical plays themselves (though one could make a case for this) but along with them in such pieces as *Médée*, a play of magic, and the two *pièces à machines, Andromède* and *la Toison d'or*, as well as *Clitandre*, a tragicomedy which is pure fancy, and, among the comedies *l'Illusion*, again a play of magic, and *le Menteur*, which is a masterpiece of illusionism. Corneille, we realize, was a man of sense, in a way hardheaded, but one who believed that the drama existed for the delight of the audience.

And quite so, he thought that explicitly tendered wisdom or a form of catharsis could, in a well conceived play, result in a profitable experience for the spectator, but the pleasure of the public was still in his opinion the playwright's first loyalty. Whatever decisions he made with respect to the rules, for instance, he made with this loyalty in mind, and such delicate issues as *vraisemblance* and *bienséance*, while recognized as complex, were resolved with relative ease on the basis of experience and common sense. The playwright had of course to be reasonable where it was possible, and regular where it was convenient, but Corneille never stood much in awe of these principles because he knew that reasonableness and regularity did not always insure dramatic satisfaction. He preferred therefore to avoid whenever he could anything which called attention to such touchy technical issues as the unities of time and place. He regretted having mentioned the passage of time in the *Cid*. In *Clitandre* as well as in *Andromède* he purposely left the place of action vague, while the endings of both the *Cid* and *Sophonisbe* were calculatedly inconclusive because he believed that the audiences could furnish their own, since the excitement was over and their interest required nothing more precise.

Corneille saw his public as an emotional and imaginative partner: he had great faith in its ability and willingness to participate in the creation of its own enjoyment by contributing to a fiction. This amounted to a conscious doctrine on his part regarding believability. The audience could be *made* to believe. It could be dazzled by the brilliance or the excitement of a scene. This had happened in the *Cid*. Scudéry had said so and Balzac had approved of it. This belief of Corneille's may indeed have originated in the Quarrel, for I do not find him expressing it before that time. In any case Aristotle stood behind him, he thought. In the *Au lecteur* of *Sertorius* we read: "Aristote . . . souffre qu'on mette quelquefois des choses sans raison sur le théâtre, quand il y a apparence qu'elles seront bien reçues, et qu'on a lieu d'espérer que les avantages que le poème en tirera pourront mériter cette grâce."[1] If an action simply had to be unbelievable, it was better to let it pass and trust to the interest of the spectators than to give a lame reason for it. The *Examen* of *Horace* says, "L'attachement de l'auditeur à l'action présente souvent ne lui permet pas de descendre à l'examen sévère de cette justesse, et ce n'est pas un crime que de s'en prévaloir pour l'éblouir, quand il est malaisé de le satisfaire."[2] Finally the whole discussion of *vraisemblance* in the *Discours*, while elaborate and legalistic, extends this cavalier attitude to the subject matter and arrives at the same point he had made in the *Au lecteur* of *Héraclius*: "la vraisemblance n'est qu'une condition nécessaire à la disposition et non pas au choix du sujet, ni des incidents qui sont appuyés de l'histoire. Tout ce qui entre dans le poème doit être croyable; et il l'est, selon Aristote, par l'un de ces trois moyens, la vérité, la vraisemblance, ou l'opinion commune. J'irai plus outre; et quoique peut-être on voudra prendre cette proposition pour un paradoxe, je ne craindrai pas d'avancer que le sujet d'une belle tragédie doit n'être pas vraisemblable."[3] I do not know of another critic in the century who had the bold-

ness to draw such a conclusion from the distinction between believability and verisimilitude. But Corneille was
not satisfied with this, and seized upon Aristotle's cou-
pling of probability and necessity to make his own definition of *le nécessaire* which was "le besoin du poète pour
arriver à son but ou pour y faire arriver ses acteurs."[4]
This, if I am not mistaken, is a virtually gratuitous interpretation of Aristotle's meaning, but it served Corneille's
purpose well.

Given this doctrine of what might somewhat clumsily
be termed the relativity of believability, one is tempted
to assert that Corneille thought of drama as some sort of
prestidigitation and not as translated reality. But here
reenters the hardheaded Norman, for if he was a fantasist,
he was also a realist, and sometimes so strict that he
seemed to give the audience credit for no imagination at
all. But this realism was based on experience. He knew
the dangers of obviously mechanical devices. He thought
that mixed meter imitated the cadence of actual conversation better than the Alexandrine, though he feared any
diction that was patently poetic because it came from the
author rather than from the character, and in general he
worked to free his dialogue of conceits and bombast. He
would have liked the time of action to be no longer than
the time of representation and the place no more extended than the stage itself. With respect to subject matter he knew that his comedies were a step in the direction
of social realism: a "style naïf" which represented "la
conversation des honnêtes gens,"[5] and of physical realism
in the case of such as *la Galerie du palais*, where he repeated the shopkeeper scene simply because he knew
that it amused the audience. He believed that the drama
in general aimed at moral realism, at "la naïve peinture
des vices et des vertus,"[6] and finally he saw the distinction between tragedy and comedy as one of *tone* pri-
marily, and saw no reason why unimportant experiences
should not be shown as happening to princes, and important (i.e., tragic) experiences as happening to ordinary men. He thought the traditional distinction by social

or moral status was only a matter of Athenian tyranno-
phobia and a matter of historical bias. Like his contemporaries however he preferred history to legend and liked
to document his serious plays. What satisfied him the
most I think was a balance of faithfulness to history with
richness of invention, such as he thought he achieved in
Pompée or in *Othon*, of which he said, "Le sujet est tiré
de Tacite, qui commence ses Histoires par celle-ci; et je
n'en ai encore mis aucune sur le théâtre à qui j'aie gardé
plus de fidélité, et prêté plus d'invention."[7] For, as he
wrote in the *Abrégé du Martyre de Saint Polyeucte*, "L'in-
génieuse tissure des fictions avec la vérité, où consiste le
plus beau secret de la poésie. . . ."[8]

Now this matter of invention was a serious one for
Corneille, so that whether we think of him as a fantasist
or as a realist, we must think of him as a conscious craftsman, sharply aware of effects, proud of his *artifice* and of
his originality and of the novelty of his product. The very
first of his plays, *Mélite*, however it may have been
marred by provincialism and ignorance (Corneille stoutly
admitted these defects—they emphasized his originality)
had at least this merit of constructive novelty. Or so he
believed when he looked back upon it. And it is certain
that he thought of himself as an innovator satisfying a
hungry public's adventurous taste. *Clitandre, l'Illusion*
(an "étrange monstre"),[9] *Rodogune* (his favorite),
*Héraclius, Don Sanche, Nicomède, Sertorius, Othon,
Agésilas* were all announced by him to be in some way
new or different. Sometimes it seemed hard to keep it up,
and he wrote in the *Au lecteur* of *Nicomède* "Voici une
pièce d'une constitution assez extraordinaire: aussi est-ce
la vingt et unième que j'ai fait voir sur le théâtre; et après
y avoir fait réciter quarante mille vers, il est bien malaisé
de trouver quelque chose de nouveau, sans s'écarter un
peu du grand chemin, et se mettre au hasard de
s'égarer."[10]

So Corneille put a high price on originality and on
virtuosity whether he was reworking old themes like the
Oedipus or the Medea, which needed toning down and

dressing up to suit the modern mode, whether he was embellishing history as in *Sertorius*, where he was forced to create two female characters almost out of whole cloth, or whether he was weaving those two arabesques *Clitandre* and *Héraclius*, so fantastically complicated, said he proudly, that no ordinary spectator could follow them at a first hearing.[11] And in the preface to *Clitandre*, having said, "Il ne faut pas moins d'adresse à réduire un grand sujet qu'à en déduire un petit,"[12] he wanted very badly to nip in the bud any notion that his first success might have been mere beginner's luck: ". . . c'est ce qui ne me tombera jamais en la pensée, qu'une pièce de si longue haleine, où il faut coucher l'esprit à tant de reprises, et s'imprimer tant de contraires mouvements, se puisse faire par aventure. Il n'en va pas de la comédie comme d'un songe qui saisit notre imagination tumultuairement et sans notre aveu, ou comme d'un sonnet ou d'une ode, qu'une chaleur extraordinaire peut pousser par boutade, et sans lever la plume. Aussi l'antiquité nous parle bien de l'écume d'un cheval qu'une éponge jetée par dépit sur un tableau exprima parfaitement, après que l'industrie du peintre n'en avait su venir à bout; mais il ne se lit point que jamais un tableau tout entier ait été produit de cette sorte."[13] The irony of it was that the success of the *Cid* was going to be attributed partly to some extra-rational quality. But then Corneille was certain that he controlled the magic too.

Now we expect this sense of craft in every artist. But it disturbs us if we find it directed more toward the effect than toward the self-justification of the work of art through some independent perfection. For then the word craft takes on a wider and less sure meaning. This appears, in some lights at least, to be what happens in the case of Corneille. His constant watching of the audience, his persistence in having them aware of the novelty and originality of his work, and his respect for *éclat* all suggest a kind of outward consciousness, if I may so describe it, which opposes and neutralizes the inward consciousness normally associated with the poet. It causes one to

wonder just how deeply he was involved either in the
fantasy or in the reality of his drama. It causes one to
wonder indeed if drama had any reality at all for him at
any level except the most superficial and the most ephem-
eral.

But it will surely be argued that Corneille cannot be
denied the category of poet. Here is precisely the difficulty. Obviously I am not going to make out that Corneille is no poet. He is several poets. He is sometimes a
lyric poet, he is sometimes an epic poet, he is sometimes
a satirical poet. He is all of these during the composition
of his plays as much as (and possibly more than) when
he is versifying the *Imitation* or adding flowers to the
Guirlande de Julie. But I should like to suggest that it is
hard to relate Corneille the poet to Corneille the playwright, or for that matter to Corneille the critic. Here
again the interplay of his theory and of his practice can
perhaps be of use to us. To what extent and at what levels did Corneille conceive of his work as poetic, if we
allow the word poetry to range from the level of versification through the level of conception to the level of
creation?

I think that at this point the fissure, the split, in Corneille should begin to appear. And it looks to me as
though it were between his intellectual and his visceral
consciousness of what he was doing.

It is certain Corneille never for a moment doubted that
he was a poet in every sense of the word. He felt it not
only in his work, but he felt it in his personality. The
vanity, for instance, which whetted the Querelle du Cid,
was not only a sort of fashionable hispanism, but it was
"vanité de poète." At the end of the preface to *Clitandre*,
for example, he said ". . . je pense n'avoir rien de commun
avec la plupart des écrivains modernes, qu'un peu de
vanité que je témoigne ici."[14] He kept up this kind of admission throughout his life, tempering it in his later days
with gratitude to God for the talent given him. He did
not seem to think highly of himself as a lyric poet, it is
true, or so he said in the *Au lecteur* to the 1652 edition of

the *Imitation* where he complained of his "peu d'habitude à faire des vers d'ode et de stances."[15] But then his remark in the preface to *Clitandre* about craftsmanship which I quoted earlier leads one to suppose that he ranked those lyric forms as lesser. Of his talent and eminence as a dramatic poet he had certainly no doubt whatever, and no one without this confidence could have criticized himself as freely as he did in the *Examens*. Yet as we know, this criticism bears almost wholly on the technique of play construction and staging. How much thought did he give to the more properly poetic aspects of his drama?

At the level of versification his thought went without question beyond the mere rhyming of dialogue. This is true for the serious plays at any rate. In appraising the finished *Médée* for instance he feared that the passages translated from Seneca were too apparently superior to his own. But he thought that in *Pompée* he had perhaps equaled Lucan, whose *force* and whose *majesté de raisonnement* he greatly admired. As a result *Pompée* appeared to him more *élevé* in its style than its predecessors, especially by the narrations, of which Achorée's in the third act was, he thought "la plus magnifique."[16] In connection with that play he made what I consider to be an informative if not crucial remark. This was in the prefatory epistle to *le Menteur*, which came immediately after *Pompée*. He wrote, "J'ai fait *Pompée* pour satisfaire à ceux qui ne trouvaient pas les vers de *Polyeucte* si puissants que ceux de *Cinna*, et leur montrer que j'en saurais bien trouver la pompe quand le sujet le pourrait souffrir; j'ai fait *le Menteur* pour contenter les souhaits de beaucoup d'autres qui, suivant l'humeur des Français, aiment le changement, et après tant de poèmes graves dont nos meilleures plumes ont enrichi la scène, m'ont demandé quelque chose de plus enjoué qui ne servît qu'à les divertir. Dans le premier j'ai voulu faire essai de ce que pouvait la majesté du raisonnement, et la force des vers dénués de l'agrément du sujet; dans celui-ci j'ai voulu tenter ce que pourrait l'agrément du sujet, dénué de la force des vers."[17] There is here a disquieting tendency to partition the elements of the plays. *La Suite du Menteur* was on the other hand not very successful, in Corneille's opinion, because of the subject matter, though it was "plus remplie de beaux sentiments et de beaux vers."[18]

To return to the serious plays, Corneille deemed the verses of *Horace* more *nets* and less *guindés* than those of the *Cid*, but those of *Cinna* more *achevés* than those of *Horace*.[19]

The case of *Andromède* was special because of the spectacle, but the author still apologized for the "manque de beaux vers."[20] He should however have had more freedom to compose because the meter was mixed. Incidentally he defended this type of verse as well as the use of *stances*, but said, "Je demeure d'accord que c'est quelque espèce de fard; mais puisqu'il embellit notre ouvrage, et nous aide à atteindre le but de notre art, qui est de plaire, pourquoi devons-nous renoncer à cet avantage?"[21] If used, however, they ought to be restricted to complaints and revery and to moments of anxiety and irresolution, but in any case they must never be affected. Corneille thought that the mixed meter of the lines spoken by Paix in the prologue of the *Toison d'Or* had come off very well.

The lines given to Viriate and Aristie in *Sertorius* seemed to Corneille, as he wrote to the Abbé de Pure while he was working on that play, "assez forts et assez nettoyés."[22] And he was well satisfied with the scene in the third act between Sertorius and Pompée where the lines, he decided, were better than those of a similar scene in *Cinna*, because they were "bien aussi forts et plus pointilleux, ce qui aide souvent au théâtre, où les picoteries soutiennent et réveillent l'attention de l'auditeur."[23]

The verses of *Nicomède, Pertharite* (even so) and *Othon* seemed worth mentioning but only to say that they were good.

Now it seems to me that all of the foregoing indicates fairly clearly Corneille's feelings about the kind of verse

he wished to write for his plays and about the place that
verse took in his conception of the drama. First of all I
have the impression that he heard his lines recited by ac-
tors, as exposition or as characterization, as narrative or
as debate more than he heard them or saw them as read
by an individual reader for the sake of their intrinsic
poetic worth. But I shall not insist upon this, for it is true
that in preparing his plays for publication he indicated
several times that the reader existed for him as distinct
from the spectator, and it is also true that he was after
all a playwright.

Secondly I note that the words which he uses to describe those lines he likes the most are such words as
fort, net, achevé, élevé, that *force* and *majesté* describe
equally the verse and the thought behind them, and that
they all suggest oratory and eloquence along with craftsmanship and clarity. They are the words which apply to
those narrative and argumentative passages of which he
was proud and which, to be sure, the public and the critics admired. But they are virtually the only words he
uses, and the remarks which I have mentioned or quoted
almost exhaust his opinions with respect to the verse in
his drama.

There is one more observation however which I should
like to notice. In the *Examen* of *Cinna* Corneille suggested that the play had succeeded because its simple
plot made it unnecessary to load the memory with past
action in order to follow the story, "C'est l'incommodité
des pièces embarrassées, qu'en termes de l'art on nomme
implexes, par un mot emprunté du latin, telles que sont
Rodogune et *Héraclius*. Elle ne se rencontre pas dans les
simples; mais comme celles-là ont sans doute besoin de
plus d'esprit pour les imaginer, et de plus d'art pour les
conduire, celles-ci, n'ayant pas le même secours du côté
du sujet, demandent plus de force de vers, de raisonnement, et de sentiments pour les soutenir."[24] This remark
like the one about *Pompée* and *le Menteur* tends to partition the dramatic elements and their functions as well,
and leads one to suspect that there existed in Corneille's

mind a separation of verse (i.e. diction) from subject
matter (i.e. plot or action), and that for him the real task
was to invent, construct, and assemble machines for
pleasing which must then be decorated and colored with
verse. The decoration must be exciting in itself of course,
but it must not on the one hand interfere with the proper
internal working of the machine, as did the *stances in-
excusables*[25] of the *Cid*, and on the other hand its function must frequently be to cover up weaknesses in the
machine as did the narration of Achorée in *Pompée*.
Nothing that Corneille says elsewhere about his verse
seems to contradict this suspicion, and the studies of
Crétin* on Corneille's imagery and metaphor rather confirm it. The poet as organizer of language seems here to
be not completely one with the craftsman as organizer of
exciting activity. There is only a working agreement between them. In the long run, I think, Corneille, perhaps
without quite realizing it, depended more on *esprit* and
art than on "force de vers, de raisonnement et de sentiments."

But this same statement about *Cinna* has still more to
tell us, for it allows us now to pass from the plane of
verse to the plane of ideas. The tendency of the statement
is not only to separate verse or diction from subject matter, but perhaps even more it tends to separate "force de
raisonnement et de sentiments" from *esprit* and *art*, suggesting that skill and intelligence have to do with plot
manipulation, with the choice and order of scenes and
with the contrivance of situations, apart from the organization and presentation of any set of ideas. And remembering his appraisal of his verse elsewhere, one would
guess that he thought of ideas in terms of dialogue in
single scenes and not in terms of the whole play, and that
he certainly was not preoccupied with the interpretation
of any coherent philosophy or morality. In short we may
not expect to get at the poetry of Corneille's drama by
way of its underlying concepts.

* See bibliography.

This I grant needs some argument, for I believe no dramatist has ever been as neatly abstracted and classified according to concepts as Corneille. Honor duty love passion reason will, the words the characters and the plays fall into line. We used to learn that the *Cid* represented duty to family, *Horace* duty to state, *Cinna* duty to monarch, and *Polyeucte* duty to God. (What duties all the other plays represented I never learned because at that time we read no further, and anyway there was nowhere left to go.) Furthermore nothing is easier than to see in Corneille the exemplification of a philosophical system. One used to speak of his stoicism, or his solipsism or his vitalism, all to be sure with some justification. Finally I hope it is unnecessary to add that there are of course ideas *in* Corneille. The problem is, what importance did he attach to them, where do they stand in relation to the whole of his drama, and to what extent do they render it poetic?

If we look to Corneille's own assertions on the matter, the plain fact is that we find very little on which to base anything positive. But we do find enough to disclose a sense of serious content. He thought of himself as presenting "des vertus morales et politiques" and "quelques-unes même des chrétiennes."[26] There is a suggestion in the dedication of *Pompée* that he was recreating "la mauvaise politique de l'Egypte."[27] In *Nicomède* he wanted to show a "grandeur de courage . . . combattue par la politique,"[28] and he said also as we know, "Mon but principal a été de peindre la politique des Romains au dehors, et comme ils agissaient impérieusement avec les rois leurs alliés. . . ."[29] And in *Attila* he wished to "opposer la France naissante au déclin de l'Empire."[30]

This is about all. He was dramatizing history, accurately as to retained fact, faithfully, he hoped, as to invention. But we find no theory of history, no theory of society, no theory of life. We are far from the ringing proclamations and sober meditations of the preface to *Cromwell* or *Racine et Shakespeare* or the introduction to the *Comédie Humaine*, where you will find all these

theories, for better or for worse, with theories of literature to match. There is no suggestion in Corneille that
his depiction of moral, political, and religious virtues
owed anything to his independent thought. As for religion, he said of himself in the *Au lecteur* of the *Imitation*
"peu de connaissance de la théologie, peu de pratique des
sentiments de dévotion."[31] He repeated this in the *Au
lecteur* of the *Louanges de la Sainte Vierge*, but added
"et ce n'est pas sans beaucoup de confusion que je me
sens un esprit si fécond pour les choses du monde, et si
stérile pour celles de Dieu."[32] There is a certain irony in
this last, considering that *Polyeucte* is his best play. But
Rodogune was his favorite, and besides, the *Imitation*
had given him endless trouble. I think the explanation
may be that he did not consider himself engaged in any
religious ideology when he wrote *Polyeucte*. "Ce n'est
qu'une pièce de théâtre,"[33] he said in the dedication. No
more I believe did he consider himself involved in any
theory of history when he was writing *Pompée* or *Attila*.
But it is obvious that he felt no lack in himself for all
that. "Les choses du monde" means the actions of men
and their motives. But the world he chose to depict required no analysis. It asked only to be described. Or I
should go even further and say it asked only to be uti-
lized.

Now I realize that much of what I have used here as
"evidence" can be explained by reference to Corneille's
modesty or by simple conventional practice. But the point
is that we have nothing else to go on, except in the domain of dramatic theory. In this domain however Corneille's attitude is analogous to the one reflected in the
preceding passages. Alfred de Vigny, we remember,
thought of a dramatic production as a machine whose
motion generated an idea which, once communicated by
the play, continued to recreate itself after the machine
had run down.[34] Corneille, I am certain, imagined no
such virtue in his drama. I have already referred to his
opinion regarding the utility of drama. He even doubted
the real operation of catharsis (which he understood

simply as the purging of desire to yield to the passions through the witnessing of a disagreeable example) and he doubted any real moral effect, except very late in his career. No wonder then at his distaste for the *sentence* and his fear of generalization. He remarked that he would always rather have an actor (he wrote "acteur"; it is sometimes hard to distinguish in him the difference between *acteur* and *personnage*) say "l'amour vous donne beaucoup d'inquiétudes" than "l'amour donne beaucoup d'inquiétudes aux esprits qu'il possède." He hastened to admit that if his works were stripped of all such generalizations they would be "bien estropiés."[35] He admitted also that generalities could be expressed with beauty, but he warned that they should be as often as possible reduced to the specific, and that they should be uttered only in moments of calm.

My point is that Corneille on the one hand wished his plays to be taken seriously, as we should certainly expect, but that on the other the element of *thought* was in his mind subordinate, whether considered as dramatized through symbols or as generated by the events of the story. Thought stands to the whole play in somewhat the same relation as verse. It embellishes the presentation, but it must not be allowed to interfere with it. Expressed ideas may indicate character, but your character is no more a rhetorician than he is a poet. He is in the literal sense of the word an actor. It is not therefore in the realm of ideas communicated explicitly or implicitly that I should look for the poetry in Corneille. Ideas, in other words, did not excite him.

How then do the plays seem to reflect something that looks like a philosophy? There is no answer to this question in Corneille's own words. Indeed it is part of my argument that he would have no answer. However one can attempt to answer for him. With the memory of his Jesuit education or from the atmosphere of the 1620's (the source makes little difference) Corneille retained certain notions of stoicism which allied themselves quite naturally with the Senecan and the Spanish drama so ad-

mired by him as by his contemporaries. They were relatively simple notions: self-consciousness, self-domination,
personal integrity through the victory of the rational will
over the passions. They were sympathetic to him, and he
knew they were sympathetic to his audience. I am probably revealing a bias when I suspect the latter reason to
have been the stronger, but I cannot think he cared
deeply about stoicism. He saw in it or took from it, along
with the characters he chose to present, those aspects
which provided a formula. The formula might read Will
(plus Reason minus Passions) equals Personal Integrity.
It is a false formula, but I am sure this never disturbed
Corneille if it ever occurred to him. It was dramatically
true: "lorsqu'on agit à visage découvert, et qu'on sait à
qui on en veut, le combat des passions contre la nature, ou
du devoir contre l'amour, occupe la meilleure partie du
poème; et de là naissent les grandes et fortes émotions qui
renouvellent à tous moments et redoublent la commisération."[36] Self-consciousness and struggle, but never any
critical examination of the formula either implied by the
play or undertaken by those who are attempting to live
it. It is never really an issue. Its significance is instrumental.

Nevertheless I would not deny that the individualism
inherent in at least one part of the stoic view appealed to
Corneille as a man and as a dramatist. He was impressed
by all manifestations of greatness, or rather strength, of
character. It is through the characters that the ideas penetrate the plays, and it was characters more than ideas
which interested Corneille and represented to him something exciting, expansive, poetic. But we shall have to be
careful again here because it is precisely at this point that
Corneille splits apart most deeply.

He looked at his subject matter first of all, I imagine, in
terms of characters. We may disregard the fact that his
serious plays have proper names for titles. This was common practice, and can moreover be misleading, since
such titles do not always tell us who is the central character. But his manner of introducing his plays shows what

he thought of them. The *Cid* is a "portrait vivant d'un héros."[37] *Horace* is "ce mauvais portrait d'Horace."[38] *Cinna* is a "tableau d'une des plus belles actions d'Auguste."[39] And later on in his career we find him insisting upon the historical accuracy of his *caractères*, so that the brief notes for the last two plays have to do only with the *caractères* of Pulchérie and Suréna.

He saw himself as recreating historical figures. In the sonnet to Campion, the author of *Hommes illustres*, he declared himself outdone, even though

J'ai quelque art d'arracher les grands noms du tom-
    beau,
De leur rendre un destin plus durable et plus beau,
De faire qu'après moi l'avenir s'en souvienne.[40]

This claim to disinterment and preservation is most enthusiastically expressed in the call to Foucquet which accompanied *Oedipe*:

Je sens le même feu, je sens la même audace,
Qui fit plaindre le Cid, qui fit combattre Horace;
Et je me trouve encor la main qui crayonna
L'âme du grand Pompée et l'esprit de Cinna.
Choisis-moi seulement quelque nom dans l'histoire
Pour qui tu veuilles place au temple de la Gloire,
Quelque nom favori qu'il te plaise arracher
A la nuit de la tombe, aux cendres du bûcher,
Soit qu'il faille ternir ceux d'Enée et d'Achille
Par un noble attentat sur Homère et Virgile,
Soit qu'il faille obscurcir par un dernier effort
Ceux que j'ai sur la scène affranchis de la mort.[41]

If Corneille's approach to his subject then was through individual figures, what determined their choice? Here he is very explicit. His conception of dramatic character seems to have been formed at the time he chose to treat Medea, whose immorality appeared to require some justification. Corneille's plea for her was purely on aesthetic grounds. "Ici vous trouverez le crime en son char de triomphe" but "dans la poésie, il ne faut pas considérer

si les moeurs sont vertueuses, mais si elles sont pareilles
à celles de la personne qu'on introduit." And with regard
to Medea's actions: "Je n'examine point si elles sont vrai-
semblables ou non . . . il me suffit qu'elles sont autorisées
ou par la vérité de l'histoire, ou par l'opinion commune
des anciens."[42]

This defense formed the basis for the conception of
character outlined in the *Discours* where Corneille, in
discussing the ever-difficult question of what Aristotle
means by good character, took it to be "le caractère brillant et élevé d'une habitude vertueuse ou criminelle,
selon qu'elle est propre et convenable à la personne qu'on
introduit." And he went on to say that Cléopâtre in
Rodogune was a criminal but that all her crimes were accompanied by a "grandeur d'âme qui a quelque chose de
si haut, qu'en même temps qu'on déteste ses actions, on
admire la source dont elles partent." The same was true
of Dorante in *le Menteur*, and spectators, said Corneille,
were forced to confess that "le talent de mentir ainsi est
un vice dont les sots ne sont point capables."[43]

The conception of character in turn was the basis for
Corneille's addition of *admiration* to the classic pity and
fear, as a "tragic" emotion. By this he meant pleased contemplation or what we should call in English admiration,
rather than wonder. But I doubt if it is necessary to make
any such distinction, for it is clear that to Corneille it was
a matter of an exciting dimension, of something bigger
than reality. It was this which he saw in Medea, and from
that time on he was to choose characters who were exciting, extraordinary, *invraisemblants*.

But it is here that we get into difficulties. The dimension is attained only by the simple extension of active or
passive force, of aggression or resistance. It is never revealed by intensive analysis. One is again troubled by
Corneille's outwardness. The same of course holds true
for the characters themselves. Their consciousness is all
directed toward combatting the disintegrating forces
which are attacking them from the outside. They are sub-
jected to a series of tests which they meet knowingly, that

is, with awareness of their danger. But these situations never cause them to ask any questions. They make only assertions or denials. Pauline fears Polyeucte's meeting with Sévère more than she does her own: "Ce n'est pas le succès que mon âme redoute."[44] Exception must be made no doubt for such as Félix and Prusias, but they are precisely the weak ones, the secondary human beings. The result of all this is that the creation of the dimension is dependent upon the complicated and extraordinary nature of the situation: what is given them to conquer, overcome, or resist. That they must conquer themselves is talked about a good deal, but the outcome of this is essentially taken for granted. The real conflict arises from the magnitude of the responsibility, assumed by such characters as Médée or Cléopâtre or Attila, imposed upon such as Rodrigue, Pauline, Nicomède or Sertorius.

Thus Corneille with one part of his mind wanted to recreate historical figures which would be portraits pleasing in their reality, with another he chose characters who would contribute an element of *invraisemblance* in a complex of *invraisemblance*. If he was attracted by outstanding personalities he was not interested in personality itself.

Yet he was probably unaware of any such limitation. Here for instance is the beginning of his acceptance speech to the Academy. It is a long period which I shall quote in full because I think it is amusing as well as enlightening: "S'il est vrai que ce soit un avantage, pour dépeindre les passions, que de les ressentir, et que l'esprit trouve avec plus de facilité des couleurs pour ce qui le touche que pour les idées qu'il emprunte de son imagination, j'avoue qu'il faut que je condamne tous les applaudissements qu'ont reçus jusqu'ici mes ouvrages, et que c'est injustement qu'on m'attribue quelque adresse à décrire les mouvements de l'âme, puisque dans la joie la plus sensible dont je sois capable, je ne trouve point de paroles qui vous en puissent faire concevoir la moindre partie."[45] After this opening chord, he goes on after all to describe the emotion of joy and its effects, but this is only to show that he can extricate himself from the peril in which he has supposed himself, by demonstrating that he should be pardoned because joy is *really* indescribable. The discourse is in a way an adumbration of Corneille's work. It is an exercise in virtuosity, an element of which has been the description of a "mouvement de l'âme," in an artificially created situation.

As a man of letters, Corneille certainly thought about and worked at the various elements of drama which we have been considering. I mean verse, ideas, character, and the rest. And I am far from suggesting that he was never successful in dealing with them. But I believe that as an artist with a set of feelings, or a heart, if you will, he did not care about any of them separately. As I have said several times, his favorite play was *Rodogune*, at the time of the *Examens* at least. We do not revere it especially for its verse, or its thought, or its characterization, which does not however keep it from being an exciting play. Here is what Corneille said of it: "Cette préférence est peut-être en moi un effet de ces inclinations aveugles qu'ont beaucoup de pères pour quelques-uns de leurs enfants plus que pour les autres; peut-être y entre-t-il un peu d'amour propre, en ce que cette tragédie me semble être un peu plus à moi que celles qui l'ont précédée, à cause des incidents surprenants qui sont purement de mon invention, et n'avaient jamais été vus au théâtre: et peut-être enfin y a-t-il un peu de vrai mérite qui fait que cette inclination n'est pas tout à fait injuste. Je veux bien laisser chacun en liberté de ses sentiments, mais certainement on peut dire que mes autres pièces ont peu d'avantages qui ne se rencontrent en celle-ci: elle a tout ensemble la beauté du sujet, la nouveauté des fictions, la force des vers, la facilité de l'expression, la solidité du raisonnement, la chaleur des passions, les tendresses de l'amour et de l'amitié; et cet heureux assemblage est ménagé de sorte qu'elle s'élève d'acte en acte. . . ."[46]

He was perhaps a little ashamed of his preference, but with characteristic independence he expressed it and explained it. What he is really saying is that basically his artistic consciousness, his affective self was stimulated most powerfully by the possibility of the "heureux assemblage," of combining, of weaving together elements of the true with elements of the fantastic and preposterous into a completely unreal, incredible but dazzling and convincing illusion. That is certainly what *Rodogune* is.

A final result of Corneille's way of conceiving the drama is that his material seldom achieves any independence, for his greatest satisfaction was in its control. This holds for the whole of it, but it is especially noticeable in the characters. They belong to history or to him, and almost never to themselves. In his discussion of them one is scarcely ever aware that they have any reality for him off the printed page or off the stage. One might make exceptions for Chimène, Rodogune, Massinisse, and a few others, but for the most part they remain material to be used, for which he shares with history the proud responsibility. But is it not true that in order to exist, a literary character must have room in which to move, to turn around and to grow? If he lacks this freedom it is understandable that his author in turn will always wear the same face, the one he has imagined for himself.

This is why I believe that if we try to understand Corneille at the level of character or ideas we shall never understand him very fully or at all variously. On the other hand I realize the difficulty of constantly stripping all the elements of their reality in order to understand him at the level of craftsmanship and illusionism. If it is at all possible, I am not sure that it is in the highest degree rewarding. But it is at this level that his extensive and his intensive powers meet.

It may be that his so competent criticism and the whole attitude reflected by it were possible because of the fissure of which I have been speaking. There is in him a lack of deep commitment which has its very interesting and sympathetic side, for it turns him into what we should probably call a liberal. It would be unfair to Corneille if we did not give him an opportunity, as it were, to explain his critical position. If we understand it together with his conception of the drama, we shall have something like a clear notion of his place in the hall of classicism.

I have said that he was a liberal. This could certainly mean that he was an individualist. I quoted earlier the passage where he said he thought himself to have nothing in common with his fellow writers except vanity. But it means more than this rather youthful conception. It means that he held, for himself as well as for others, to a more or less relativistic standard. He was not a radical, but he was satisfied with his own experience for guide. He was therefore a moderate and a pragmatist. In the dedicatory epistle to *la Suivante* he declared his independence: "Chacun a sa méthode; je ne blâme point celle des autres, et me tiens à la mienne: jusques à présent je m'en suis trouvé fort bien; j'en chercherai une meilleure quand je commencerai à m'en trouver mal. . . . Les jugements sont libres en ces matières, et les goûts divers."[47] And in the *Au lecteur* to *Héraclius* we read "Aussi ne donné-je ici mes opinions qu'à la mode de M. de Montagne, non pour bonnes, mais pour miennes. Je m'en suis bien trouvé jusqu'à présent; mais je ne tiens pas impossible qu'on réussisse mieux en suivant les contraires."[48] And by the time of the *Discours* he is still saying, as he does in the conclusion to the last of them, "Quoi qu'il en soit, voilà mes opinions, ou si vous voulez, mes hérésies touchant les principaux points de l'art; et je ne sais point mieux accorder les règles anciennes avec les agréments modernes. Je ne doute point qu'il ne soit aisé d'en trouver de meilleurs moyens, et je serai tout prêt de les suivre lorsqu'on les aura mis en pratique aussi heureusement qu'on y a vu les miens."[49]

As the above passage suggests, this liberalism meant also a certain freedom from tradition. In the preface to *Clitandre* he had said, "Je me donne ici quelque sorte de liberté de choquer les anciens, d'autant qu'ils ne sont plus en état de me répondre, et que je ne veux engager personne en la recherche de mes défauts. Puisque les sciences et les arts ne sont jamais à leur période, il m'est permis de croire qu'ils n'ont pas tout su, et que de leurs instructions on peut tirer des lumières qu'ils n'ont pas eues. Je leur porte du respect comme à des gens qui nous ont frayé le chemin, et qui après avoir défriché un pays fort rude, nous ont laissé à le cultiver."[50] And I hope it is unnecessary to repeat that he thought of himself as a pioneer, so that still, near the end of his career, he could say of *Agésilas*, "La manière dont je l'ai traitée n'a point d'exemple parmis nos Français, ni dans les précieux restes de l'antiquité. . . . Les premiers qui ont travaillé pour le théâtre, ont travaillé sans exemple, et ceux qui les ont suivis y ont fait voir quelques nouveautés de temps en temps. Nous n'avons pas moins de privilège." He quoted Horace in praise of the Romans who took other paths than the Greeks, and continued: "Leurs règles sont bonnes; mais leur méthode n'est pas de notre siècle; et qui s'attacherait à ne marcher que sur leurs pas, ferait sans doute peu de progrès, et divertirait mal son auditoire."[51] This passage I have quoted at some length because it combines Corneille's modernism with his pragmatism and also suggests that he was quite willing to make use of ancient (and recent) authority when it seemed practical.

His liberalism implies also a certain freedom from the rules. And here again the pragmatism makes itself felt. His method was from the beginning one of compromise. In the *Au lecteur* of *la Veuve* he explained how he had decided that the unity of time could be interpreted so that his play of five acts took five days, and he observed that of the six plays he had written up to that time three had followed the unities and three had not. He judged this enough. But his compromise and his independence and his practicality all were expressed more vigorously in the dedication of *la Suivante* which, as we have seen, was a veritable manifesto; but it was for himself alone: this is not the century of schools and programs. In this letter he said, "J'aime à suivre les règles; mais loin de me rendre leur esclave, je les élargis et resserre selon le besoin qu'en a mon sujet, et je romps même sans scrupule celle qui regarde la durée de l'action, quand sa sévérité me semble absolument incompatible avec les beautés des événements que je décris. . . . Cependant mon avis est celui de Térence: puisque nous faisons des poèmes pour être représentés, notre premier but doit être de plaire à la cour et au peuple, et d'attirer un grand monde à leurs représentations. Il faut s'il se peut, y ajouter les règles, afin de ne déplaire pas aux savants, et recevoir un applaudissement universel; mais surtout gagnons la voix publique; autrement notre pièce aura beau être régulière, si elle est sifflée au théâtre, les savants n'oseront se déclarer en notre faveur, et aimerons mieux dire que nous aurons mal entendu les règles, que de nous donner des louanges quand nous serons decriés par le consentement général de ceux qui ne voient la comédie que pour se divertir."[52]

About ten years later he repeated this opinion in the avertissement to the *recueil* of 1648 where he said of the unity of time, "Je crois que nous devons toujours faire notre possible en sa faveur, jusqu'à forcer un peu les événements que nous traitons, pour les y accomoder; mais si je n'en pouvais venir à bout, je la négligerais même sans scrupule, et ne voudrais pas perdre un beau sujet pour ne l'y pouvoir réduire."[53] It is the public that counts; it is the *beau sujet* that counts. But he has no special animus against the rules or the idea of rules, or against Aristotle. Let those who will quarrel over these points. At the conclusion of the first *Discours* he writes, "J'écris sans ambition et sans esprit de contestation, je l'ai déjà dit. Je tâche de suivre toujours le sentiment d'Aristote dans les matières qu'il a traitées; et comme peut-être je l'entends à ma mode, je ne suis point jaloux qu'un autre l'entende à la sienne. Le commentaire dont je m'y sers le plus est l'expérience du théâtre et les réflexions sur ce que j'ai vu y plaire ou déplaire." Again the independence and the pragmatism and the moderation. The individualism comes out with special sharpness a few lines further on when he says "J'ajoute à ces trois *Discours* généraux l'examen de chacun de mes poèmes en particulier, afin de voir en quoi ils s'écartent ou se conforment aux règles que j'établis."[54] It must have given him a particular satisfaction to write those words almost a quarter of a century after the quarrel of the *Cid*. Now he was the artist, the critic, the judge, and the legislator all rolled into one.

I shall not go into the detail of these very interesting and readable *Discours*. But I should like to point out that they represent the greatest attempt at mediation of the century. They are a document of the highest legalism. Corneille recognized that laws must be reinterpreted to meet changed conditions. He realized that they must be interpreted in the spirit and not in the letter, because they are framed by human beings at various stages of a civilization which changes, and because they are applied to an activity whose instrumental values change with the times and whose ultimate value cannot be stated in absolute terms. Corneille feared the absolute, and perhaps in the long run he saw tradition and precept not as a code of law but as a body of opinion.

Now this fear found itself inevitably involved in the problem of perfection. In the *Discours de la tragédie*, for instance, he discussed two conditions for the excitement of pity and terror: (1) the use of a single protagonist (the tragic hero), and (2) the exploitation of close personal relationships between protagonist and antagonist, between patient and agent. Perfection in tragedy, he said, might consist in adhering to these two conditions, but neither of them is "d'une nécessité absolue." He saw immediately the difficulty in this distinction, and tried to meet it: "Quand je dis que ces deux conditions ne sont que pour les tragédies parfaites, je n'entends pas dire que celles où elles ne se rencontrent pas soient imparfaites: ce serait les rendre d'une nécessité absolue, et me contredire moi-même. Mais par ce mot de tragédies parfaites j'entends celles du genre le plus sublime et le plus touchant, en sorte que celles qui manquent de l'une de ces deux conditions, ou de toutes les deux, pourvu qu'elles soient régulières à cela près, ne laissent pas d'être parfaites en leur genre, bien qu'elles demeurent dans un rang moins élevé, et n'approchent pas de la beauté des autres, si elles n'en empruntent de la pompe des vers, ou de la magnificence du spectacle, ou de quelque autre agrément qui vienne d'ailleurs que du sujet."[55]

I do not pretend to understand this except as a manipulation of words in the face of an impossible problem. Is it not the liberal who distrusts perfectionism as he fears absolutism? And would one expect him to be a perfect dialectician? Or is "tragédie parfaite" *true* tragedy?

At any rate what Corneille is doing (and what he does all through the *Discours*) is mediating between accepted theory and modern (his own) experience. He affirms this explicitly in the course of the discussion to which I have just referred when he says, "Cela posé, trouvons quelque modération à la rigueur de ces règles du philosophe [Aristotle, of course, who was no playwright], ou du moins quelque favorable interprétation, pour n'être pas obligés de condamner beaucoup de poèmes que nous avons vus réussir sur nos théâtres."[56] And he affirms it in the conclusion to the last *Discours* when he says, as I have already noted, "Je ne sais point mieux accorder les règles anciennes avec les agréments modernes."

He carried out this mediation in his practice as well, for in trying to satisfy the savants along with the public (Court and popular) taste, he produced a combination which was externally one of erudition and theatricality, of high oratorical seriousness and melodrama, but also one of fantasy and realism, and which was internally one of morality and brutality, of self-control and egoism, of *politesse* and intrigue. But however many lines or planes this mediation might follow, Corneille's drama, it seems to me, is still a combination, an *heureux assemblage*. Thus his situations, his heroes and his philosophy all appear to require quotation marks around them. There is perhaps nothing surprising about this, considering his devotion to *invraisemblance*. It is the effect of his never yielding to his material. Just as his characters seemed to have little reality for him, so his whole drama seemed unreal, and never engaged his whole poetic being except, as I have said, at the level of the combination. This is why one ought always to speak not of Corneille's tragedy, but of his pseudo-tragedy.

He himself spoke of his *tragédies* however, and as far as I can make out he was never aware that he was not creating a modern counterpart of Greek tragedy. If this had not been so, it would probably be unnecessary to take up the question. It is really unfair to demand that Corneille or anyone else write true tragedy, and we can appreciate him more justly if we do not look for it in his plays, some of which are excellent drama. To be sure, if we are going to judge all serious drama by the standards of Sophocles and Shakespeare many fine dramatists will appear deficient. But the fact remains that Corneille (he may himself have unconsciously felt this) lacked the tragic sense. What I have already said about his practice may have pointed to this lack. In his criticism it becomes quite obvious. He misunderstood entirely the antique drama which he was trying, with his liberalism and his pragmatism, to modernize. He never, for instance caught the significance of recognition, which he called an "ornement." It did not occur to him that it might represent the sudden awful revelation of what we are. Likewise, the tragic hero escaped him altogether. To him the hero was simply any superior individual in a dangerous and important situation as agent or patient, who could be as wholly good as Polyeucte or as wholly bad as Cléopâtre. The symbolism of the Greek conception was therefore quite lost to him. The fantastic paradox of determinism and responsibility, the interplay of divine creativity and animal destructiveness which we commonly regard as the condition of humanity, none of this seems ever to have impressed itself upon his artistic or his critical consciousness.

If there is any irony in Corneille then, it is not tragic. His irony is the irony of the immediate situation, where normal everyday human values are upset, where the forces of vitality are at play and reign for their own sake, but where nothing more is involved than ethical values. Tragic irony, it seems to me, must transcend this purely human plane and engage the metaphysical, with all the resulting incongruity and mystery. One is of course immediately tempted to say that Corneille's irony is essentially comic. In fairness to him I should say that if he seems to have been pulled more and more back to the processes of comedy after he had abandoned the form, he was not altogether unaware of the tendency, for his last two plays but one are called *comédies héroïques.* Basically I do believe he never left the comic plane, and it is not astonishing that he was able to conceive in theory the genre of the *drame*, that is, the serious play about ordinary people.* His *tragédies* are of course serious in tone, because ethical problems are worth respectful contemplation, but this plane of ethics was passed successfully in only one of them. This was in *Polyeucte,* and it is widely considered his masterpiece. It is the one play where, as I see it, the edge is not taken off the interest by doubt as to the reality of the problem and as to the means of its solution. All the elements work together in harmony toward an end which, consciously or not, we regard as valid or at least as respectable. Here then Corneille's fantasy meets with the miraculous and the most incredible becomes the most credible. But this is the last of the major serious works, and it is still untragic, perhaps because of the very harmony which informs it.

This play *Polyeucte* provides a nexus for the explanation, if one is needed, of Corneille's non-tragic character. We might say, to be sure, that the times were not ripe, or that modern public taste never really demands tragedy, or that stoicism is naturally untragic, and this may all be true, but I think one answer at least lies in Corneille's religious consciousness. Quietly, without dramatic conversion or critical mystic experience he was probably the most consistently devout of all the Grands Classiques.

* In the discourse on *tragédie.* See above, pp. 50-51.

He was active in his parish, he read his breviary every day, and he worked slowly at the translation of the *Imitation* and other devotional works. He seems to have rejoiced in a calm faith which left his mind secure in the absolute reality of the other world. But this very security, I should think, would work against the possibility of a tragic sense, for it would tend to keep the metaphysical world quite separate from "les choses de ce monde," that is, from the ethical world. So that no matter how well Corneille thought he knew this ethical world, it would remain without depth and, I suspect, without reality and so without ultimate importance. Now Corneille could write his best play about this very theme and as it were transcend himself. But I do not see how he could write a tragedy when there was apparently so little doubt in his mind about the order of the universe. Tragedy, unless I am mistaken, requires some sense of something unexplained, unfinished, cosmically disquieting even if ultimately believed to be just. There must be present some intuition of evil which at times carries up into the source of good and renders imperfect a nonetheless deeply felt relationship between the metaphysical and the ethical world. I see nothing of this in Corneille. His metaphysics and his ethics, like Descartes',* remain unrelated unless, as in the case of *Polyeucte*, they are in *total* harmony.

If this is true, one has a right then to ask where Corneille's religious verse stands, and in particular where the *Imitation* stands in relation to his temperament. I confess I find the question of his religious verse a puzzling one. In the first place he had extreme difficulty with the *Imitation*. The technical problem was almost insoluble. The repetitions, the lack of continuity, the homely terms all gave him so much trouble that he found it impossible to work at it without frequent periods of rest. But this did not keep his translation from being an impressive achievement, where the tone and incantatory spirit of the origi-

* See J. Maritain, *The Dream of Descartes*, N.Y., Philosophical Library, 1944.

74

nal shine through an incredible variety of verse patterns
worked out with a relatively limited vocabulary.

Yet one cannot help wondering again what his feeling
was about the poetry of the original material. He seemed
to have understood the necessity of retaining its simplicity. But I think he regarded this as an obstacle rather
than an advantage, and was moved by considerations of
piety rather than beauty. Once more he spoke as though
"l'agréable" were something to be laid on like color, and
one begins to understand that he did not think of beauty
as inherent in subject matter, as coming from the inside,
but instead as the result of application and extension. "Ce
n'est pas que je ne sache bien que l'utile a besoin de
l'agréable pour s'insinuer dans l'amitié des hommes; mais
j'ai cru qu'il ne fallait pas l'étouffer sous des enrichisse-
ments, ni lui donner des lumières qui éblouissent au lieu
d'éclairer. Il est juste de lui prêter quelques grâces, mais
de celles qui lui laissent toute sa force . . . et l'accom-
pagnent sans le dérober à la vue."[57] Here at least was a
body of matter for which he had some respect. He could
not treat it as he had the material for his drama. Unfortunately it lay so completely in the domain of the metaphysical that his approach to it was bound to be less than
poetic. Underneath all the versification therefore lay the
fact that "ces matières ont si peu de disposition à s'accommoder avec notre poésie, qu'elles me lassent incontinent et m'obligent à me reposer plus souvent que je ne
voudrais."*

But if the approach was different, the process was
similar. It was one of extension. It was determined for
one thing by the necessity of rendering each separate
thought of the original in a developed stanza of some sort.
I will illustrate what I mean by taking the very first sentence of the *Imitation*, which in the Latin is "Qui sequitur
me, non ambulat in tenebris, dicit Dominus," Corneille
writes:

* *Oeuvres, ed.cit.*, VIII, 23; for Corneille's general opinion concerning verse renderings of sacred matter, see his letter to Voyer
d'Argenson, *Oeuvres*, X, 444ff.

"Heureux qui tient la route où ma voix le convie,
Les ténèbres jamais n'approchent qui me suit,
Et partout sur mes pas il trouve un jour sans nuit
Qui porte jusqu'au coeur la lumière de vie."[58]

An earlier variant made it into a *dizain*, which is the unit of the first chapter, each paragraph of the original calling for a ten-line stanza regardless of its length in the Latin, so that the original, "Ista est summa sapientia, per contemptum mundi tendere ad regna coelestia," becomes a ten-line stanza precisely as does the paragraph following, which is much longer. Throughout the whole the ten-line stanza is the maximum formal unit and is reserved for those chapters where the paragraphs are generally long. Each chapter is committed to a single form except where there is dialogue, and here the form shifts with the person speaking, or where the Alexandrine couplet is used, and here the stanza form is abandoned, the lines being broken up unevenly according to the thought of the original. But even here the four-line group is almost exclusively the minimum, although I shall mention one separate couplet, from a dialogue,

A ces mots, tout saisi d'un transport extatique,
Ma joie et mon amour te diront pour réplique:[59]
etc.

The original of this is "Et dixi."
Occasionally the conception of the original gives the translation a certain grandeur, but Corneille must always elaborate it. So that "O pondus immensum! o pelagus intransnatabile, ubi nihil de me reperio quam in toto nihil!" becomes,

O néant! o vrai rien! mais pesanteur extrême,
Mais charge insupportable à qui veut s'élever!
Mer sans rive où partout chacun se peut trouver,
Mais sans trouver partout qu'un néant en soi-même![60]

The notion of weight is twice expressed and once explained (by "à qui veut s'élever"). The compression obtained by the presence of *nihil* twice in the same phrase, ending with the second one, is lost by dividing the *néant* between the beginning and the end of the whole stanza, though there is an attempt at compensation for this by the repetition and inversion of "partout" and "trouver." But the point is missed. One set of words cannot substitute for another merely by being used in a similar fashion. The possibilities of the fine *intransnatabile* are neglected, being at best split up between "charge insupportable" and "mer sans rive," so that the image is blurred if not completely effaced. Finally the cry of the first person is eliminated, the sense being carried over from the preceding stanza. All of these alterations lose the intensity of the original: the thought is stretched out and the expression distended in the service of some greater dignity. This in spite of Corneille's wish to retain the simplicity of the Latin.

The same could be said of the *Louanges de la Sainte Vierge*, the *Office de la Sainte Vierge*, the *Sept Psaumes Pénitentiaux*, the *Vêpres des Dimanches et Complies*, and the various hymns which he put into French verse. Here however the problem was somewhat different since most of this was in verse to begin with, or in a poetic form at least. But note his remark about the *Louanges* in connection with the question of authorship: "Elle n'a pas l'élévation d'un docteur de l'Église; mais elle a la simplicité d'un saint, et sent assez le zèle de son siècle, où, dans les hymnes, proses et autres compositions pieuses que l'on faisait en latin, on recherchait davantage les heureuses cadences de la rime que la justesse de la pensée. L'auteur de celle-ci a voulu trouver l'image de la Vierge en beaucoup de figures du Vieil et Nouveau Testament: les applications qu'il en a faites sont quelquefois un peu forcées; et quelqu'aide que j'aie tâché de lui prêter, la figure n'a pas toujours un entier rapport à la chose."[61] He put the eight-line stanzas of the original into *dizains* with the possibility of various lengths of meter. The fact that the first line of each stanza in the original begins with a letter which makes an acrostic of the Ave Maria was a challenge which Corneille ignored.

Here is a fairly successful rendering of a hymn from the *Vêpres des dimanches et complies*. It is the *Te lucis ante*, the regular hymn for the compline, which is the last hour of the divine office, and the night prayer of the Latin church, so that its themes are "sleep and waking, life and death, sin and grace." This is the Latin:

> Te lucis ante terminum,
> Rerum creator, poscimus,
> Ut solita clementia
> Sis praesul ad custodiam.
>
> Procul recedant somnia,
> Et noctium phantasmata,
> Hostemque nostrum comprime,
> Ne polluantur corpora.
>
> Praesta, Pater omnipotens,
> Per Jesum Christum Dominum,
> Qui tecum in perpetuum
> Regnat cum sancto spiritu.

This is Corneille's version:

> En ces derniers moments du jour qui nous éclaire,
> Auteur de l'univers, nous t'osons demander
>   Qu'avec ta clémence ordinaire
> Jusques à son retour tu daignes nous garder.
>
> Repousse loin de nous l'insolence des songes,
> Les fantômes impurs que le démon produit:
>   Retiens ce père des mensonges;
> Qu'aucune indignité ne souille notre nuit.
>
> Fais-nous, Père éternel, fais à tous cette grâce,
> Nous t'en prions au nom de ton fils Jésus-Christ,
>   Qui règne en cet immense espace
> Où tu règnes toi-même avec le Saint-Esprit.[62]

78

Obviously this is not great poetry, but it retains most of the directness, reverence and simplicity of the Latin. "Père des mensonges" is unfortunate, but I cannot object to the decorous substitution of "nuit" for *corpora*. Corneille on the whole was more fortunate with the hymns, which are almost all in quatrains in the original as well as in the French. The Psalms because of the greater variety of tone and of subject matter, and perhaps because of the form also, gave him more trouble. They seem labored and stiff. Again the standard for the translation was the quatrain, but frequently again the need for extension distorts the original. As an example of this, here is the rendering of *De profundis clamavi ad te, Domine; Domine, exaudi vocem meam*:

Des abîmes profonds où mon péché me plonge,
    Jusqu'à toi j'ai poussé mes cris;
Tu vois mon repentir et l'ennui qui me ronge:
Seigneur, ne reçois pas mes voeux avec mépris.[63]

Furthermore Corneille deviates so frequently from the sense of the Psalms as translated into the French prose which accompanies the verse that one wonders if he did not base himself upon another version.

I am aware that my treatment of Corneille's sacred verse is less than full and that it may be less than fair. I hope nevertheless that it has served its purposes here. One of them is to lead me into the conclusion of this chapter. There are several reasons for dwelling upon it. First of all, though it is certainly not for us a major aspect of Corneille's art, still it occupied many years of his literary life and quantitatively it is not negligible, filling as it does two volumes of the standard edition of his works. And if we are to know what the man was we must pay somewhat more attention to this verse than the manuals of literature generally do. But a more important reason is that, given Corneille's devotion to religion, one might expect this kind of undertaking to summon up his best, his most poetic part. But it does not. It does however provide another example of the essentially extensive rather than intensive nature of his craft. Lest this distinction be misunderstood I might say I realize that intensity or intension in poetry can produce all sorts of expansive results. One enters so deeply into the matter as it were that one shoots out beyond. My point is that Corneille did not understand or sense this sort of poetic activity, as Racine so definitely did. I do not mean of course that Racine's talent was only intensive. The very best poets I think must operate in both directions, meeting and reinforcing themselves at countless points. This is why I said at the beginning of this chapter that the greatest artists suggest the whole of themselves no matter from what direction they are approached.

Along with this characteristic of Corneille, others are suggested by the sacred verse. There is, for one, his conception of beauty as not inherent in subject matter. I believe that this was always his tendency. But I think it was especially so in the case of the religious matter, for it is quite clear as he speaks of it that there is a distinction in his mind between beauty and truth, and that for him this matter represented truth. For some, truth and goodness and beauty are one and the same thing. I believe Corneille was able to think of them at best only in combination, but preferably one at a time. Beauty furthermore resided in or resulted from the treatment of the subject, and it was here that Corneille could best identify himself with his work, but of course he was sadly limited in the religious domain. It is significant that he wrote no original religious poetry, as such. Translation and paraphrase allowed him to dedicate his talent to his devotion, but he could go no further, for it was a serious business.

All of this then seems to support the notion that the domain of Corneille's real poetic activity was the world of the theater, a world apart from ideas, from metaphysics, from religion, and even, I think, apart from ethics or psychology, for all of these were used merely as elements or ingredients to combine his mechanisms that seem almost human, his convincing improbabilities. For Corneille was not much interested in the state of this world, and he was unconcerned about the state of the next. He was not interested in philosophy or in theology. He was interested in magic.

III: The Amateur Spirit

MÉRÉ, LA ROCHEFOUCAULD, AND PASCAL

BALZAC and Chapelain were professional men of letters in the sense that the written word and the choices confronting the conscious artist were the stuff of their existence and presented to them the problems to which they devoted their lives, whether in the service of officialdom like Chapelain, or as the semi-recluse like Balzac. In the case of Corneille the profession is obvious. But we know that the discussion of literary questions and even the exercise of the art was not limited to such as these. Such activity fell within the sphere of interest of the nonprofessional but cultivated man even more than it does today.

Now we have seen how much Balzac and Chapelain defended the ideals of naturalness, simplicity, and *honnêteté* against the grammarians. And we have seen how Corneille cheerfully allowed himself to take from Aristotle what he recognized and from experience what he chose. In the case of the nonprofessional the fear of categorization is even greater. Good examples of this type are the Chevalier de Méré, La Rochefoucauld, and Pascal. I hope that the reader will understand the sense in which I consider them nonprofessionals. La Rochefoucauld was a noble, and Pascal, if he could be classed professionally at all, would have to be placed among the scientists or with the religious rather than with the men of literature as such. All three of these express what I call the amateur spirit. Because so much of this spirit is already evident in Balzac and even in Chapelain, and because it will be possible to find it in other later critics and writers, it seems to me that it must be taken seriously if the real texture of the literary sensibility of the age is to be recaptured.

1. THE PROFESSIONAL AMATEUR:
THE CHEVALIER DE MÉRÉ

IT IS with a somewhat divided mind that I introduce now the shadowy figure of Antoine Gombaud, Chevalier de Méré. This acquaintance of the great is important in the history of French literature mostly because he might have influenced Pascal. If he was the imaginary *esprit fort* to whom that incomparably superior man was addressing himself, we owe him I suppose a certain debt. If, as he claimed, he "converted" Pascal to a recognition of a world beyond mathematics, we owe him something for that too. But I incline with his editor Boudhors to the belief that it was Pascal who converted him by leading him to see, rather late in life, the spiritual basis of *honnêteté*. I freely admit a prejudice here, for I find the Chevalier de Méré in the long run a not very attractive person.

Oddly enough as we know him through his published works he has almost no dimension in his personality. To begin with, his dependence upon his connection with other significant people of his time takes away from his individuality, as we see him today. For a long time he was a kind of curiosity, and not very well identified even as such. For instance Moreau in his edition of the works of Balzac in 1854, after calling him George Brossin (confusing him with another unrelated Chevalier de Méré) described him thus: "Bel esprit et homme du monde; ses écrits, aujourd'hui oubliés, portent l'empreinte d'une morgue et d'une suffisance insupportables. Il n'y a rien de plus curieux en ce genre qu'une lettre sur les mathématiques qu'il écrivit à Pascal."[1] Just as he had no visible or at least mentionable means of support in his lifetime, so now he is a dependent. But even more, this teacher of the art of pleasing and of being pleased wanted to be his own best example. Expert card player, expert swordsman, expert horseman, connoisseur of all good things, he carried the theory and practice of anti-professional *honnêteté* so far that he really violated them and became that self-canceling, that lonely being, the professional amateur.

Yet in spite of all this he did of course have a personality. If it is almost wholly absent from his published works, as I say, it does appear in the *Propos* of 1674-1675, published by M. Boudhors in the *Revue d'Histoire littéraire* from 1922 to 1925. From these very disconnected notes, taken presumably by a disciple, he emerges as an individual, but not as a very sympathetic one. He was sixty-seven years old at that time, something of a back number, so that his conversation is largely reminiscent, and he was rather on the defensive. The general tone of the remarks may be gathered from the following thrust: "La plupart de ces gens qu'on appelle de grands hommes ont été de grands sots."[2] The word *sot* occurs again and again, applied to great and small. His tongue was sharp.

His defensiveness, if defensiveness it is, gives him a creditable vigor and independence however. He preferred Homer to Virgil, about whom he had serious reservations as he did about Horace. He thought very little of Cicero. He admired Tasso greatly. Corneille was, personally at least, a *sot*, and Racan *niais*. He liked to insist on the weaknesses of his first mentor Balzac, and he criticized very strongly the lack of sense in much of Voiture. La Rochefoucauld impressed him not at all (the *Maximes* were *torcheculs*) and he preferred, as we might expect, Bouhours to Boileau whom he thought pedantic like Cicero. Most of those whom he condemned were lacking, I suppose, in that kind of *justesse* which he specially favored and believed himself to possess. "Il y a des choses enveloppées et embrouillées, qu'on a de la peine à séparer, et c'est où je réussis le mieux."[3] Precisely what he meant by this remark will become clear I hope during the course of this chapter.

For Méré is significant in this way: he was one individual who attempted to live aesthetically. He represents what one man in the Seventeenth Century in France wanted to be, in himself and by himself. He wanted to have no other *raison d'être* than his feeling, thinking, judging, and acting self. He maintained that he had not even any desire to teach what he knew, except how to play the Spanish card game of *hombre*. But of course he was bound to make a theory of his being, and to communicate that theory. And so it is that he treats more fully than anyone else the very matters with which we are dealing in this study. He was the Doctor of the *agréments*. Where for others the question was incidental, ineresting enough and perhaps even close to the heart, for Méré it was life. He is himself in a way the most extended and explicit expression of a way of looking at things. We cannot ignore him, for in him we may see how the texture of a society affected a man who was and who wanted to be simply—a man. Others had a theory of the epic or of the universe; he had a theory of activity. It naturally carried with it a theory of artistic and critical excellence, which is what pertains here.

His works are not extensive. They include, as published in 1930 by Charles-H. Boudhors,[4] six *Conversations* on education (1668-1669); a *Discours de la Justesse* (1671); three *Discours: Des Agrémens* (1676), *De l'Esprit* (1677) and *De la Conversation* (1677); a rendering of an episode from Tasso, *Les Aventures de Renaud et d'Armide* (1678); the *Oeuvres Posthumes* (1700) containing two discourses on *La Vraie Honnêteté*, one on *L'Eloquence et de l'Entretien*, one on *La Délicatesse dans les choses et dans l'Expression*, and two on *Le Commerce du Monde*; two poems attributed to him. There are also the *Lettres* in two small volumes, first published in 1682.[5]

The titles of these discourses give the range of the matter. The letters increase it somewhat, but not greatly.

It is not hard to make a broadly organized presentation of Méré's "system." Some danger of repetition results from the tendency to fine distinctions. This is inherent in the system, though it is not easy always to see how much these distinctions are worth. As with La Rochefoucauld one is sometimes tempted to pass over them, and to suppose that in some cases if a contradiction emerges there is nothing to be done about it. It would be wise to say at the outset that in discussing the *agréments* we slip easily from literature to personality and behavior and back again. Here is a good example of what I mean: in the *Propos* Méré is reported as saying, "Il y a un art dont je ne fais pas grand cas; que c'est celui des mots. Mais il y en a un des agréments, comme l'art de Térence, de Virgile, de Mme de Longueville et Mme de Lesdiguières, dont je fais grand cas."[6] Or more succinctly, "Ninon a quelque chose de ces belles stances de Malherbe."[7] Almost everyone in the century tended to do this, and there is always the danger that a remark applicable to personal attractiveness or beauty would not carry over into literature. Because Méré is interested in the detail of the question generally, the danger is correspondingly greater. But for the sake of clarity I shall refrain from insisting upon the specific application of this or that remark. We are more than justified in so doing by the fact that Méré in the discourse on the *agréments* said, "toutes les choses qu'on trouve à son gré, ont quelque rapport entre elles, du moins en ce qui fait qu'on les trouve à son gré, et le goût qu'on prend de ce qui plaît dans une chose, donne à connaître ce qui doit plaire dans une autre; et comme il faut qu'elle soit pour être agréable."[8]

For Méré, the world is divided into that which is easily discernible and explicable and that which is veiled, secret, and difficult to demonstrate. I might as well say now that he preferred the latter division, and believed that it deserved preference. It is that part which has to do, after all, with love, be it *eros* or *agape*, and he was an *amateur*.

There are therefore two kinds of discernment: "Il y a deux sortes de justesse: l'une paraît dans le bon tempérament qui se trouve entre l'excès et le défaut. Elle dépend moins de l'esprit et de l'intelligence que du goût et du sentiment; et quand l'esprit y contribue on peut dire (si vous me permettez de le dire ainsi) que c'est un esprit de goût et de sentiment: je n'ai point d'autres termes pour expliquer plus clairement, ce je ne sais quoi de sage et d'habile qui connaît partout la bienséance, qui ne souffre pas que l'on fasse trop grand, ou trop petit, ce qui veut être grand, ou petit; et qui fait sentir en chaque chose les mesures qu'il y faut garder. . . . L'autre Justesse consiste dans le vrai rapport que doit avoir une chose avec une autre, soit qu'on les assemble ou qu'on les oppose; et celle-ci vient du bon sens et de la droite raison: pour peu qu'on y manque ceux qui ont le sens net y prennent garde, ou du moins ils en sont persuadés sitôt qu'on les en avertit. C'est que cette sorte de justesse s'exerce sur la vérité simple et nue, qui n'est point sujette au plus ni au moins, et qui demeure toujours ce qu'elle est."[9]

This passage, from the *Discours de la Justesse*, I have quoted at length because it illustrates in simple fashion the relationships which obtain in Méré's view of discernment: taste and feeling and a *je ne sais quoi* operating in the field of the mean, of the *bienséances*, where the values are shifting; good sense and "right reason" operating in the field of relationships where the values are fixed. The first type of *justesse* tends to consider things in themselves, while the second wants to generalize. Hence *les règles* mean more to the second. In *De la Conversation* Méré explained this tendency and committed himself to a preference. "Il y a deux sortes d'Étude, l'une qui ne cherche que l'Art et les Règles; l'autre qui n'y songe point du tout, et qui n'a pour but que de rencontrer par instinct et par réflexions, ce qui doit plaire en tous les sujets particuliers. S'il fallait se déclarer pour l'une des deux, ce serait à mon sens pour la dernière, et surtout lors qu'on sait par expérience ou par sentiment, qu'on se connaît à ce qui sied le mieux. Mais l'autre n'est pas à négliger, pourvu qu'on se souvienne toujours que ce qui réussit vaut mieux que les Règles. C'est aussi de là que les meilleures sont prises."[10]

The Pascalian turn to this distinction is undeniable. And indeed in the *Propos* Méré used the terms *esprit métaphysique* and *esprit mathématique* in opposition to each other.[11] There is no need to go into the question of influence or of the origin of the terms. Just why they never appear in the Chevalier's written works is, as M. Boudhors points out,[12] unexplained. However the famous letter to Pascal,[13] and a passage from the *Seconde*

Conversation[14] express in more extended fashion his distaste for the mathematical spirit.

The measured preference then, is evident. One may now go on to ask how it affects Méré's conception of the artist, the work of art and the critic.

The artist.

Genius will not be all, though innate capabilities certainly distinguish an élite. Here again the dichotomy: "Il y a deux sortes d'esprits. Les uns qui sont en petit nombre, comprennent les choses d'eux-mêmes. Ce sont eux qui ont cherché dans les idées de la nature et qui ont inventé ou perfectionné les arts et les sciences."[15] This is the creative mind; the other kind does not invent, but it understands. It is the critical mind. However, if the first kind is a "présent du Ciel" and a "lumière naturelle qui ne se peut acquérir" it can nevertheless be perfected and in that sense acquired.[16]

Furthermore talent can accomplish much without genius, even though talent should not be confused with mental superiority.[17] In a letter to the Duchesse de Lesdiguières[18] we read, "Pour ce qui est des Arts dont vous me parlez, la peinture, la Musique, la Poésie, et l'éloquence, il ne faut pas douter que pour en acquérir la perfection, il ne soit à desirer cet esprit. Cependant parce que l'imagination, et plusieurs autres parties de l'âme, et même du corps peuvent beaucoup contribuer à tous ces talents on y peut exceller sans avoir le génie du premier ordre. Je suis même persuadé qu'on peut surpasser tous les autres dans le plus grand et le plus beau métier du monde, et ne pas avoir cet esprit. A-t-on vu quelqu'un qui se pût vanter d'avoir égalé César dans la guerre? et néanmoins je doute un peu si nous le devons mettre au plus haut rang des esprits." This passage suggests Méré's theory of the passions, if we may call it such. In the *Discours des Agrémens* he objected to the standard view of the passions as harmful because (granted it were possible to be rid of them) "celui qui ne souhaiterait rien, et qui ne serait sensible à quoi que ce soit, trouverait la vie ennuyeuse, et déplairait à tout le monde et à soi-même. D'ailleurs ce sont principalement les passions qui font exceller les meilleurs ouvriers. Car quand on le veut ardemment, on en cherche les plus sûrs moyens. Et c'est par ce grand soin qu'on se rend habile en tout ce qu'on entreprend."[19]

Yet talent or genius by themselves are not always enough. To a suggestion, conveyed by a correspondent, that if he did not leave gambling for a quieter life he would soon lose all his eloquence as well as all his money, Méré replied that indeed of late his luck had fallen off, that a good deal depended on it, and that "il ne suffit pas non plus d'avoir ce génie extrêmement rare, cet esprit d'invention pour découvrir partout d'excellentes choses que nul autre n'ait jamais pensées. Il faut encore pour cela que l'heure des faveurs soit venue, et que le Ciel regarde tendrement ceux qui lui sont chers. Car l'invention est un présent du Ciel, mais comme une pension qu'on ne touche pas quand on veut. . . . Car il n'y a point d'art pour l'invention, quoi qu'on y fasse du progrès à force de s'y exercer, et toutes les règles qu'on en voit ne servent qu'à se charger d'impertinences."[20]

So, besides genius, which is inherent ability, there are the passions and Fortune to be taken into account in the reckoning of the factors necessary to the best artistic achievement. In the passage just quoted there was a suggestion that the rules did not count for much. Méré never liked to admit that skill could not be acquired without genius, but his natural bent was to be suspicious of rules, and of maxims. He wrote in *De l'Esprit*, "Ce ne sont pas les règles ni les maximes, ni même les sciences qui font principalement réussir les bons ouvriers, et les grands hommes. Ces choses-là peuvent beaucoup servir pour exceller, et même il me semble qu'elles soient nécessaires; mais on peut les avoir et ne rien faire que de fort commun si le reste manque."[21] The point is that general rules, "qui ne regardent rien en particulier" can teach nothing, so that a painter might know a great deal more than

Raphael and still be very mediocre if he lacked that master's genius.[22]

Now in all of the foregoing there is no intimation that mere unregulated self-expression could be the source of beauty. Méré believed in order and in clarity. But this order and this clarity are of a special kind. As he wrote to Mme de Lesdiguières, "Tous les esprits bien faits aiment l'Ordre, et si quelques-uns de ceux qui cherchent l'embarras sont estimés habiles gens, c'est une fausse prudence. . . . On ne voit rien de beau ni d'agréable à moins que l'ordre n'y soit observé."[23] Order, in fact, is Nature; and Méré appends a little poem:

> Tout ce merveilleux règlement
> Des Astres qui vont fièrement
> Autour de la terre immobile,
> Nous font voir assez clairement
> Quand la nuit est pure et tranquille,
> Que le maître fut bien habile,
> Qui leur donna ce mouvement.[24]

If one limited one's knowledge of Méré's opinions to the above-quoted statement and poem (we will disregard the safe cosmology as well as the quality of the verse), one might suppose him to be the most orthodox and traditional of classicists. But if one stops to think of this starry order one realizes that clear and visible though it may be, its source and the means of its operation are ultimately unknown. Now Méré does not make the illustration as explicit as I do, but here is what follows: "Encore que la diversité plaise et délasse, il faut avoir l'oeil à ne pas tomber dans la confusion, et garder en toutes les choses dont nous disposons un ordre secret et naturel qui les démêle, qui les distingue, et qui les fasse paraître si à propos et si bien placées, que ce soit toujours dans le temps et de la manière qu'on le peut souhaiter."[25]

The order then is secret and natural. It is not necessarily the order of exactitude. Rather the contrary. In a letter to Balzac Méré tells how he criticized a distinguished person's ode for being in that exact order, as though its author had intended to "mettre en rimes les Gazettes d'Allemagne plutôt que de composer une Ode à la manière de Pindare, ou d'Horace, ou de Malherbe."[26] To be sure, the ode is a specially privileged form.

The work of art.

What does this order produce? Once more the division into two. Méré distinguished constantly between *beauté* and *agrément*, or *grâce*. No great insight is needed to guess his preference. However one must be careful about this distinction because he took care to say that *beauté* and *agrément* were really but different modes of the same quality. He did not want to say that *agrément* was not beautiful. But when an object is admired for its visible *éclat*, its quality is called *beauté*, whereas if its attractiveness is hidden, as it were "en retraite," and hard to define, it is called *agrément* or *grâce*.[27]

As we might expect, *agrément* is felt rather than rationally apprehended. Beauty is felt too, but its causes are visible. And in trying to explain for instance why of two beautiful women one should be more *agréable* than the other, the observer is reduced to merely stating the effect upon his own feelings.[28]

Agrément is something apart from perfection. It is a more personal quality: "en matière d'agrément chacun a son goût, et si vous le remarquez, ce qui d'ordinaire plaît, ne vient pas tant de la perfection, que d'un certain tempérament, qui s'accomode à nos sentiments naturels. C'est cette proportion qui charme sans que l'on s'aperçoive d'où cela vient."[29] This idea was expressed more specifically with regard to literature in a letter to an unidentified correspondent, "Si nous lisons un Ouvrage de Poésie ou d'éloquence, qui ne soit pas loin de la perfection, et qu'il y paraisse un tour simple et naïf, nous ne l'aimons guère moins que la même perfection."[30]

It is thus that the effect of the *agréments* is practically beyond our control. Several times Méré likens it to that of a "poison subtil qui fait tomber en langueur," so that "ces Agréments secrets, dont on ne peut découvrir la cause, sont aussi les plus dangereux. Ce sont les personnes qui les ont, qui tiennent le plus au coeur. On ne les saurait oublier, parce qu'elles plaisent toujours quand elles ne feraient que des fautes. J'ai pris garde en la plupart des arts à ces sortes d'Agréments. . . ."[31]

The *agréments* appeal to the heart. They must, along with beauty to be sure, be distinguished from those qualities which appeal rather to the mind and which include a certain kind of *bienséance*, rather more moral and social than aesthetic, I expect, for we saw that the intuitive spirit, the "feeling mind" was more skillful at knowing "ce qui sied bien" than the *esprit mathématique*. Méré says categorically that "les agréments et les bienséances ne sont pas une même chose," that one can exist without the other, and that the former are for love and the latter for esteem.[32] I should think it might be possible to make a distinction here between "ce qui sied bien" or "rightness" and "les bienséances" or "correctness." The reader will agree that this is cutting it fine, but that is what Méré does. One more short quotation can sum the matter up. It is from the *Discours des Agrémens*,[33] "On ne saurait être assez persuadé que la beauté qui n'a point de grâce n'est pas faite pour être aimée, et que les choses qui plaisent sans être belles, sont plus à rechercher que celles qui sont belles sans Agrément."

There is a further distinction which Méré makes and which seems to be rather dear to him. Since it is also peculiar to him, I must at least make a note of it. This has to do with "le bon air." He speaks of it in the *Discours des Agrémens*: "Le bon air qui me semble très difficile est tout-à-fait nécessaire aux Agréments, et c'est même une espèce d'Agrément."[34] But it ought not to be confused with the *agréments*, for its causes are less hidden and can be more easily learned. Yet it is less perceptible than beauty, and pleases "ceux qui ont le goût fait." An illustration can be made from architecture (it reminds us of La Rochefoucauld's example[35]): "La grandeur sied bien en plusieurs choses, comme dans les spectacles. Il me semble aussi qu'elle a bonne grâce pour les édifices des Princes, mais ce qu'on en voit de plus grand en apparence n'est pas ce qu'on doit le plus admirer. Le Louvre est plus grand que Versailles, mais Versailles est plus beau, plus noble, et plus agréable que le Louvre, et même il sent plus cette véritable grandeur qui plaît aux personnes de bon goût."[36]

"Le bon air" then would stand somewhere between *beauté* and *agrément*. Insofar as it has to do with what is external, apparent to the eye and impressive, it leans toward the former, but since it does not depend upon formal requirements it partakes of the latter. "Il ne faut pas tant songer à la régularité qu'au bon air," said the Chevalier in the *Propos*.[37] And the concept is applicable to literature and to eloquence. In his judgment of Demosthenes and Cicero one can see its relationship to other requirements for excellence which he has pondered. He wrote to Balzac,[38] "Il me semble que tout ce que l'éloquence a de plus noble et de plus aimable, vient d'observer toute sorte de bienséance, et que pour être parfaitement éloquent, on ne saurait être assez honnête homme. Mais c'est à quoi, si vous y prenez garde, les plus grands Orateurs ont le moins songé. Je lis quelquefois Démosthène et Cicéron, et quand cela m'arrive, si j'ose dire ce qui se passe en moi, les choses de mauvais air qui me rebutent de ces grands hommes sont en plus grand nombre que celles que je suis bien aise d'y voir." He disliked their professionalism. "Je voudrais qu'on ne pût deviner le métier d'un homme à l'entendre parler. . . ."[39] He found something mean, bourgeois in Cicero: "Pour la pureté des sentiments, je vois qu'elle consiste à n'avoir que des affections que l'honneur inspire, et celle des pensées à ne penser rien qui ne soit agréable et de bon air. . . . J'observe . . . que ses termes magnifiques n'expriment le plus souvent que de petites choses, ce qui me semble le contraire du bon air et de ces beautés secrètes, qui veulent plus d'effet que de parade."[40]

Here, then, in this rather long quotation, is the familiar link between *bienséance, honnêteté*, antiprofessionalism, secret beauty, *agréments*, "le bon air," and true eloquence.[41] There is no need, I imagine, to point out how much of all this is in Pascal.

Related also is the notion, again familiar, of negligence, "Mais pour ce qui regarde Homère, laissons-le dormir de temps en temps pourvu qu'il nous divertisse toujours. . . . Qui voudrait examiner cet Horace si ennemi de la négligence, et qui veillait tant sur ses vers, on y trouverait des choses de si mauvais air et si dégoûtantes qu'Homère ne les eût pas voulu dire en dormant."[42] And the notion of easy grace, "je ne sais quoi de libre ou d'aisé."[43] And finally the notion of *urbanité* which by now we may guess Méré considered more the possession of the French than of the Romans,[44] and which he described thus to an unidentified correspondent, the Maréchale de ****, "Il me semble que cette urbanité n'est point ce qu'on appelle de bons mots, et qu'elle consiste en je ne sais quoi de civil et de poli, je ne sais quoi de railleur et de flatteur tout ensemble. . . . Mais c'est une de ces choses qui se sentent mieux qu'on ne les fait entendre, et qui s'apprennent plus aisément par des exemples que par des raisons."[45] A variation on this theme appeared in the *Discours des Agrémens* and brought with it still another term, "Ce que j'aime le mieux, et qu'on doit selon mon sens le plus souhaiter en tout ce qu'on fait pour plaire, c'est je ne sais quoi qui se sent bien, mais qui ne s'explique pas si aisément, et je ne sais de quelle façon me faire entendre si je ne me sers du mot de gentillesse."[46]

The reader will perhaps be conscious of the frequent appearance, in all of these attempts at definition and distinction, of the phrase "je ne sais quoi." Now none of them has reflected very strongly any clearly grasped substantive conception.[47] But Méré used the phrase so much more frequently than any of the other critics or artists whom we examine in this study that one expects him at any moment to give it this clear substantive meaning. And he does. In a letter to Monsieur de Luns[48] he criticized the length and laboriousness of a book which his correspondent had sent him, and said, "On fait bien de travailler quand on le peut, et même encore plus que cet

Auteur, pourvu que la peine qu'on se donne à bien écrire,
tende principalement à rencontrer le bon air. Sans cela
tout le reste est peu considérable. Sur quoi j'ai à vous
dire . . . que dans les manières de l'esprit, et même dans
les expressions, ce qu'on entend par le je ne sais quoi,
consiste en de petites choses qui ne s'apperçoivent pas
aisément. Et néanmoins ce n'est pas le je ne sais quoi
pour tout le monde. Quelques-uns en connaissent la
cause, et savent d'où cela vient. Cette cause secrète, et
qui n'aime à se montrer qu'à peu de personnes produit
de grands effets, et tout ce qui tient le plus au coeur." I
cannot avoid the feeling here that Méré was excluding
poor M. de Luns from a little circle of initiates to which
Méré naturally considered he himself belonged.

And yet, in spite of all the difficulty surrounding this
matter of what pleases, Méré did, like Pascal, see certain
qualities or principles which could be definitely stated as
requirements. These were the standard moderation,
unity, proportion, and symmetry.[49] In accordance with
the principle of unity for instance he was opposed to the
mixing of the genres, or of tones, though he admitted
that he had at one time thought it possible.[50] It is not to
be supposed then that he surrendered entirely to a vague
criterion of individual satisfaction, though, as we shall
see, his leanings were markedly in that direction.

The critic.

This brings us at long last to Méré's conception of the
critic's position in the business of artistic living. His opinions on the nature of minds already provide a background. The critic will obviously have the mind capable
of feeling what has to be felt rather than understood. We
are after all in the domain of taste. It is Méré's domain.
It is a world which he certainly did not create, but it is
one which he came to inhabit so thoroughly that he identified himself completely with it.

But taste itself is mysterious. "Il serait fort à propos,"
wrote Méré in *De la Conversation*, "de dire bien clairement ce que c'est que ce bon goût, mais on le sent mieux

qu'on ne le peut exprimer. C'est une expression figurée qu'on a prise de goûter ce qu'on boit, et ce qu'on mange. On voit beaucoup plus de gens de bon esprit, que de bon goût; et j'en connais qui savent tout, et qu'on ne saurait pourtant mettre dans le sentiment de ce qui sied bien. J'en connais aussi dont le raisonnement ne s'étend pas loin, et qui ne laissent pas de pénétrer subtilement tout ce qui regarde la bienséance. Cela parait fort étrange, et par où trouver la cause d'une si grande disproportion? je croirais aisément que c'est un sens intérieur peu connu; mais dont les effets en sont bien sensibles."[51] In the *Quatrième Conversation* it was described as "je ne sais quel sentiment qui va plus vite, et quelquefois plus droit que les réflexions."[52]

Taste is mysterious, but immensely important. "Je ne vois rien de si rare, ni qu'on doive tant rechercher, que d'avoir du goût, et de l'avoir fin, surtout dans les choses qui concernent l'esprit et les agréments."[53] Some people have naturally good taste; many have bad taste. But it can be improved because, says Méré with a turn which is reminiscent of Pascal's perfect model, one may exercise it in observing good things, and "toutes les bonnes choses se ressemblent par une conformité de perfection."[54]

But this is still not easy, because the right judgment has to be free of prejudice,[55] and even more difficult (we think once more of La Rochefoucauld), free of self-interest which distorts almost everyone's judgments.[56] "Qui sera donc capable de bien juger? Les Dieux qui n'ont besoin de rien, et les hommes qui se passent de tout, et qui connaissent la nature des choses. . . ."[57]

There is a more positive approach which Méré suggests as a means of avoiding these difficulties, and this is to keep one's attention on the thing itself. "Il me semble que pour juger sainement si une chose est agréable, on ne la doit considérer qu'en elle-même. . . . C'est un grand avantage pour ne s'abuser en rien que de pouvoir regarder les choses comme elles sont, sans avoir égard à celles qui les environment . . . la moindre circonstance impose, et . . . pour ne se pas tromper en ce qui plaît ou qui déplaît, on a besoin d'un discernement bien juste."[58]

The rules do not help as they ought. In a letter to Costar, where Méré was arguing, precisely, for the independent judgment, he wrote, "D'où croyez-vous qu'en lisant des Vers, il arrive à toute heure qu'on s'ennuie incontinent, quoique tout y paraisse beau et régulier? Pour moi, je m'imagine que cela vient de quelques laideurs secrètes qui ne se communiquent qu'au sentiment, et que ces gens si Doctes qui d'ordinaire ont beaucoup d'Art et peu de goût ne les sentent pas. Car je prends garde que ceux qui s'attachent fort aux règles n'ont que bien peu de goût, et c'est pourtant le bon goût qui doit faire les bonnes règles pour tout ce qui regarde la bienséance."[59] He again expressed and tried to explain his distaste for, or distrust of, the rules in a letter to Mme de Lesdiguières from which I have already quoted in connection with his belief in order. He was in fact trying to explain that by order he did not mean scholastic division and subdivision according to the book. "Les règles sont en aversion à tout le monde, et je crois qu'on en peut donner deux raisons. La première que nous avons un sentiment de liberté duquel nous ne pouvons nous défaire. En effet ce qui nous est aisé quand nous le faisons sans contrainte, nous devient quelquefois insupportable si nous y sommes forcés.* La seconde est que nous n'aimons ordinairement que les choses qui nous semblent naturelles, et quoique les Sciences le soient, les règles pourtant ne le sont pas."[60]

Now this whole view of things was based largely on his own way of going about criticism, and he was more than willing to admit it. In that same letter to Costar where he was pleading against judgments based on authority, he wrote to excuse himself from giving up his "sentiments trop délicats," which Costar had advised him to do. He admitted, sarcastically, that "pour moi qui n'estime les choses que par mon goût, je me trouve souvent en danger d'en rebuter une bonne ou d'en admirer une

---

* Compare a similar opinion of Gomberville in his preface to *Polexandre*, 1638.

mauvaise parce qu'on ne m'en a pas averti."[61] But, he went on, how does one judge the judgment of an authority? By another authority? But the process is infinite (cf. Pascal), until one is, after all, finally reduced to accepting one's own private feeling, and "pour connaître le vrai mérite des écrits on fait mieux en les lisant d'examiner ce qui se passe en soi-même sans prévention."[62]

Furthermore he was happy to suppose that (since he was no professional critic) his opinions counted for nothing, so that he felt perfectly free to have them.[63] If he condemned Virgil, Virgil would continue to be praised by others, "et puis je ne juge de rien, je dis seulement ce que je sens, et l'effet que chaque chose produit dans mon coeur et dans mon esprit. Je voudrais que chacun sans épiloguer en usât de même; parce que le sentiment quand il agit sans réflexion est d'ordinaire un bon juge de la bienséance et des agréments. . . ."[64]

But he did not deny that he was a "difficult" critic, because it meant also that he was a sincere one. He wrote to Balzac, "J'aime extrêmement cette sincérité que vous me conseillez, et peut-être ne l'ai-je que trop et que je m'en devrais corriger; parce qu'à dire le vrai je suis quelquefois si bizarre en mes sentiments que je dois souvent craindre de choquer mes amis à qui je me communique dans une extrême franchise. Quand je puis connaître les choses par moi-même, je m'en rapporte à personne et je sens d'ordinaire je ne sais quoi au-dessus de ce qui me paraît le plus excellent."[65]

So the Chevalier de Méré criticizes and theorizes about criticism as an individual apart, apprehending the imperfect shadows of a secret reality, and prizing even so the secrecy if not the imperfection.

A summary of what he believed can be drawn from his own letter to an unknown correspondent. It is a long passage but it should be less tiresome than any I could make myself. "Si vous me demandez ce que j'entends par ces choses rares, je vous réponds que celles que j'aime le mieux et qui me touchent le plus vivement ce sont les subtiles, les hautes, et les tendres; les subtiles viennent

d'un discernement fin et juste; les hautes d'une intelligence qui s'étend partout, et les tendres d'un coeur humain et sensible. Je mets encore en ce nombre une raillerie honnête, qui réjouit sans choquer personne; elle
procède d'un esprit agréable et d'une humeur enjouée.
De ces quatre caractères dépend tout ce qu'il y a de plus
exquis dans le plus beau commerce, et dans les meilleurs
Auteurs. De sorte que c'est presque tout pour être éloquent que de penser d'une manière fine et sublime,
d'avoir le coeur plein de sentiments nobles, et de savoir
inspirer la joie, et divertir en honnête homme. Mais par
la fréquentation des honnêtes gens et par la lecture des
bons Auteurs, vous pouvez observer quantité de choses
pour vous achever dans l'éloquence: comme un air galant
et du grand monde en tout ce que vous direz: je ne sais
quoi de naïf, et principalement pour ce qui regarde les
moeurs et la vie: une façon adroite et délicate à vous insinuer: un ordre secret et naturel qui ne sente ni l'art ni
l'étude: une netteté de pensées et d'expression qui ne
laisse rien d'embarrassé."[66]

The morality or at least the ethics of this advice leave
something to be desired. Can it be, as M. Boudhors suggests, that the aim of all Méré's thinking is so hollow that
it nullifies or stultifies the effect of the thought? This is
believable. But this does not keep that thought from being amply expressive of the century, especially when we
add to it this last pronouncement on the perfect artist and
the perfect critic: "Il me semble aussi que le plus parfait modèle, et celui que nous devons le plus imiter,
aimait tout ce qui se faisait de bonne grâce, comme ces
excellents parfums qui furent répandus sur lui; et peut-
on rien s'imaginer de plus agréable que ses moindres discours et ses moindres actions. . . . Quand je pense que le
Seigneur aime celui-ci, et qu'il hait celui-là sans qu'on
sache pourquoi; je n'en trouve point d'autre raison qu'un
fond d'Agréments qu'il voit dans l'un et qu'il ne trouve
pas dans l'autre, et je suis persuadé que le meilleur
moyen, et peut-être le seul pour se sauver, c'est de lui
plaire."[67]

2. THE HIDDEN HEART:
LA ROCHEFOUCAULD

I CAN think of no body of work in modern French literature which has made a greater mark in proportion to its
volume than the writings of La Rochefoucauld. This becomes even more true when limited to the *Maximes*, of
course. These carefully turned comments on human behavior, composed almost as a game, exchanged with Mme
de Sablé for recipes for soup or for maxims of her own,
were gathered together, passed around among friends,
we suppose, and published in 1665 only after a pirated
edition had (genuinely this time?) forced the author's
hand. After they were published they were reworked,
culled, and added to through four more editions until
1678, which edition forms the basis for the definitive one.[1]

Besides the *Maximes*, however, there are the *Réflexions*, discovered some years after La Rochefoucauld's
death, but not published in their entirety until well along
in the Nineteenth Century. Some of the ideas which are
pertinent to this study appear in these longer passages,
though they are often only more extended observations
previously or subsequently squeezed into maxims.

There are finally the *Mémoires* and the letters. Since
these would be of value to the student of literary sensibility only in confirming a general conception of La
Rochefoucauld's character, we shall limit our attention
to the *Maximes* and the *Réflexions*.

La Rochefoucauld, if one judges him rightly by his
writings, was more exclusively and explicitly preoccupied with morality than any of his great lay contemporaries. So we must, at first glance at least, be prepared to
find him rather thin when it comes to questions more
specifically literary. Yet one can, I think, extract from
him enough to put together something that looks like an
aesthetic position, if not a system. And this will not be
all guesswork, for he is not absolutely lacking in reflec-
tions which bear directly on the subject. But even if these
were absent one could infer much, especially from those

of his remarks which have to do with *esprit, jugement,* and *goût.*

His general opinion one could certainly infer. If there is any good in beauty, how could La Rochefoucauld's man know it? And when I say La Rochefoucauld's man, I mean the man of the Seventeenth Century. In the conclusion to the *Réflexion* XVII *(Des événements de ce siècle)*[2] we read this dismal judgment: "Si le siècle présent n'a pas moins produit d'événements extraordinaires que les siècles passés, on conviendra sans doute qu'il a le malheureux avantage de les surpasser dans l'excès des crimes. La France même, qui les a toujours détestés, qui y est opposée par l'humeur de la nation, par la religion, et qui est soutenue par les exemples du prince qui règne, se trouve néanmoins aujourd'hui le théâtre où l'on voit paraître tout ce que l'histoire et la fable nous ont dit des crimes de l'antiquité. Les vices sont de tous les temps; les hommes sont nés avec de l'intérêt, de la cruauté et de la débauche; mais si des personnes que tout le monde connaît avaient paru dans les premiers siècles, parlerait-on présentement des prostitutions d'Héliogabale, de la foi des Grecs, et des poisons et des parricides de Médée?" This complaint would not have much value if the assumptions behind it did not affect his thinking about the whole man. Man is born self-loving. This is enough to distort his every opinion. There is no reason to suppose those opinions would be anything but more distorted than ever in La Rochefoucauld's own society.

The *Maximes* are deliberately set forth in disorder for the sake of variety and of anti-professional *honnêteté,* but also apparently because La Rochefoucauld thought it too difficult to try to arrange them except by an index. Consequently any "system" must be, as with Pascal, the result of patching together various maxims and longer observations. I might say here that when I make use of posthumous or suppressed maxims I am aware of the risk involved. But I believe that those which I use seem to have been kept from publication for reasons of *bienséance* (artistically as well as morally speaking) rather

than belief. This is true especially with anything having
to do with religion, and there seems to be no reason for
supposing that his religious beliefs, whatever their depth
(or lack of it), were any more unorthodox than the Jansenistic pessimism which pervades his entire thought.

The structure of this thought is not a complicated one,
though certain inconsistencies may at times make it appear so. Man is moved by two principal general forces,
one external, Fortune; the other internal, the state of the
emotions. "La fortune et l'humeur gouvernent le monde."[3]
La Rochefoucauld speaks sometimes of "la fortune" and
sometimes of "les fortunes," but I think this need not
cause us any difficulty. In the same way he speaks mostly
of "l'humeur," but one maxim very clearly describes the
effect of "les humeurs,"[4] and others confirm his conventional psychosomatic view, as for instance, "La force et
la faiblesse de l'esprit sont mal nommées; elles ne sont, en
effet, que la bonne ou la mauvaise disposition des or-
ganes du corps." *Réflexion* xii *(De l'origine des mala-
dies)*[5] turns this notion around and makes the passions
responsible for bodily ills. Then, in a sense, fortune and
the emotions are interoperative, though in a roundabout
way, "Le calme ou l'agitation de notre humeur ne dépend pas tant de ce qui nous arrive de plus considérable
dans la vie, que d'un arrangement commode ou désagréable de petites choses qui arrivent tous les jours."[6] The
complexity of our entire volitional mechanism is correspondingly greater.

Besides the two major forces of *fortune* and *humeur,*
there are numerous others at the social level which control our impulses. They can again be characterized as
external and internal. Externally, opinion and custom
guide our choices while internally, pride and self-esteem
motivate them. Self-esteem is really the villain of the affair, and this quality is the only one which La Rochefoucauld describes at length. Its constant and silent effi-
ciency is magnificently recreated in unsurpassed Baroque
prose in the suppressed maxim no. 563. As for the rest
he is concerned principally with their effect. The only

principle which one can observe is the shifting and hidden mingling and interchange of values.

One may not predict, then, which of an infinite number of values will predominate in a world ruled by judgments based on the state of the individual's fortune, his petty or grand interest or his metabolism, in a society governed by greed, laziness, and fear. All of this is so out of control that, briefly, "on est quelquefois aussi différent de soi-même que des autres."[7]

Yet the faculties of taste, judgment, and intellect seem to deserve attention. For in spite of the inconstancy of fortune and of human nature there are degrees of understanding and degrees of worth. Minds can be typed and graded. La Rochefoucauld indulged in this *précieux* passion for distinction. He had for instance a special dislike of the petty mind, the *esprit de détail*. "Ceux qui s'appliquent trop aux petites choses deviennent ordinairement incapables des grandes."[8] They furnish sad examples of prejudiced ignorance, "La petitesse de l'esprit fait l'opiniâtreté, et nous ne croyons pas aisément ce qui est au delà de ce que nous voyons."[9] Indeed, mediocre minds condemn what is beyond their comprehension. At one point La Rochefoucauld seemed to think that the *esprit de détail* really belonged to a separate category: "La complexion qui fait le talent pour les petites choses est contraire à celle qu'il faut pour le talent des grandes."[10] This maxim was suppressed, possibly because it was too pat. Furthermore, the idea expressed in the *Réflexion* xvi (*De la différence des esprits*)[11] seems to contradict it, for there, the *esprit de détail*, when combined with "grandes vues" can produce a mind infinitely superior to the average.

Such contradictions are almost inevitable if the game of categorizing types of personality is carried far enough. The *Réflexion* to which I have just referred carried those distinctions up to a point where the shifting meaning of the word *esprit* itself had to be recognized. *Bel esprit, esprit adroit, bon esprit* are all different. *Esprit utile* can be distinguished from *esprit d'affaires* as *esprit fin* from *esprit de finesse*, and *esprit de feu* from *esprit brillant*. By *esprit de finesse*, incidentally, La Rochefoucauld meant not at all Pascal's intuitive mind, but a petty intriguer. The *esprit fin*, however, comes closer to Pascal: "il plaît toujours; il est délié, il pense des choses délicates et voit les plus imperceptibles."[12]

There are then types of mind, and there is a superior mind, and these can be distinguished. But it is possible to go further and differentiate various faculties of the mind. Here the possibilities of contradiction are even greater. No. 97 of the *Maximes* reads, "On s'est trompé lorsqu'on a cru que l'esprit et le jugement étaient deux choses différentes: le jugement n'est que la grandeur de la lumière de l'esprit; cette lumière pénètre le fond des choses, elle y remarque tout ce qu'il faut remarquer, et aperçoit celles qui semblent imperceptibles. Ainsi il faut demeurer d'accord que c'est l'étendue de la lumière de l'esprit qui produit tous les effets que l'on attribue au jugement." It is interesting again to set this against Pascal's profound distinction between the two faculties. The maxim was much retouched and, as the G. E. F. edition says, La Rochefoucauld never seemed quite able to make up his mind on the matter, for at least two other maxims, nos. 258 and 456, neither of them suppressed, imply the opposite. The first of these, "Le bon goût vient plus du jugement que de l'esprit," links the question of taste with the *esprit de finesse* in the Pascalian sense, via *jugement*, and touches the domain of literary criticism closely. The validity of supposing a special faculty of taste allied to a special faculty of judgment was coming to be more and more recognized. The aesthetic position implied needed generations of critics to elaborate it, but I am not certain that the possibilities of contradiction have been lessened since La Rochefoucauld's day. Moreover he was as aware of the slipperiness of the word *goût* ("ce terme de goût a diverses significations, et il est aisé de s'y méprendre")[13] as he was of the danger in the use of the word *esprit*. *Goût*, he knew, can mean enjoyment, or it can mean a capacity for judging: these two, he knew also, are not necessarily complementary.

My reason for insisting upon these distinctions is this: that La Rochefoucauld, while proclaiming the unconscious subjectivity and inconstancy of human judgments, nonetheless believed in a superior mentality and in a superior critical faculty, perhaps distinct from intelligence as ordinarily conceived. Yet his conclusion, if we can call it one, was based on no scholastic division and subdivision. He recognized the extreme delicacy of the subject. But, if a necessary secrecy hides the deep sources of this complexity, and if, as he said, even the *grand esprit* is often at the mercy of his emotions,[14] and if, because the details of things are almost infinite, "nos connaissances sont toujours superficielles et imparfaites,"[15] still, there exists an underlying order and an underlying truth. There is something for the superior mind to know, and for the superior critic to understand.

This order and this truth too are perhaps veiled in secrecy, but they exist. Truth is always equal to itself (though this may not be said of the mind that perceives it) no matter where it is found.[16]

And even those two forces which control our judgments have their hidden regularity, and I come back to that maxim, no. 297, on the humors which I mentioned earlier, "Les humeurs du corps ont un cours ordinaire et réglé qui meut et qui tourne imperceptiblement notre volonté; elles roulent ensemble, et exercent successivement un empire secret en nous, de sorte qu'elles ont une part considérable à toutes nos actions sans que nous le puissions connaître."

As for Fortune, she has her law of compensation. "Quelque différence qui paraisse entre les fortunes, il y a néanmoins une certaine compensation de biens et de maux qui les rend égales."[17] But even more, "Quelque incertitude et quelque variété qui paraisse dans le monde, on y remarque néanmoins un certain enchaînement secret et un ordre réglé de tout temps par la Providence, qui fait que chaque chose marche en son rang et suit le cours de sa destinée."[18] I am led to believe that the suppression of this maxim was not the result of doubt, by comparing it to the striking, unsuppressed, and at first glance rather uncharacteristic no. 69, which reads, "S'il y a un amour pur et exempt du mélange de nos autres passions, c'est celui qui est caché au fond de notre coeur, et que nous ignorons nous-mêmes." Finally there is no. 523, to be sure posthumous: "Une preuve convaincante que l'homme n'a pas été créé comme il est, c'est que, plus il devient raisonnable, et plus il rougit en lui-même de l'extravagance, de la bassesse et de la corruption de ses sentiments et de ses inclinations."

I believe I have said enough to indicate that La Rochefoucauld's cynicism was not universal, and that behind the overwhelming complexity of what we might call subject-object relationships he saw a fixed reality which he thought was at least partially visible to some rare minds who might have the necessary kind of *esprit* or *jugement*. It is to be noted I think, that where Pascal would say that the heart knows this hidden truth, La Rochefoucauld would make *goût*, or the *jugement* behind it, the knowing faculty. The heart meant something else to him. "L'esprit est toujours la dupe du coeur,"[19] and the heart is the seat of contrariness and confusion.

Now the general view of things which I have here set forth as La Rochefoucauld's is carried over into the realm of aesthetics. It goes without saying that taste fluctuates as capriciously as inclination everywhere else. "Il y a une révolution générale qui change le goût des esprits, aussi bien que les fortunes du monde."[20] But this does not mean that there is no basis for good taste. "La vérité est le fondement et la raison de la perfection et de la beauté. Une chose, de quelque nature qu'elle soit, ne saurait être belle at parfaite, si elle n'est véritablement tout ce qu'elle doit être."[21] This maxim, the first part of which was originally composed by one of La Rochefoucauld's maxim-making circle, expresses the familiar principle of *bienséance*. *Réflexion* III *(De l'air et des manières)*[22] examines in some detail its relationship to the natural, with regard to behavior in general. But there is in judging, too, a kind of *bienséance*, and it is based on the faithful classic implements of reason and good sense. "Il faut que la raison et le bon sens mettent le prix aux choses, et déterminent notre goût à leur donner le rang qu'elles méritent et qu'il nous convient de leur donner. . . ."[23] And one could put La Rochefoucauld even further into the toils of standard classicism by quoting the passage from the *Réflexion* x, which I have already mentioned, where he distinguished between "goût qui nous porte vers les choses" and "goût qui nous en fait connaître et discerner les qualités en s'attachant aux règles."[24]

But what are the rules, and how does one follow them? All that La Rochefoucauld tells us suggests that this is also a mystery. Our taste is trustworthy only when we ourselves are not involved in our judgments,[25] and of course such objectivity is rare. The *Réflexion* xii (*Du faux*)[26] begins with the confusion of values in matters of taste, "On craint encore plus de se montrer faux par le goût que par l'esprit." And it concludes with the suggestion that *esprit* can tell us anything and therefore nothing.[27] What is the judgment to do if "il y a des faussetés déguisées qui représentent si bien la vérité, que ce serait mal juger que de ne s'y pas laisser tromper"?[28]

Nevertheless beauty like truth remains equal to itself. Two houses however different they may be, if they have the beauty which fits them respectively, are equally beautiful. The example from La Rochefoucauld's own experience: Liancourt, a private residence, equals the grander princely Chantilly. And beauty is real, even though in women, for instance, it may be momentarily eclipsed by another kind of "beauté éclatante, mais ir-régulière."[29] But this is merely the effect of vagaries of taste and the accident of light.[30] Thus again a real value can be obscured by an internal and an external cause. And in this case the implication is that real beauty is regular. But even so it must be distinguished from per-fection. The passage on *vérité* as the basis of perfection and beauty, which I quoted above, seems to insist upon the separation in repeating "de la perfection *et* de beauté" and "belle *et* parfaite." And in the maxim 627 La Rochefoucauld wrote, in the edition of 1665, after which he suppressed it, "Il y a de belles choses qui ont plus d'éclat quand elles demeurent imparfaites que quand elles sont trop achevées." Obviously there is something not quite right with this maxim. If an object is *too* "achevé," is it therefore perfect? But the general notion behind it is in the same spirit as no. 240 which has, to be sure, to do with people, and not things: "On peut dire de l'agrément, séparé de la beauté, que c'est une symétrie dont on ne sait point les règles, et un rapport des traits ensemble, et des traits avec les couleurs, et avec l'air de la personne." More generally still, "Il y a des gens dégoûtants avec du mérite, et d'autres qui plaisent avec des défauts." Of the first of these two maxims "l'annotateur contemporain" (as reported by Duplessis in the edition of the Bibliothèque Elzévirienne, Paris, 1853) said "Bonne définition, qui revient au *je ne sais quoi.*" Of the second he said, "Vrai—cela vient de je ne sais quoi."*

That La Rochefoucauld remained in doubt as to the finality of some of his observations is certainly suggested by the number of maxims having to do with beauty and taste which he either suppressed or never published. But his doubt, I insist, was of their finality rather than of their truthfulness. One would, I think, destroy an untrue maxim, if one ever completed it. What I have left to say is based almost wholly on the *Réflexions*. There is no way of telling what he thought of these. But once more, it seems to me that the passages to which I shall refer are not really out of key with the rest of his thought.

The whole complex of beauty, *agrément* and perfection as applied to works of art is pretty well summed up in the *Réflexion* XVI (*De la différence des esprits*), "Bien que les productions de l'esprit soient infinies, on peut, ce me semble, les distinguer de cette sorte: il y a des choses si belles, que tout le monde est capable d'en voir et d'en

* The G.E.F. edition reports only the first of these comments.

sentir la beauté; il y en a qui ont de la beauté et qui en-
nuient; il y en a qui sont belles, que tout le monde sent
et admire, bien que tous n'en sachent pas la raison; il y
en a qui sont si fines et si délicates, que peu de gens sont
capables d'en remarquer toutes les beautés; enfin il y en
a d'autres qui ne sont pas parfaites, mais qui sont dites
avec tant d'art, et qui sont soutenues et conduites avec
tant de raison et tant de grâce, qu'elles méritent d'être
admirées."[31]

It is indeed too bad that La Rochefoucauld gave no
examples for this passage, though such a lack is certainly
characteristic of him. Maxims are pure generalities
mostly, and in the *Réflexions* the examples are practically
all from history or politics; that was where his education
and his experience lay. But one wonders to what category he would have assigned the *Cid*, for instance, and
where he would have put Homer, Virgil, Ronsard, and
Malherbe. Even without these, however, the passage is
rich in implications and a whole treatise on aesthetics
could be developed out of it. As it stands it is very clear-
cut: no basic value distinction on the grounds of perfection; beauty implies something beyond perfection; but
enjoyment requires something beyond beauty, and this
quality is *felt*, not only admired or understood intellectu-
ally.

Now if we wish to pass from the indefiniteness of the
object and of the critical act to the capacity of the critic,
the transition is easy if we return to the *Réflexion* x on
taste, where La Rochefoucauld lists an analogous order
of capability. Some individuals have bad taste in all
things, others only in some. Some follow tastes which
they know are bad. Some let chance and their friends
determine their likes and dislikes. Others are slaves to
their own tastes and prejudge accordingly. But, "Il y en
a qui sont sensibles à ce qui est bon, et choqués de ce qui
ne l'est pas; leurs vues sont nettes et justes, et ils trouvent
la raison de leur goût dans leur esprit et dans leur discernement." However, besides these, "Il y en a qui, par

une sorte d'instinct, dont ils ignorent la cause, décident de ce qui ce présente à eux, et prennent toujours le bon parti. Ceux-ci font paraître plus de goût que d'esprit, parce que leur amour-propre et leur humeur ne prévalent point sur leurs lumières naturelles; tout y est sur un même ton. Cet accord les fait juger sainement des objets, et leur en forme une idée véritable; mais à parler généralement, il y a peu de gens qui aient le goût fixe et indépendant de celui des autres: ils suivent l'exemple et la coûtume, et ils empruntent presque tout ce qu'ils ont de goût."[32] So the conclusion is fairly hopeless. It is rare, almost impossible to find the kind of "bon goût qui sait donner le prix à chaque chose, qui en connaît toute la valeur, et qui se porte généralement sur tout."[33] Our knowledge is too limited, we are too much involved, too subject to self-esteem and to emotional states, which create in us a "nombre infini de changements et d'incertitudes," so that our taste is eventually so little under control that "nous méconnaissons enfin ce que nous avons vu et ce que nous avons senti."[34]

It should not be hard to see that in the world and in the century as it was seen by La Rochefoucauld, if rational criticism was the ideal, there was not much room left for it, and that some of the space which it might have occupied was already taken up by the interoperation of mysterious rightness with instinctive taste and feeling. The rightness exists. It is not a relative quality. And it surely has to do with nature and fitness and ease. "La bonne grâce est au corps ce que le bon sens est à l'esprit."[35]

But the requirements for this rightness remain mysterious, if not inherently, then certainly to all practical purposes. If there is contradiction here, it is similar to and probably derives from the contradiction seen by Gilbert in the maxim on Providence, which he thought had been retired because it opposed the rest of La Rochefoucauld.[36] But the contradiction was deep in La Rochefoucauld and it was proper to the century.

3: BLAISE PASCAL

"La manière d'écrire d'Epictète, de Montaigne et de Salomon de Tultie est la plus d'usage, qui s'insinue le mieux, qui demeure plus dans la mémoire, et qui se fait le plus citer, parce qu'elle est toute composée de pensées nées sur les entretiens ordinaires de la vie. . . ."[1]

So we read in the Pensées* and so Pascal himself— Salomon de Tultie—wrote, filling his notes with illustrations from such various ordinary activities as tennis, hunting, travel, dreams, painting, architecture, the theater, and so on. Literature takes its place along with these. It would be surprising if it were otherwise.

Actually, however, I do not believe that Pascal was much interested in literary problems except for two reasons. One of these was that they afforded in their elusiveness examples of human complexity and instability. The other was that Pascal himself was clearly conscious of his own effects as a composer of concise, balanced, and startling pensées, or as a fashioner of sustained and colorful argument. The passage which I quoted above of course indicates this consciousness.

One finds in him therefore almost no mention of individual novelists, dramatists or poets, and very little discussion of formal problems. He was concerned with the mechanism of pleasure and with the means of persuasion.

And I think that in answer to any question about literary or artistic activity Pascal would first of all wish to make clear that he put a relatively low price on the products of the imitative and imaginative spirit. "Quelle

* My quotations from the Pensées are taken from the readings of Z. Tourneur in his edition for the Bibliothèque de Cluny, 2 vols., Paris, printed 1938. My references are however to the Brunschvicg edition of the Oeuvres. Tourneur's and Brunschvicg's readings do not always correspond. A table of concordance between Brunschvicg and Tourneur can be found in Tourneur's Edition paléographique of the Pensées, Paris, J. Vrin, printed 1942. The arrangement in this last edition differs from that of Tourneur's Cluny edition. However, a table of concordance between Brunschvicg and both Tourneur editions may be found in the "little" Brunschvicg edition, Pensées et opuscules, Paris, Hachette, printed 1946.

vanité que la peinture, qui attire l'admiration par la res-
semblance des choses dont on n'admire point les originaux!"[2] Praise which is bestowed upon the display of skill
has a corrupting effect: "L'admiration gâte tout dès
l'enfance. 'Oh! que cela est bien dit! Oh! qu'il a bien fait!
Qu'il est sage!' "[3] And what is the significance of this
sort of activity? "Si le foudre tombait sur les lieux bas,
etc., les poètes et ceux qui ne savent raisonner que sur
les choses de cette nature, manqueraient de preuves."[4]
If a man be defined by what he does he is thereby dimin-
ished: "Poète et non honnête homme."[5] Definition itself
reduces. Pascal was his own best example here, for what
should he be called? A mathematician, a physicist, a
polemist, a Christian apologist, or simply a thinker?
Ironically a recent biographer, Zacharie Tourneur, ex-
asperated by the exaggerations of many *Pascalisants* denied him practically everything but the quality of mag-
nificent poet.[6]

But let us suppose we are to speak about literature.
Do we even know what we are talking about? Are we
not in this respect as in others the slaves of custom and
the dupes of the imagination? Whence comes our notion
of beauty? "L'imagination dispose de tout; elle fait la
beauté, la justice et le bonheur, qui est le tout du
monde. . . ."[7] "Comme la mode fait l'agrément, aussi
fait-elle la justice."[8] How is one ever to know what constitutes a really independent judgment? "Qu'il est difficile de proposer une chose au jugement d'un autre, sans
corrompre son jugement par la manière de la lui proposer! Si on dit: 'Je le trouve beau; je le trouve obscur—ou
autre chose semblable,' on entraîne l'imagination à ce
jugement ou on l'irrite au contraire." It is better to say
nothing, except that even this silence has its effect, "tant
il est difficile de ne point démonter un jugement de son
assiette naturelle, ou plutôt, tant il en a peu de ferme et
stable!"[9]

We do not even know what we are looking for. The
famous passage on *beauté poétique* understands that we
look for pleasure in art, but "Comme on dit beauté

poétique, on devrait dire aussi beauté géométrique et beauté médicinale; mais on ne le dit pas. Et la raison en est qu'on sait bien quel est l'objet de la géométrie et qu'il consiste en preuves et quel est l'objet de la médecine et qu'il consiste en la guérison; mais on ne sait pas en quoi consiste l'agrément, qui est l'objet de la poésie."[10] The word then merely covers up our confusion and if we knew what *agrément* was, we would abandon the term "beauty." Certain "beauties" even are the result of human frailty: "La faiblesse de l'homme est la cause de tant de beautés qu'on établit, comme de savoir bien jouer du luth. . . ."[11]

It is extraordinarily difficult to find any fixed point of judgment. "Ceux qui sont dans le dérèglement disent à ceux qui sont dans l'ordre que ce sont eux qui s'éloignent de la nature, et ils la croient suivre; comme ceux qui sont dans un vaisseau croient que ceux qui sont au bord fuient. Le langage est pareil de tous côtés. Il faut avoir un point fixe pour en juger. Le port juge ceux qui sont dans un vaisseau. Mais où prendrons-nous un port dans la morale?"[12]

The process of being pleased or persuaded is complicated by the interference of *fantaisie*, which upsets the natural transition from reasoning to feeling upon which the writer might be expected to rely: "Tout notre raisonnement se réduit à céder au sentiment. Mais la fantaisie est semblable et contraire au sentiment; de sorte qu'on ne peut distinguer entre ces contraires: l'un dit que mon sentiment est fantaisie, l'autre que sa fantaisie est sentiment. Il faudrait avoir une règle. La raison s'offre, mais elle est ployable à tous sens, et ainsi il n'y en a point."[13] So that even if one had the means to reach the conative springs of one's audience, one could never be certain of having done so: "En sachant la passion dominante de chacun on est sûr de lui plaire, et néanmoins chacun a ses fantaisies, contraires à son propre bien, dans l'idée même qu'il a du bien; est c'est une bizarrerie qui met hors de gamme."[14]

Now all of this presupposes the need for a "point fixe," a "règle." Indeed Pascal believed that such existed, and he would have been logically forced to it even if he had not specially wanted it, because so much of his thinking is built upon the notion of two extremes, between which there must be a mean. "Si on est trop jeune, on ne juge pas bien; trop vieil, de même. Si on n'y songe pas assez; si on y songe trop on s'entête et on s'en coiffe. Si on considère son ouvrage incontinent après l'avoir fait on en est encore tout prévenu; si trop longtemps après, on (n') y entre plus.[15] Trop et trop peu de vin. Ne lui en donnez pas, il ne peut trouver la vérité. Donnez-lui-en trop, de même.[16] Quand on lit trop vite ou trop doucement on (n')entend rien."[17]

Nature however demands the mean, and she works through society to enforce it. "L'extrême esprit est accusé de folie, comme l'extrême défaut; rien que la médiocrité n'est bon. C'est la pluralité qui a établi cela et qui mord quiconque s'en échappe par quelque bout que ce soit. Je ne m'y obstinerai pas. Je consens bien qu'on m'y mette, et me refuse d'être au bas bout; non pas parce qu'il est bas mais parce qu'il est bout; car je refuserais de même qu'on me mit au haut. C'est sortir de l'humanité que de sortir du milieu. . . ."[18] This principle seems to dominate in the very constitution of human nature: "La nature nous a si bien mis au milieu que si nous changeons un côté de la balance, nous changeons aussi l'autre—'Je fesons,' 'zôa trékei.'"* Cela me fait croire qu'il y a des ressorts dans notre tête qui sont tellement disposés que qui touche l'un touche aussi le contraire."[19]

Thus, as between the contrariness of the two infinities, there is, or ought to be some mean point of rightness. But where is it? "Je n'ai jamais jugé d'une même chose exactement de même. Je ne puis juger d'un ouvrage en le faisant. Il faut que je fasse comme les peintres, et que

---

* "Je faisons" and "animals runs": i.e. if somewhere in human speech a plural verb is found to be used with a singular subject, then somewhere also will be found a singular verb used with a plural subject.

je m'en éloigne.—Mais non pas de trop—De combien
donc?—Devinez!"[20] And who can find it? "Qui tient le
juste milieu, qu'il paraisse et qu'il le prouve!"[21]

Yet in spite of these difficulties, we persist in retaining
the notion of perfection. It is surely associated with the
mean point. It is a point where the opposite extremes are
conciliated and where nature is satisfied. "Il y a un certain modèle d'agrément et de beauté qui consiste en un
certain rapport entre notre nature, faible ou forte, telle
qu'elle est, et la chose qui nous plaît."[22] But we have to
be careful here, for our model may be bad as well as
good. The only difference is that there is only one good
model while there are countless bad ones. But everyone
judges everything according to a model. It is an idea of
perfection in general. It is a notion of what constitutes
beauty. "Tout ce qui est formé sur ce modèle nous agrée:
soit maison, chanson, discours, vers, prose, femme, oi-
seaux, rivières, arbres, chambres, habits, etc."[23]

The only trouble is that "on ne sait pas ce que c'est que
ce modèle naturel qu'il faut imiter; et à faute de cette
connaissance, on a inventé de certains termes bizarres:
'siècle d'or,' 'merveille de nos jours,' 'fatal,' etc.; et on
appelle ce jargon 'beauté poétique.' "[24] And because
there is a multiplicity of badness, because there are an
infinite number of points to one side or the other of the
mean, deviation is easy. "Le mal est aisé, il y en a une infinité; le bien presque unique."[25] In this last remark Pascal is not in the realm of aesthetics but in the realm of
morality. But I think the reader will understand by now
that Pascal's devices are applicable in both realms. As
for the good model of beauty, easy though it may be to
miss it, "ceux qui ont le goût bon" dislike whatever does
not imitate it.[26]

It is also possible to say what some sources of pleasure
and of excellence are. Identification with self,[27] conflict,[28]
and symmetry[29] are sources of pleasure. The most effective sources of excellence are simplicity, clarity, and
naturalness, especially when they are combined with
grandeur. "Jésus-Christ a dit des choses grandes si simple-

ment, qu'il semble qu'il ne les a pas pensées, et si nette-
ment néanmoins, qu'on voit bien ce qu'il en pensait. Cette
clarté jointe à cette naïveté est admirable."[30] Naturalness
is the mark of humanity. "Quand on voit le style naturel,
on est tout étonné et ravi; car on s'attendait de voir un
auteur, et on trouve un homme; au lieu que ceux qui ont
le goût bon et qui, en voyant un livre, croient trouver
un homme, sont tout surpris de trouver un auteur. *Plus
poetice quam humane locutus es.*"[31] At the basis of this
simplicity and this naturalness will be the writer's sincerity, that is, his real concern for what he is trying to
say. "Ceux qui font les antithèses en forçant les mots font
comme ceux qui font de fausses fenêtres pour la symétrie.
Leur règle n'est pas de parler juste, mais de faire des
figures justes."[32] In other words, "Tout ce qui n'est que
pour l'auteur ne vaut rien. 'Ambitiosa recidet orna-
menta.' "[33]

This seems to suggest that for Pascal the idea was more
important than the expression of it, but he would not let
himself fall into that dangerous assumption. The disposition of words was in fact the writer's real task. "Les mots
diversement rangés font un divers sens, et les sens diversement rangés font différents effets."[34] "Qu'on ne me
dise pas que je n'ai rien dit de nouveau; la disposition
des matières est nouvelle. Quand on joue à la paume,
c'est une même balle dont on joue l'un et l'autre; mais
l'un la place mieux."[35] The right use of words depends of
course upon the underlying thought: "Il y a des lieux où
il faut appeler Paris 'Paris,' et d'autres où il la faut appeler 'Capitale du Royaume.' "[36] But there is no set rule
of style: "Quand dans un discours se trouvent des mots
répétés, et qu'essayant de les corriger, on les trouve si
propres qu'on gâterait le discours, il les faut laisser, c'en
est la marque. Et c'est là la part de l'envie, qui est
aveugle, et qui ne sait pas que cette répétition n'est pas
faute en cet endroit; car il n'y a point de règle générale."[37]

The final importance in Pascal's mind of the choice and
disposition of words and their relation to the thought is
perhaps best expressed in this remark, "Un même sens

change selon les paroles qui l'expriment. Les sens reçoivent des paroles leur dignité, au lieu de la leur donner."[38]

There are sources of pleasure then and there is style, but what it all comes down to is the familiar criterion of basic correspondence to the truth: "Il faut de l'agréable et du réel; mais il faut que cet agréable soit lui-même pris du vrai."[39] And in this correspondence there will reside a unity where, again, all contradictions are resolved, "On ne peut faire une bonne physionomie qu'en accordant toutes nos contrariétés, et il ne suffit pas de suivre une suite de qualités accordantes sans accorder les contraires, pour entendre le sens d'un auteur il faut accorder tous les passages contraires." Pascal was thinking here principally of the Bible, as he indicated in the continuation of the passage. But he made the application general because he was using it as an example. "Tout auteur a un sens auquel tous les passages contraires s'accordent, ou il n'a point de sens du tout."[40]

But when one says "basic correspondence to the truth" one means: to all the elements involved in the business of pleasing or persuading; and the variations of these are infinite. That is why there are no known rules for style. However there is the familiar principle of *bienséance*: that the expression should fit the thought of the writer or speaker and also the thought of the audience. The nature of the audience is then of real importance. But then the question arises: if, as we have seen, the act of judging one's own or another's work is so difficult, given the inconstancy of human nature, how is one to know anything about this audience, and so how is one to please it? "On croit toucher des orgues ordinaires en touchant l'homme. Ce sont des orgues à la verite, mais bizarres, changeantes, variables (Ceux qui ne savent toucher que les ordinaires) ne feraient pas d'accords sur celles-là; car il faut savoir où sont les (marches? touches?)."[41] I have quoted this remark in all its incompleteness because it shows Pascal as he pondered the precise means of expressing this notion of a being who can be played upon, if the player can find the proper mechanism. Is it however even a mechanism? "Qu'est-ce qui sent le plaisir en nous? est-ce la main, est-ce le bras, est-ce la chair? est-ce le sang? On verra qu'il faut que ce soit quelque chose d'immatériel."[42]

One can however make some positive suppositions. The audience must be supposed to be capable of some sort of understanding and sympathy. "Il faut plaire à ceux qui ont les sentiments humains et tendres."[43] If they lack this sympathy they will look for the wrong kind of attractiveness: "On ne consulte que l'oreille, parce qu'on manque de coeur. Sa règle est l'honnêteté."[44] "Ces gens manquent de coeur, on n'en ferait pas son ami."[45] One addresses one's self to the heart, but also to common sense. In commenting on those who expressed their disdain of Christianity, Pascal quoted their affected worldliness: "Cela n'est pas du bon air," and said, "Cela montre qu'il n'y a rien à leur dire, non par mépris, mais parce qu'ils n'ont pas le sens commun. Il faut que Dieu les touche. Les gens de cette sorte sont académistes, écoliers; et c'est le plus méchant caractère d'hommes que je connaisse."[46]

In short one addresses one's self to the *honnête homme*, the man of heart, of sense, and of taste. Yet how indefinable these qualities are!

Beauty and rightness exist. There is a mean, there is a model, there is good taste, there is *honnêteté*. But there seem to be no rules. Confusion, uncertainty, tyranny, and anarchy reign in the kingdom of beauty and eloquence. What is the explanation of this state of affairs? If it is to be found at all, it is to be found only by going beyond style and ordinary eloquence, to an understanding of the deep order of things, to a higher *bienséance*. The confusion comes as the result of looking for the wrong qualities in the wrong orders. "Diverses chambres: de forts, de beaux, de bons esprits, de pieux, dont chacun règne chez soi, non ailleurs. Et quelquefois ils se rencontrent, et le fort et le beau se battent sottement à qui sera le maître l'un de l'autre; car leur maîtrise est de divers genre. Ils ne s'entendent pas, et leur faute est de vouloir régner partout. Rien ne le peut, non pas même la force;

elle ne fait rien au royaume des savants; elle n'est maîtresse que des actions extérieures."[47]

Tyranny is wishing to dominate outside one's own order. "La tyrannie est de vouloir avoir par une voie ce
qu'on ne peut avoir que par une autre. On rend différents
devoirs aux différents mérites: devoir d'amour à l'agrément, devoir de crainte à la force, devoir de créance à la
science. . . . Ainsi ces discours sont faux et tyrraniques:
'Je suis beau, donc on doit me craindre. Je suis fort, donc
on doit m'aimer.' "[48]

Here in shadow are the three orders which exist so
centrally in Pascal's thought that they work themselves
into almost everything he says. For our purposes the order of charity or of the heart can be spoken of, as Pascal
does on occasion, as the order of the will. It is the conative order. Persuasion seeks to attain its audience as much
through the will as through the reason, the order of cognition. These might seem like unrewarding exchanges of
terms were it not for the fact that the order of charity,
considered as such takes us beyond the business of *agrément* and persuasion. But it is well to remember that
Pascal uses both *charité* and *volonté* to describe the order
of the heart as opposed to the mind, of judgment as opposed to analysis.

These orders may be seen to operate in all human beings, one supposes. But individuals can be dominated by
one or the other. It is important that this be remembered,
and that the special domains of the separate orders be
kept in mind. If a man is truly wise, for instance, he may
be allowed a pride which would be unbecoming in another, for his order is the order of ultimate good. "Il y a
trois ordres de choses: la chair, l'esprit, la volonté. Les
charnels sont les riches, les rois; ils ont pour objet le corps.
Les curieux et savants; ils ont pour objet l'esprit. Les
sages; ils ont pour objet la justice. Dieu doit régner sur
tous, et tout se rapporter à lui. Dans les choses de la
chair règne proprement la concupiscence; dans les spirituelles, la curiosité proprement; dans la sagesse, l'orgeuil
proprement. Ce n'est pas qu'on ne puisse être glorieux

pour les biens ou pour les connaissances, mais ce n'est pas
le lieu de l'orgeuil; car, en accordant à un homme qu'il
est savant, on ne laissera pas de le convaincre qu'il a tort
d'être superbe."[49] So that the intelletual, provided he es-
teems his attainments properly, rejoices in his own proper
satisfaction: "Les grands génies ont leur empire, leur
éclat, leur grandeur, leur victoire et leur lustre, et n'ont
nul besoin des grandeurs charnelles où elles n'ont point
de rapport. Ils sont vus, non des yeux, mais des esprits;
c'est assez." Likewise the saint transcends the intellectual: he is seen not by minds or bodies, but by God and
the angels.[50]

In one's own domain one can have one's own rightness.
"Diverses sortes de sens droit: les uns dans un certain
ordre de choses, et non dans les autres ordres, où ils ex-
travaguent."[51]

At this point it becomes necessary to remember that
the word *ordre* has a somewhat elastic sense. It means
always the arrangement of values: which things come
first, and the sequence of cause and effect. But it is used
in connection sometimes with metaphysical economy,
sometimes with human economy (individually and so-
cially speaking) and sometimes with rhetorical economy.
In the first sense one tends to think of it almost as an area;
in the second, one thinks of it in terms of categories of
minds or personalities or social types; in the third, one
thinks of the ordering, the disposition, the sequence of
thought and word.

It is right, I think, that the word should be used so, for
the *meanings* of the various aspects of the human condition, nature, and activity all merge into one another. A
good example of this merging is the passage, "L'ordre.
Contre l'objection que l'Ecriture n'a point d'ordre. Le
coeur a son ordre; l'esprit a le sien, qui est par principes
et démonstration. Le coeur en a un autre. On ne prouve
pas qu'on doit être aimé, en exposant d'ordre les causes
de l'amour; cela serait ridicule. Jésus-Christ, Saint Paul
ont l'ordre de la charité, non de l'esprit, car ils voulaient
échauffer non instruire."[52] Here Pascal is thinking of the

sequence of ideas and expressions with respect to emotional persuasion, but the subject matter of the remark
itself takes it into the realm of the metaphysical. Another
example of the merging is "La vraie éloquence se moque
de l'éloquence; la vraie morale se moque de la morale,
c'est-à-dire que la morale du jugement se moque de la
morale de l'esprit, qui est sans règles. Car le jugement est
celui à qui appartient le sentiment, comme les sciences
appartiennent à l'esprit. La finesse est la part du jugement, la géométrie est celle de l'esprit. Se moquer de la
philosophie, c'est vraiment philosopher."[53] Here we pass
from rhetoric to morality to psychology to philosophy.
This is the way Pascal's mind seems to operate, and that
is why one can take almost any remark in the *Pensées* as
a starting point and work from it through the others without losing the thread of the thought.

One may gather also, from the two passages which I
have just quoted, that in spite of each order having its
own particular fitness, its own *bienséance*, Pascal conceived them in a hierarchy. The separateness of the orders is one of value as well as of being; all the order of
nature is not equal to the least mind, nor the whole order
of mind equal to the least impulse of charity.[54] "La distance infinie des corps aux esprits figure la distance infiniment plus infinie des esprits à la charité, car elle est sur-
naturelle."[55]

I have dwelt upon this question of the orders and the
merging of levels within a hierarchy because what seems
to me to be Pascal's final position with respect to the arts
of persuasion and pleasing emerges quite simply from the
main body of his thought, whatever the sources of his
remarks may have been.* We may observe now a further
aspect of this position in the two fragments known as *De
l'esprit géométrique* and *De l'art de persuader*. In the
first of these Pascal, describing the geometric method of

* Cf. Z. Tourneur, *"Beauté poétique." Histoire critique d'une
pensée de Pascal et de ses annexes.*, Paris, Vrin, 1933, and the review of this book by J. Dedieu in the *Rev. d'hist. litt.*, 1935, pp.
130 ff.

proof, limited himself to that part of geometry which demonstrates convincingly truths already known. But, he said, before embarking upon his description of the geometric method, he was bound to give an idea of a "méthode encore plus éminente et plus accomplie, mais où les hommes ne sauraient jamais arriver: car ce qui passe la géométrie nous surpasse; et néanmoins il est nécessaire d'en dire quelque chose, quoiqu'il soit impossible de la pratiquer."[56] This "véritable méthode" or "véritable ordre," as he called it, would consist in defining everything and proving everything. But this finality is humanly unattainable, for everything defined presupposes antecedent terms by which it is defined, and these terms in their turn depend for definition upon preceding ones, "et ainsi il est clair qu'on n'arriverait jamais aux premières. Aussi, en poussant les recherches de plus en plus, on arrive nécessairement à des mots primitifs qu'on ne peut plus définir et à des principes si clairs qu'on n'en trouve plus qui le soient davantage pour servir à leur preuve. D'où il paraît que les hommes sont dans une impuissance naturelle et immuable de traiter quelque science que ce soit dans un ordre absolument accompli."[57]

It is of course geometry which understands this limitation since it never defines or demonstrates what is simple and clear to all men: space, time, motion, etc., but does define and demonstrate all the rest. Thus it performs its function in a mean order, an order violated by all who try to define and prove everything as well as by all who neglect to define and prove what is not self-evident.[58] There is therefore no reason to abandon it simply because it cannot prove everything, for within its order it is admirable and perfect. The terms which it assumes without proving, while simple and clear, are still incapable of proof, not because they are difficult but precisely because they are simple. These terms which are at the same time the object of geometry are principally motion, number, and space. Time, by its relation to motion is also included. They are all indefinable, and those who attempt to define them "se perdent eux-mêmes et s'égarent dans des embarras inexplicables."[59]

Now these objects of geometry have certain properties in common, the principal one being that they are all doubly infinite and infinitely divisible. Pascal proceeded to demonstrate, for the benefit of those who might not understand but who would be capable of understanding. The non-geometrically minded, however intelligent they might be, would always have difficulty in conceiving these properties. But, Pascal concluded, "ceux qui verront clairement ces vérités pourront admirer la grandeur et la puissance de la nature dans cette double infinité qui nous environne de toutes parts, et apprendre par cette considération merveilleuse à se connaître eux-mêmes, en se regardant placés entre une infinité et un néant d'étendue, entre une infinité et un néant de nombre, entre une infinité et un néant de mouvement, entre une infinité et un néant de temps. Sur quoi on peut apprendre à s'estimer à son juste prix et former des réflexions qui valent mieux que tout le reste de la géométrie même."[60]

The infinitely divisible and indefinable reality, the "véritable ordre," the universal mean, and the final ontological and moral implication, all these notions show a combination of absolutism and relativity which, extending as it does from nature to the moral order, will have its reflection in Pascal's aesthetic sensibility. It is symbolic that the point discussed in the *Esprit géométrique*, namely the infinite divisibility of space, number, motion and time, was the subject of a disagreement between Pascal and Méré, wherein the conflict of the *esprit géométrique* with the *esprit de finesse* was evident. Méré could not believe in infinite indivisibility, nor, as a matter of fact, if we are to credit the letter supposedly written to Pascal around 1658-1659,[61] could he believe in the usefulness of the concept of infinity itself. "Je vous apprends (he wrote) que dès qu'il entre tant-soit-peu d'infini dans une question elle devient inexplicable, parce que l'esprit se trouble et se confond. De sorte qu'on trouve mieux la vérité par le sentiment naturel que par vos démonstrations."[62] But the point at issue was really the utility of the geometrical method. Whether or not this letter could have had any effect on Pascal, we know that he never abandoned the concept of infinity (his whole conception of reality was involved), but he did concede the *ultimate* uselessness of the mathematical order. "J'aurais bien pris ce discours d'ordre; comme celui-ci: pour montrer la vanité de toutes sortes de conditions, montrer la vanité des vies communes, et puis la vanité des vies philosophiques, pyrrhoniennes, stoïques. Mais l'ordre n'y serait pas gardé. Je sais un peu ce que c'est et combien peu de gens l'entendent. Nulle science humaine ne le peut garder. Saint-Thomas ne l'a pas gardé. La mathématique le garde: mais elle est inutile en sa profondeur."[63] The treatise on geometry shows him in a position to make this admission.

Now, if we pass to the second of the fragments, the *Art de persuader*, we shall see this issue arise once more. It was natural that Pascal should carry over the geometrical method into the art of persuasion, since it was a method which within limits was capable of absolute proof. The treatise begins with the classic statement that persuasion is effected by appealing to two human faculties: the understanding (*entendement*) and the will (*volonté*).[64] The latter appeal Pascal described as unworthy because it means catering to self-interest and the baser passions— unless one is thinking of sacred matters, which are an entirely different proposition and not to be discussed, for God, in order to confound presumptuous man, appeals in this way. Therefore the appeal to the understanding ought to be the only path to persuasion for man to take. But the fact remains that men are more moved through the heart and the will, by what pleases them, than through the mind, and this fact must be faced.

Of the ideas which must be persuasively communicated some are sure to take root if they are based on admitted truth or if they appeal to the audience's interest, but if they conflict with this interest then the task becomes more delicate, and the audience's personality must be taken into account so that the ideas can be presented in their most attractive form. "De sorte que l'art de persuader consiste autant en celui d'agréer qu'en celui de convaincre, tant les hommes se gouvernent plus par caprice que par raison!"[65] Now one can give rules for the "art de convaincre" provided principles are agreed upon. "Mais la manière d'agréer est bien sans comparaison plus difficile, plus subtile, plus utile et plus admirable; aussi, si je n'en traite pas, c'est parce que je n'en suis pas capable; et je m'y sens tellement disproportionné, que je crois la chose absolument impossible.

"Ce n'est pas que je ne croie qu'il y ait des règles aussi sûres pour plaire que pour démontrer, et que qui les saurait parfaitement connaître et pratiquer ne réussît aussi sûrement à se faire aimer des rois et de toutes sortes de personnes, qu'à démontrer les éléments de la géométrie à ceux qui ont assez d'imagination pour en comprendre les hypothèses. Mais j'estime, et c'est peut-être ma faiblesse qui me le fait croire, qu'il est impossible d'y arriver."[66]

The extreme difficulty of explaining this so admirable and useful "manière d'agréer" is caused, Pascal believed, by the instability of the principles of pleasure and the changeableness, variety, complexity, and unpredictability of the individuals with whom one has to deal. Yet its principles do exist even if it is impossible to demonstrate them, so that it corresponds in a way to the "véritable ordre" as the "manière de convaincre" obviously corresponds to the geometric method. And if it is true that the majority are convinced more through the heart than through the head, it follows that the successful pleader is going to have to depend upon some inner sense of *agrément* most of the time, and the usefulness of the geometric method when left to itself seems decidedly limited.

The connection of the two fragments just examined with the distinction between the *esprit de géometrie* and the *esprit de finesse* is quite obvious. The passage which opens the *Pensées* in the Brunschvicg edition carries into the domain of epistemology the same separation of orders. Geometry is specialized and to one side, as it were, but basically simple and clear. The world of the *esprit fin* is all about us, but its principles are complicated and numerous and require perception. Geometers reason perfectly well in their field, but are blind to what is all around them. *Esprits fins* have trouble turning aside and concentrating on geometric principles. But what they see, in their world, they see as a whole and seize its meaning immediately. "Les choses de finesse" are not easy to see: "On les voit à peine, on les sent plutôt qu'on ne les voit; on a des peines infinies à les faire sentir à ceux qui ne les sentent pas d'eux-mêmes; ce sont choses tellement délicates, et si nombreuses, qu'il faut un sens bien délicat et bien net pour les sentir, et juger droit et juste selon ce sentiment, sans pouvoir le plus souvent les démontrer par ordre comme en géométrie, parce qu'on n'en possède pas ainsi les principes, et que ce serait une chose infinie de l'entreprendre. Il faut tout d'un coup voir la chose d'un seul regard, et non pas par progrès de raisonnement, au moins jusqu'à un certain degré."[67] The geometric mind wants to begin by defining and to proceed by principles. In the order of the *esprit fin* this is not possible. The mind itself performs these operations, but "tacitement, naturellement et sans art, car l'expression en passe tous les hommes, et le sentiment n'en appartient qu'à peu d'hommes." For the *esprit de finesse* the definitions and principles necessary to the *esprit de géométrie* are sterile and distasteful. He has not the patience to think in abstractions, he is by way of being an empiricist, while the geometric mind cannot work without clear-cut explanations of everything.[68] Pascal takes care to make it clear that he speaks only of the minds who are only one of these things, with the implication that it is possible to be both, as indeed he himself was. But it is fairly obvious, when all the ways of stating the distinction are taken into account, that the combination of the two is, as Pascal says, extremely rare, and that we are dealing with two distinct types of mind working in distinctly different orders.

"*Véritable ordre, coeur* or *volonté, manière d'agréer, esprit de finesse,* these all seem to be related in the same order of things. It is an order of wisdom. To repeat part of a passage which I quoted earlier, "la finesse est la part du jugement, la géométrie est celle de l'esprit."[69] This order has its mode which is not that of other orders, but the operation of this mode cannot be demonstrated. It can only be demonstrated that there *is* such an order, but it is outside cognition, and you cannot explain one order by the procedure proper to another. Yet I believe that for Pascal it represented an order of permanence and an order of the whole. He placed it, I think, above the order of reasoning, in his hierarchy, though perhaps somewhat against his better judgment. It is evident from the manuscript of the passage in the *Pensées* on the two *esprits* that his reworkings were almost all in the direction of less absolute distinction than his first *élan* had set up. He inserted (like La Rochefoucauld) a "le plus souvent" and an "au moins jusqu'à un certain degré" to soften the generalizations; he substituted "des géomètres" for "les géomètres," and most revealing of all, at the end of the third paragraph, he substituted "et le sentiment n'en appartient qu'à peu d'hommes" for the original "et le sentiment n'en appartient qu'aux grands hommes."*

It is tempting to attach this order, which might be called the perceptive order, to the order of charity, but I think this can be done only indirectly. By perceptive order I do not mean simply the order of vision, but the order of feeling, or I should say the economy of felt values, including of course moral values as well as aesthetic values. To make this clear, let me quote another passage from the *Pensées*: "Ceux qui sont accoutumés à juger par le sentiment ne comprennent rien aux choses de raisonnement, car ils veulent d'abord pénétrer d'une vue et ne sont point accoutumés à chercher les principes. Et les autres, au contraire, qui sont accoutumés à raisonner

---

* For a typographical representation of this reworking see Tourneur, ed. cit., Cluny, no. 349, II, 84-86, or the *Edition paléographique*, pp. 63-64.

par principes, ne comprennent rien aux choses de sentiment, y cherchant des principes et ne pouvant voir d'une
vue."[70] Here, as elsewhere, the figure of seeing belongs to
the faculty of feeling. And, to return to the hierarchy
(and to repeat a quotation again), "la vraie morale se
moque de la morale, c'est-à-dire que la morale du jugement se moque de la morale de l'esprit, qui est sans
règles. Car le jugement est celui à qui appartient le sentiment, comme les sciences appartiennent à l'esprit."[71]

Thus, "voir d'une vue," *sentiment, jugement,* "morale
du jugement," "vraie morale" are interdependent, and of
the same order.

We have come rather far afield, and it is time to return
to the starting point. It is clear, I think, that Pascal recognized an order of things to which real beauty and real
eloquence belong, and in which real judgment operates.
If this order seems to be related to the order of charity, it
is because it has always been possible to speak of art in
terms applicable to religion (we have seen this affinity
in other discussions), but it is also because for Pascal persuasion and the ability to convince emotionally meant the
ability to lead his subject to a realization of the vanity
of human things and to the desire for God. Thus, while
several elements of an aesthetic can be pulled out of his
thought, they reside there only in fragmentary form. He
was not interested in the problem for its own sake any
more than he was interested in the problem of good government or the problem of personality, the elements of
which can also be found in the *Pensées.* Moreover it was
precisely not his intention to develop a theory: "J'écrirai
ici mes pensées sans ordre, et non pas peut-être dans une
confusion sans dessein. C'est le véritable ordre, et qui
marquera toujours mon objet par le désordre même. Je
ferais trop d'honneur à mon sujet, si je le traitais avec
ordre puisque je veux montrer qu'il en est incapable."[72]

Yet the "véritable ordre" is one in which eloquence,
beauty, and taste have their being *according to the rules.*
The rules have to do with the mean, with the conciliation
of opposites, with symmetry ("en ce qu'on voit d'une

128

vue")[73] and unity. But they can never be known as the mind conceives knowing: that is, they can never be *proved*. "Nous avons une impuissance de prouver, invincible à tout le dogmatisme. Nous avons une idée de la vérité, invincible à tout le pyrrhonisme."[74] And so, "nous connaissons qu'il y a un infini, et ignorons sa nature: comme, nous savons qu'il est faux que les nombres soient finis; donc il est vrai qu'il y a un infini en nombre; mais nous ne savons pas ce qu'il est. . . ."[75]

In this same way we know that there is a model but we do not know its nature. Art is in the order of the infinite to this extent: that we know its existence but not its nature because it has extent like ourselves, but not limits as we have. We know its existence almost more by the obvious untruth of its opposite than by any obviousness of its truth. There are so many bad models.

The faculty which understands the existence of the real rules, and which operates according to them, is the *sentiment*. This itself provides, for the critic, the *règle*, the secret watch with which to tell the time, the moment of *bienséance* and *honnêteté*. But nothing is easier than to go wrong in this order, for nothing resembles *sentiment* so much as its opposite, *fantaisie*. And the whole difficulty of the problem might be summed up in this passage: "Les choses ont diverses qualités, et l'âme diverses inclinations; car rien n'est simple de ce qui s'offre à l'âme, et l'âme ne s'offre jamais simple à aucun sujet. De là vient qu'on pleure et qu'on rit d'une même chose."[76] What becomes in reality of the *séparation des genres*? Perhaps this is why in the long run the discussion of problems of taste and beauty is fruitless, and why it were more profitable to listen to the heart and really know (i.e. not "know" at all) what can be known and what is worth knowing, in the order of charity.

Pascal conformed to the idea of Seventeenth Century French Classicism insofar as he prized unity and symmetry, simplicity and naturalness, *honnêteté* and *bienséance*. Indeed he understood these criteria better than anyone in the century, but he raised them all to a level where they scarcely mean what is ordinarily meant by them. He related them to a conception of wholeness and differentiation, of relativity and absoluteness much more vast and much more mysterious than any held by his contemporaries. Yet it is my belief that those contemporaries themselves thought in the same direction, if they went less far. And it is my hope that these studies support that belief.

IV: The Secret of the Practitioners

LA FONTAINE, MOLIÈRE, AND RACINE

IT WOULD be folly to attempt to understand what was happening to literature and to literary sensibility in the Seventeenth Century without paying attention to the artists who worked in the atmosphere of this sensibility while they contributed to it. I have already had much to say about Corneille. He might of course have been included in the present chapter, but he seemed to be more useful in reinforcing the understanding of Balzac and Chapelain. Even so, the individualism revealed and proclaimed by him was restated in one way or another by his three great successors. Their positions with respect to literary creation show a sense of independence and freedom which is not only expressed in their prefaces but is also reflected in their work. In the case of La Fontaine and Molière this is frequently done directly as they touch upon literary subject matter. But in the case of all three of the artists treated in this chapter this sense of freedom can be said to inform their work as a whole and to explain their lasting vitality.

As it will be seen, La Fontaine, Molière, and Racine all by one means or another make it impossible for the critic to fix them, to pin them down to a point of view, to reduce them to any completely satisfactory aesthetic or philosophical formula. They all succeed in achieving this freedom for themselves and for their work by a conscious evasion and a clever dispersal of responsibility. Thus, for instance, La Fontaine's hedonism, Molière's naturalism, and Racine's manicheanism need to be considered in the light of aesthetic as well as philosophical or theological objectives. The kind of objectivity implied by those attitudes may be found to harmonize admirably with the deep purposes of the artist.

131

I do not intend, however, anything like a full analysis of these writers. But it is necessary at least that their consciousness of their artistic integrity be shown, for they are at once the proof and the example of the literary ideals of the time. For this reason, as well as for reasons of chronology loosely applied, they occupy the center of this volume.

1. THE INDEPENDENCE OF LA FONTAINE

JEAN DE LA FONTAINE probably remains in our modern imaginations as the most authentic artistic personality among the Grands Classiques. His distracted (or simply cold-blooded) irresponsibility in his personal life contributes a good deal to such a conception of him; his reputation for simplicity and honesty complicates it rather pleasantly, while his final repentance and mortification render it altogether satisfactory. It is added to of course by his independence in matters of literature, and it is finally fixed by the self-exposure that colors his work. We like our artists to be sincere, brave, and a little mad. La Fontaine seems to fill the bill.*

But he satisfied his own generation too, and one might therefore hope to learn something of the poetic sensibility of the age by knowing what this artistic personality really was. So I propose now to discuss La Fontaine's aesthetic consciousness, as well as his artistic conscience.

At the outset we should remind ourselves that he was not only the fabulist of *La Cigale et la fourmi*. He was and is appreciated almost as much for the licentious verse *Contes*. He wrote a considerable amount of lyric poetry in a variety of metrical forms. He was the author of the charming prose and verse "nouvelle" *Psyché*, of the verse idyll *Adonis*, and of numerous combined prose and verse letters including the too little read *Voyage en*

---

* See, for example, F. Gohin's chapter on La Fontaine the artist in his *L'Art de La Fontaine dans ses fables*, Paris, Garnier, 1929, pp. 1-37, and this same critic's sketch of his character in *La Fontaine, études et recherches*, Paris, Garnier, 1937, pp. 1-17.

Limousin, about which I shall have more to say later. He tried his hand at comedy, opera, and ballet. One might almost say that his talent was at the disposal of anyone who could use it or enjoy it: he wrote a long religious poem for Port-Royal, and one on the virtues of quinine at the request of a protectress. In short he led a full literary existence for a period of about forty years, and if the fables and the tales were his masterpieces they were not his whole life.

We should also remember that he came to his life work late, reaching full stature as a literary person only when he was nearing fifty, so there will be no real alteration and very little progression in his ideas until almost the end when he is converted. What progression there is will be observed in the focusing of his thoughts as he found his talent more surely in the years after Vaux.

Finally we should realize that this so open, so *distrait*, so amiably helpless "bonhomme" lived as calculated an existence as one could possibly imagine. To be sure, this calculation was in the service of a thoroughly respectable ruling passion: verse-making. At the end of his life, when he was seventy-three and had turned to the Church, he was making hymns and writing to his dear friend Maucroix, "Je mourrais d'ennui si je ne composais plus."[1] And some thirty years earlier a passage from the *Voyage en Limousin* runs, "On laisse, en sortant du Bourg-la-Reine, Sceaux à la droite, et à quelque lieues de là Chilly à la gauche, puis Montléry du même côté. Est-ce Montléry qu'il faut dire, ou Montlehéry? C'est Montlehéry quand le vers est trop court, et Montléry quand il est trop long."[2]

Everything La Fontaine did, everything he wrote was designed to protect the preoccupation suggested by these lines. To this protective sense we owe the *Fables*. To it perhaps we may attribute the character of La Fontaine's whole way of thinking and feeling about literature and art, about criticism, about his own work, and even about himself.

In 1663, when he was forty-two years old and had been publishing for nine years, he took a trip into the

Limousin in connection with the break-up of the Foucquet clique to which he had been attached. Along the way he wrote to his wife the series of letters which is called the *Voyage en Limousin*. They were a mixture of prose and verse and, as was the custom, only semi-private. They would be read aloud or passed around. They could not be expected then to expose any side of La Fontaine which he would not willingly show to the world. But then, as I have said, it seems that there was no side to hide, no secret. Yet I think these letters do reveal a La Fontaine of whom perhaps he himself was not conscious. They are the letters of a man who looks about him and who has the normal curiosity of the tourist concerning his traveling companions, his accommodations, the country and the places through which he passes or where he stops, and the natural, architectural or artistic "points of interest" which he is privileged to see. He philosophizes over the ruins of Etampes, damaged in the Fronde; he sleeps through the Beauce, "pays ennuyeux, et qui, outre l'inclination que j'ai à dormir, nous en fournissait un très beau sujet."[3] He goes to look at the sunset from the bridge at Orléans; he visits the church at Cléry; he appreciates the view from Amboise, and admires the château at Blois for its lack of symmetry and regularity. But the most detailed description of the whole trip is his account of the town and the château of Richelieu.[4] He made a special excursion from Port-de-Piles to see it. What he said about it seems especially revealing. He felt a certain responsibility for making a full report of his side trip, but he apologized for his faulty memory and for his lack of architectural and mythological background: "Vous savez mon ignorance en matière d'architecture et que je n'ai rien dit de Vaux* que sur des mémoires." However, he went cheerfully ahead and described the architecture, the gardens, the decoration of the interior of the château, and the paintings, statues, and furnishings which were on exhibit there. I shall mention only a few of his observations to show how he looked at things. Michelangelo's

* In the *Songe de Vaux*, see below, pp. 137-139.

"slaves" for instance he liked for their apparent incompleteness as much as in spite of it. He described a Perugino painting in some detail but limited himself to the subject matter, which he said was a "combat burlesque et énigmatique" between Pallas and Venus.

He saw a series of paintings done in collaboration by Claude and Drevet which represented the four elements. He was not certain of the authorship but did not care very much who had done them and said after describing them briefly, "Si vous me demandez ce que tout cela signifie, je vous répondrai que je n'en sais rien."

He contemplated for a moment a Titian, a Magdalen which he said was "l'original de cette dondon que notre cousin a fait mettre sur la cheminée de sa salle" and which he described as "une Magdelaine du Titian, grosse et grasse, et fort agréable: de beaux tétons comme aux premiers jours de sa pénitence, auparavant que le jeûne eût commencé d'empiéter sur elle." He apologized a little for speaking thus irreverently, "aussi n'est-ce pas mon fait que de raisonner sur des matières spirituelles: j'y ai eu mauvaise grâce toute ma vie," so he begged leave to omit mention of the other religious subjects, except to express his admiration for the skill and patience of a mosaic representing St. Jerome.

He noticed some busts and statues "parmi lesquelles on me nomma Tibère et Livie; ce sont personnes que vous connaissez, et dont M. de la Calprenède nous entretient quelquefois."

But his greatest enthusiasm was for what he claimed to be "le principal ornement de Richelieu," a rich mosaic and encrusted table whose central decoration was an enormous agate, or onyx.*

Finally he admired the gardens and the park with its dark alleys. They inspired in him a poetic meditation on the greatness of Cardinal Richelieu. Then, after tipping an employee who had obviously been expecting it, he took his leave. It was late in the day and he was tired.

* This would seem to be the table now shown in the Galerie d'Apollon of the Louvre.

The rest of the *Voyage*, related in the last of the letters which we possess, describes the country, the towns, the food and the people (including family connections) in the region around Poitiers and Limoges.

Now these letters were conscious prose and verse compositions designed to please. The writer must therefore avoid pedantry or professionalism, and he must not get intense about his subject matter. But if we admit this, what impression of La Fontaine's aesthetic sensibility do we nevertheless receive? One could say this much: he was certainly not unconscious of the presence and beauty of nature. He was aware of the existence of people and of their appearance. He was interested in the products of the human spirit such as architecture, decoration, furniture, sculpture, and painting. But when he looked at all of this, what did he see? Monumentality, richness, and technical skill; historical and literary associations, and in representational art, realism. There is some consciousness of external form, but I see in him little concern for the expression of individuality, little feeling for technique, for texture, or for mood, for what we might call the personality of a work of art. If he judged, it was from the outside, and often frankly at second hand. If he pondered, it was mostly the connection of what he saw with something else that he remembered. There seems to be no identification of his feeling self with anything that he sees. Things remain objects.

It may well be that this detachment, average in our day, was all one could expect of a Seventeenth Century man, even the most sensitive. But it is my impression that it was peculiar to La Fontaine, in that it dominated his work and his life.

His general literary standards appear to have been set from the beginning of his career, and I cannot see that contact with other literary figures of his age altered them, or that his life in the age itself had any noticeable effect on them. His ideals and his models had all come to inhabit his thought before 1661 when Foucquet was arrested and the Vaux dream ended. The *avertissement* of

the almost preprofessional *Eunuque*, his first published
work, shows that as far as his formal taste was concerned
he had very little to learn from Racine or Boileau. This
play, based on the Terence comedy, appeared in 1654, La
Fontaine being then thirty-three years old. The *avertissement* begins, "Ce n'est ici qu'une médiocre copie d'un excellent original. Peu de personnes ignorent de combien
d'agréments est remplie l'Eunuque latin. Le sujet en est
simple, comme le prescrivent nos maîtres; il n'est point
chargé d'ornements inutiles et détachés; tous les ressorts
y remuent la machine, et tous les moyens acheminent à la
fin. Quant au noeud, c'est un des plus beaux et des moins
communs de l'antiquité. Cependant il se fait avec une
facilité merveilleuse, et n'a pas une seule de ces con-
traintes que nous voyons ailleurs. La bienséance et la
médiocrité, que Plaute ignorait, s'y rencontrent partout."[5]

Simplicity, clarity, unity, ease, fitness and naturalness,
they are all here, the ideal qualities of a work of literature, found in an ancient model. Nothing could be more
correct, nothing could be more expressive of the aspira-
tions of the generation of 1660.

Yet as we know, it was not merely in copying Terence
that the Classic school was to achieve its greatness. Likewise this is not the whole La Fontaine. The fantasy on
love poetry called *Clymène* (composed sometime between 1658 and 1661, that is, during the Vaux period)
added modern models to the ancient and joined the
French tradition to the classic. Malherbe, Marot and
Voiture now accompany Horace in serving as inspiration.
They are, with the later addition of Rabelais (though
there is already a reminiscence of him here) the "maîtres"
whom La Fontaine will claim for the rest of his life.[6]

One is impressed, in the *Clymène*, with the poet's attention to tone, or mode. He had a sharp ear. Was his
consciousness of poetic values limited to this, as his sense
of plastic meanings stopped at the external shapes? His
defense of poetry in the *Songe de Vaux*, written during
this same period, reflects some such limitation. It adds
to but in no way extends or deepens his conception of

literature. Poetry debates against architecture, painting, and horticulture, mostly in rather bad Alexandrines. The plea is that immortal poetry creates the Gods and heroes whom architecture only houses in palaces which crumble; that horticulture can grow no flowers more beautiful than poetry can describe, and that painting can represent much less than poetry can, for poetry can even paint a painting.[7] So the creative, descriptive, and analytical virtues are praised, though in very general terms, and nothing is said about the moral value of literature, or about inspiration, or about insight. Granted the necessities of the whole *Songe* (praise of the beauties of Vaux) and those of the particular fragment on poetry, which proceeds by comparison, I can find nothing in it to indicate that La Fontaine had any but the most conventional ideas about his vocation.

What I have said up to now has been meant to sketch a sort of basic La Fontaine, a natural versifier with a classic taste and a keen ear, but with an essentially narrative and descriptive mind. In other words the passages I have mentioned suggest a technical equipment for poetry but not a temperamental equipment for high, that is, for lyric and heroic poetry. Now I think that La Fontaine knew this and I think that in spite of it he still aspired to high poetry. The degree of his aspiration could only have made him more acutely conscious of his limitations and of the limitations of his epoch. His natural urge to versify led him then to organize his talents to their best advantage. This was part of his calculation. We know from his statements at the beginning of the *Psyché*, in the *avertissement* to the *Adonis* and in the *avertissement* to the *Songe* that he considered himself as working in the heroic if not the lyric genres, and we know from the *avertissement* to the *Songe* that by about 1670 he regretted that they no longer appealed to the public. By that time of course he was committed to the *conte* and the fable.

The attraction of La Fontaine's talent toward the pole of the fable is quite noticeable by the time of the composition of the *Songe de Vaux,* in connection with which I have already mentioned the stiff Alexandrines of the debate on the arts. One need only turn the page to the fragment which follows in order to find a wholly different kind of poetry. It is the *Aventure d'un Saumon et d'un Esturgeon.* This little dream of two fish who explain with dignity to the poet how they have been sent by Neptune as ambassadors to Foucquet is set forth in fresh free verse which treats an absurd impossibility as though it were the most natural thing in the world. The conception is simple and the tone is of a seriousness suited to the elevated mission of the animals, but of course, therefore, fundamentally burlesque. So the mock dignity of the poem allows such phrases as "le fier Borée, auteur de maint orage," or "le dieu/ De l'humide et vaste lieu" or "Monarque de l'eau salée" to mingle with the realistic criticism of a passage such as "Si les gros nous mangeaient, nous mangions les petits/ Ainsi que l'on fait en France."[8]

All of the La Fontaine whom we are accustomed to think of is in the *Aventure* fragment: the animals who talk ("même les poissons"), the narrative in free verse, the mingling of the heroic and the realistic tones, the satire, gracefully cynical. La Fontaine did not invent this kind of thing, and he owed his understanding of the tone largely to Voiture,* but he was to make it his own. It was his way, as perhaps it was one of the century's ways, of accommodating the heroic. It was the way of the burlesque, of the *galant,* of what La Fontaine called *gaieté,* by which he meant, as he explained,[9] something more than the persuasion to laughter.

I am not here concerned with determining the precise moment at which La Fontaine discovered the limitations of his equipment, or those of his times (they are perhaps one and the same thing), for it is quite enough to say

---

* One thinks especially of the famous letter to the Duc d'Enghien—purporting to be from a carp to a pike (*Lettres,* ed. Uzanne, Paris, 1880, II, pp. 126ff.) but also of the tone of Voiture's verse and its affiliation with Marot.

that the Vaux period was his apprenticeship. I am however concerned with the results of such a discovery, if
discovery it was, and the effect of it upon his work. If
the practice of the burlesque or the *galant* allowed him
to write with a kind of impunity in the grand style, this
was still not enough to distinguish him from any number of his contemporaries. There were other ways of capi-
talizing upon his limitations, and the free form of the
conte and the fable permitted these. As La Fontaine
made use of them, it seems to me that they all in the long
run derive from, or add up to that *detachment* which I
mentioned earlier, a detachment which allowed him to
exploit, above all, himself.

One of the first steps was to externalize the sense of
limitation by admitting it.

> Comme la force est un point
> Dont je ne me pique point,
> Je tâche d'y tourner le vice en ridicule,
> Ne pouvant l'attaquer avec des bras d'Hercule,
> C'est là tout mon talent, je ne sais s'il suffit.
> (*Le Bûcheron et Mercure*) [10]

This admission, be it noted, plays a double role. It neutralizes the limitation, but it also makes use of the poet
himself. This is what I mean when I say that La Fontaine
is exploiting himself. Somewhere he had learned the
value of openness. Years later in the *Ballade* for the birth
of the Duc de Bourgogne he still claimed that his muse
aspired only to modest efforts, and later on to this same
prince he wrote "chanter sur la musette c'est mon
talent."[11]

But, quite naturally, the limitation can be further ex-
ploited by being attached to a principle. And so we read
at the beginning of *L'Âne et le petit chien,*

> Ne forçons point notre talent;
> Nous ne ferions rien avec grâce.[12]

And in the preface to the first collection of fables the oc-
casional omission of the moral is justified by the advice

of Horace, for "Cet auteur ne veut point qu'un écrivain s'opiniâtre contre l'incapacité de son esprit, ni contre celle de sa matière."[13] A subject demands a manner and a manner demands a temperament. *La Montagne qui accouche* points again to a Horatian moral:

> Je me figure un auteur
> Qui dit, "Je chanterai la guerre
> Que firent les Titans au maître du tonnerre."
> C'est promettre beaucoup, mais qu'en sort-il souvent?
> Du vent.[14]

One is not surprised then to see La Fontaine specially attracted to certain other traditional literary virtues. One of these was studied negligence, and again the form of the *conte* and the fable allowed it, even demanded it. The *avertissement* for the 1665 edition of the *Contes* and the preface to the 1666 edition both expressed the necessity of avoiding strict versification or "narrations étudiées" in any but the grand subjects.[15] As for the fables, that same *Bûcheron et Mercure* began (it was addressed to a friend),

> Votre goût a servi de règle à mon ouvrage,
> J'ai tenté les moyens d'acquérir son suffrage.
> Vous voulez qu'on évite un soin trop curieux,
> Et de vains ornements l'effort ambitieux.
> Un auteur gâte tout quand il veut trop bien faire.[16]

This willful negligence, this air of insouciance naturally goes hand in hand with the quick touch and the easy eclecticism of the free soul, and connects the sense of tonal distinction and tonal unity with the detachment inherent in La Fontaine's character. "Les longs ouvrages me font peur,"[17] he said in the epilogue to the first book of fables. And in the *Discours* addressed to La Rochefoucauld occurs the Musset-like line, "Les ouvrages les plus courts sont toujours les meilleurs."[18] So in the preface to the 1666 *Contes* he explained how he cut down some of his material to avoid "la longueur et l'obscurité."[19]

And since one spends little time on any single topic, variety follows, and conversation is a "parterre où Flore épand ses biens." In the *Discours à Mme de la Sablière* we read,

> Sur différentes fleurs l'abeille s'y repose,
> Et fait du miel de toute chose.[20]

La Fontaine of course is the bee: "A beaucoup de plaisirs je mêle un peu de gloire."[21] He was as well Poliphile, as he called the narrator in the *Psyché*.* He was the lover of all things, "jusqu'au sombre plaisir d'un coeur mélancolique,"[22] dwelling upon nothing for long but liking everything, and so, as I say, remaining detached, uninvolved, uncommitted in any direction except literarily; and even there he would not like to be thought of as taking himself very seriously. I sometimes wonder if the completeness with which La Fontaine committed himself publicly at the time of his conversion† was not a reverse reflection of this life-long refusal to let himself be caught by any of his affections—except that all-absorbing one of making verse.

There is another way of describing La Fontaine's self-exploitation, and this is to say that in openly revealing himself he forces his readers to share some of the responsibility for their enjoyment of his art. His attitude toward criticism was correspondingly liberal. The *goût du siècle* is his rule and *plaire* is his only aim. About the critics themselves he never had much to say, his most violent statement against criticism being the moral of the *Serpent et la lime*:

> Ceci s'adresse à vous, esprits du dernier ordre,
> Qui n'étant bon à rien, cherchez surtout à mordre.
> Vous vous tourmentez vainement.

* On the question of the identity of the four characters in the framework of the *Psyché*, see *Oeuvres diverses de La Fontaine*, Bibliothèque de la Pléiade, ed. P. Clarac, Paris, 1942, pp. 817-18 and 820.

† Cf. G. Michaut, *La Fontaine*, II, chap. 30, pp. 304ff.

Croyez-vous que vos dents impriment leurs outrages
　　　Sur tant de beaux ouvrages?
Ils sont pour vous d'airain, d'acier, de diamant.[23]

But his principal defense was that there would always be criticism and that, as *Contre ceux qui ont le goût difficile* maintained, there is no pleasing everybody. He reacts all in all less violently than Racine or Corneille or Molière.

Quite consistently, therefore, La Fontaine thought that literary judgments were a matter of individual taste, not swayed by analytical discourse. In the preface to *l'Eunuque* from which I have already quoted he said further, "Je ne prétends pas . . . empêcher la censure de mon ouvrage, ni que ces noms illustres de Térence et de Ménandre lui tiennent lieu d'un assez puissant bouclier contre toutes sortes d'atteintes; nous vivons dans un siècle et dans un pays où l'autorité n'est point respectée: d'ailleurs l'État des belles-lettres est entièrement populaire; chacun a droit de suffrage et le moindre particulier n'y reconnaît pas de plus souverain juge que soi."[24] This was written, or at least published, only a year after the Fronde to be sure, but when it is added to Corneille's, Gomberville's, and Méré's opinions concerning restrictions, one feels safe in attributing it to something more than the political state of the nation at the time. Besides, La Fontaine makes a special category for the Republic of Letters.* Finally, he continued to hold this view: fifteen years later in the preface to *Psyché* he said, "Ce n'est pas à force de raisonnement qu'on fait entrer le plaisir dans l'âme de ceux qui lisent."[25] And in the *Avertissement* to the *Songe de Vaux* he said, "Que j'aie bien fait ou non . . . je m'en dois remettre au goût du lecteur plutôt qu'aux raisons que j'en pourrais dire."[26]

His own taste, the taste of the public, and the air of insouciance all come together in the preface to *Psyché*.

---

* Cf. Boileau's statement concerning freedom in the Republic of Letters in the preface to the first edition of his collected works (see below, p. 203) and also Barbier d'Aucour's *Sentiments de Cléante*, 1671-1672, ed. of 1776, pp. 377-78.

There he discussed the difficulty of finding just the right tone before deciding that the taste of the times was for the *galant* and for *plaisanterie*, so that "il a fallu badiner depuis le commencement jusqu'à la fin: il a fallu chercher du galant et de la plaisanterie. Quand il ne l'aurait pas fallu, mon inclination m'y portait, et peut-être y suis-je tombé en beaucoup d'endroits contre la raison et la bienséance."[27] This is really a curious passage, for in a sense it puts the blame on the audience, but at the same time asserts the will of the author. The little avant-propos to the *Songe de Vaux* expresses this independence in a different and equally interesting fashion: "Le lecteur si bon lui semble peut croire que l'Aminte dont j'y parle représente une personne particulière; si bon lui semble que c'est la beauté des femmes en général; s'il lui plaît même, que c'est celle de toutes sortes d'objets. Ces trois explications sont libres. Ceux qui cherchent en tout du mystère, et qui veulent que cette sorte de poème ait un sens allégorique, ne manqueront pas de recourir aux deux dernières. Quant à moi je ne trouverai pas mauvais qu'on s'imagine que cette Aminte est telle ou telle personne: cela rend la chose plus passionnée, et ne la rend pas moins héroïque."[28]

However, La Fontaine's taste had nothing extreme about it. He admired as we saw the regularity of Terence. We know that he respected Malherbe and disliked Ronsard. Yet, "le secret de plaire ne consiste pas toujours en l'ajustement ni même en la régularité; il faut du piquant et de l'agréable si l'on veut toucher. Combien voyons-nous de ces beautés régulières qui ne touchent point et dont personne n'est amoureux?"[29] He liked the irregularity of Blois* and the supposed imperfection of

---

* The abbé Michel de Marolles, in a discourse defending the city of Paris against critics of its disorder and irregularity said, after mentioning the Place Royale (now the Place des Vosges) and the Place Dauphine as contrary evidence, "Ce n'est pourtant pas à mon avis, qu'une proportion si régulière fasse toujours un si bel effet à la vue. Les diverses Architectures, plaisent souvent davantage et marquent je ne sais quoi de plus riant et de plus nombreux . . ." Marolles, *Mémoires*, Amsterdam, ed. of 1755, II, 279. The date

the Michelangelo slaves. He understood the mystery of
attractiveness, of the *je ne sais quoi*, and the *Psyché* for
instance contains an episode involving two women where
the theme is precisely regular beauty conquered by irregular charm.[30] This opposition, incidentally, was carried over into real life in the description of Mademoiselle
de La Vallière given by the Abbé de Choisy in his
Mémoires.[31] He wrote, "Mademoiselle de La Vallière
n'était pas de ces beautés toutes parfaites qu'on admire
souvent sans les aimer. Elle était fort aimable, et ce vers
de La Fontaine 'Et la Grâce plus belle encore que la
Beauté' semble avoir été fait pour elle." The line of verse
is from the *Adonis* and the full passage runs,

Rien ne manque à Vénus, ni les lis, ni les roses,
Ni le mélange exquis des plus aimables choses,
Ni le charme secret dont l'oeil est enchanté,
Ni la grâce plus belle encore que la beauté.[32]

(The Princess Palatine thought similarly of Mademoiselle
de La Vallière, and wrote in one of her letters, that her
look had a charm which it was not possible to describe;
that her eyes were more beautfiul than those of Mme de
Montespan, although her teeth were bad; that her whole
demeanor was modest, and that her slight limp, even,
was not unbecoming to her.[33]) But even here, I hope it is
by now unnecessary to say, La Fontaine was not so independent as he seems, for he was in a well-established
tradition. Or perhaps it would be more correct to say that
his independence easily adopted this tradition. In this
connection I should like to mention a most interesting
piece which has been attributed to La Fontaine as well
as to others.* This is the anonymous preface to the

---

of the discourse is probably 1656. For another reference to this
dispute over the Paris of the period see below, p. 239n.
  * See Ch.-H. Boudhors, *Oeuvres complètes de Boileau*, Paris,
Belles Lettres, 1934-1943, *Epîtres*, p. 263; also F. Gohin, *La
Fontaine, études et recherches*, Paris, Garnier, 1937, pp. 177ff. and
P. Clarac, *Oeuvres diverses de La Fontaine*, Paris, Bibliothèque de
la Pléiade, 1942, p. 773 [the preface itself] and p. 935; also P.
Clarac, *La Fontaine, l'homme et l'oeuvre*, Paris, Boivin, 1947, p. 53.

Recueil de poésies chrétiennes et diverses, which is of 1671 (the *achevé* is of 1670). La Fontaine had a part in the editing of this collection; just how great a part we do not know. If he did compose the preface, then he was much more explicit in his distrust of the rules than in anything I have here quoted. Personally I do not feel that it is by La Fontaine. The tone and the vocabulary remind me more of Méré. In any case it is an additional document of the sort we have been considering, though it should appear less startling than some critics seem to find it.* Its insistence upon the ultimate vanity of poetic theory, and upon the necessity for *sentiment* and *goût* were neither a novelty nor an archaism in 1670.

To return to La Fontaine, all that I have said concerning this question might be summed up by the famous passage from the preface to the first *Fables*, "On ne considère en France que ce qui plaît, c'est la grande règle et pour ainsi dire la seule."[34]

It is thus that La Fontaine turned natural inclinations or disinclinations into advantages, into positive characteristics. So in justifying himself he was able to talk about himself, and as his adoption of a certain tone had allowed him to satisfy his penchant for the heroic, so this easy confiding both protected him and allowed him to satisfy his lyric leanings. If we stop to think of it, we do not read La Fontaine's fables at all for the morality, but we read them for the sense of the presence of a strongly individual narrator and commentator. And how frequently this sense is satisfied by the poet's reminding us that it is he who is telling the story; and this is even done sometimes by the simple overt reversion to personal experience, as in the conclusions to *La Laitière et le pot au lait*[35] and to *Les Deux pigeons*.[36]

The same is true, but perhaps less noticeable because of the form, of the *contes*. Boileau pointed out the fact in the *Dissertation sur la Joconde*.† He quoted this passage:

* Gohin and Clarac, *opera cit., l.c.*
† See below, p. 206 note, for the question of the authorship of the *Dissertation*.

Marié depuis peu; content, je n'en sais rien.
    Sa femme avait de la jeunesse,
  De la beauté, de la délicatesse:
Il ne tenait qu'à lui qu'il ne s'en trouvât bien.[37]

And Boileau made the following comment: "S'il eût dit simplement que Joconde vivait content avec sa femme, son discours aurait été assez froid; mais par ce doute où il s'embarrasse lui-même, et qui ne veut pourtant dire que la même chose, il enjoue sa narration, et occupe agréablement le lecteur."[38]

La Fontaine was undoubtedly aware of the literary value of this honesty. There is a hint that he realized its practical value as well in a letter to the duchesse de Bouillon where he wrote a poem which he partly used again in that conclusion to *Les Deux pigeons*, already referred to. I shall quote the whole poem so that the reader may if he wishes compare, though I am interested here mainly in the lines which I italicize. Notice, however, how it praises irregular beauty.

    Peut-on s'ennuyer en des lieux
Honorés par les pas, éclairés par les yeux
    D'une aimable et vive princesse,
A pied blanc et mignon, à brune et longue tresse?
Nez troussé? c'est un charme encor selon mon sens:
C'en est même un des plus puissants.
Pour moi, le temps d'aimer est passé, je l'avoue,
    Et je mérite qu'on me loue
    De ce libre et sincère aveu,
Dont pourtant le public se souciera très peu:
Que j'aime ou n'aime pas, c'est pour lui même chose;
    Mais, s'il arrive que mon coeur
Retourne à l'avenir dans sa première erreur,
Nez aquilins et longs n'en seront pas la cause.[39]

(It is amusing to note that in the fable, published some years after this letter was written, La Fontaine, well in his fifties, only asked the question "Ai-je passé le temps d'aimer?" instead of admitting it as he does in this "libre et sincère aveu.")

147

Thus, in the various ways which I have tried to indicate, La Fontaine capitalized on his limitations and on his personality, protected himself and escaped being fixed or pigeonholed in this century so inclined to clearcut distinctions. It was by constantly admitting his peculiarities, by involving the public in his procedures and by uninvolving himself, that, as Mornet said, "il a glissé si subtilement et si aisément entre les lois qu'il a toujours été libre sans paraître l'avoir cherché."[40] Perhaps, though, the literary and social laws were not as stringent as Mornet's statement seems to imply.

Whatever La Fontaine's relation to these laws may have been, however, I cannot help thinking that his honesty, his *bonhomie*, even his distraction, were somehow deliberate, and that, like many another artist, he acted himself: he played the part of Jean de La Fontaine, and played it as far as posterity is concerned with the utmost success. Or, to invert the notion, it seems to me that his life was, like his work, a series of *mensonges* or *feintes*, as he was fond of calling his tales and his fables, which were at the same time true:

> Et même qui mentirait
> Comme Esope et comme Homère
> Un vrai menteur ne serait.
> Le doux charme de maint songe
> Par leur bel art inventé
> Sous les habits de mensonge,
> Nous offre la vérité.
> (*Le Dépositaire infidèle*)[41]

So the line between illusion and reality is very thin as is was for the whole century, and this gives La Fontaine a sort of Protean quality. It is for this reason that the poet whose principal monument is a collection of rhymed fables recited by school children should be thought of as an epic poet and also (I believe more justly) as his generation's almost unique lyric poet. Boileau tried to explain this quality. Here is what he said in the *Dissertation sur la Joconde*: "Tout ce qu'il dit est simple et naturel: et ce que j'estime surtout en lui, c'est une certaine naïveté de langage que peu de gens connaissent, et qui fait pourtant tout l'agrément du discours; c'est cette naïveté inimitable qui a été tant estimée dans les écrits d'Horace et de Térence. . . . Ces sortes de beautés sont de celles qu'il faut sentir, et qui ne se prouvent point. C'est ce je ne sais quoi qui nous charme, et sans lequel la beauté même n'aurait ni grâce ni beauté. Mais, après tout, c'est un je ne sais quoi. . . ."[42]

2. THE INDIVIDUALISM OF MOLIÈRE

MOLIÈRE's critical position is one of the most balanced and most explicit in the century. It is in harmony with the "philosophy" of his comedy, and it helps to explain how his reasonable view of life finally leaves much to faith. For, if La Fontaine can change his shape, Molière can turn himself inside out.

His theory of comedy is to be found principally in the *Critique de l'Ecole des femmes*, and in *Les Femmes savantes*, but here and there in his prefaces there are some illuminating statements.

I expect that personally his ideas can be explained by the fact that of all the major figures of the century he was the most professional, and that he was as much a man of the theater as he was a man of letters. We are apt to forget how much of his drama was given over to ballet and how many of his plays remained unversified. It should be remembered that *Les Femmes savantes* was preceded by *Les Fourberies de Scapin* and followed by *Le Malade imaginaire*. These are his last plays. He acted in them and directed them as he had done all of his life. He must have had very little time for leisurely, careful composition. He remained dependent upon and devoted to the traditional immediacy of the *commedia* and the farce.

Ironically though, his dignity was such that he had very early to face serious criticism. I do not say he did not enjoy being taken seriously. I believe he was ambitious. But this is part of the inverted nature of his whole being and destiny, that Sganarelle should be the greatest writer of comedy since Aristophanes. His deepest faith was really in the largely instinctive reaction of the *parterre*. "Apprends, Marquis, je te prie, et les autres aussi, que le bon sens n'a point de place déterminée à la comédie; que la différence du demi-louis d'or et la pièce de quinze sols ne fait rien du tout au bon goût; que debout ou assis, on peut donner un mauvais jugement; et qu'enfin, à le prendre en général, je me fierais assez à l'approbation du parterre, par la raison qu'entre ceux qui le composent, il y en a plusieurs qui sont capables de juger d'une pièce selon les règles, et que les autres en jugent par la bonne façon d'en juger, qui est de se laisser prendre aux choses, et de n'avoir ni prévention aveugle, ni complaisance affectée, ni délicatesse ridicule."[1] This faith, expressed here in the *Critique*, is extended in the same play to include all judgment: "Moquons-nous donc de cette chicane où ils [the rule critics] veulent assujétir le goût du public, et ne consultons dans une comédie que l'effet qu'elle fait sur nous. Laissons-nous aller de bonne foi aux choses qui nous prennent par les entrailles, et ne cherchons point de raisonnements pour nous empêcher d'avoir du plaisir."[2]

This famous passage is directed against all thoughtful criticism. Nevertheless Molière wished also to assert that he had a very solid respect for the taste of the Court. Clitandre says to Trissotin the *bel esprit* in the *Femmes savantes*:

Vous en voulez beaucoup à cette pauvre cour,
Et son malheur est grand de voir que chaque jour
Vous autres beaux esprits vous déclamiez contre elle,
Que de tous vos chagrins vous lui fassiez querelle,
Et, sur son méchant goût lui faisant son procès,
N'accusiez que lui seul de vos méchants succès.
Permettez-moi Monsieur Trissotin, de vous dire,
Avec tout le respect que votre nom m'inspire,

Que vous feriez fort bien, vos confrères et vous,
De parler de la cour d'un ton un peu plus doux;
Qu'à le bien prendre, au fond, elle n'est pas si bête
Que vous autres Messieurs vous vous mettez en tête;
Qu'elle a du sens commun pour se connaître à tout;
Que chez elle on se peut former quelque bon goût;
Et que l'esprit du monde y vaut, sans flatterie,
Tout le savoir obscur de la pédanterie.[3]

Clitandre's speech here is practically a verse rendering of one of Dorante's speeches in the *Critique*.[4] Like its prose prototype it sets off good taste against pedantry. If we add the satire of *précieux* fadism with which Molière is full, we can say that his literary creed was about as follows: the instinctive judgments of the *parterre* are generally trustworthy; but there is such a thing as intelligent and experienced taste, which is not to be confused with an overdelicate insistence on the requirements of a momentarily fashionable enthusiasm, nor with an *esprit de chicane* resulting from the application of criteria based on irrelevant knowledge.

In all of this the rules occupy a relatively unimportant place. Molière's position was pragmatic like Corneille's. "Mais les rieurs ont été pour elle," he said of *L'Ecole des femmes*,[5] and in the preface to *Les Fâcheux*, "Ce n'est pas mon dessein d'examiner maintenant si tout cela pouvait être mieux, et si tous ceux qui s'y sont divertis ont ri selon les règles."[6] Furthermore his conception of the drama was a theatrical one, which means that much depends on the ephemeralities of the performance, while rules are for the written play. In the *avis au lecteur* of *L'Amour médecin* he said "Il n'est pas besoin de vous avertir qu'il y a beaucoup de choses qui dépendent de l'action. On sait bien que les comédies ne sont faites que pour être jouées."[7] Indeed he had claimed to be really not interested in the printing of *Les Précieuses ridicules*; ". . . comme une grande partie des grâces qu'on y a trouvées dépendent de l'action et du ton de la voix, il m'importait qu'on ne les dépouillât pas de ces ornements et je trouvais que le succès qu'elles avaient eu dans la représentation était assez beau pour en demeurer là."[8]

Even if we take this with a grain of salt, I think Molière felt apart from the literary world and in a sense rival to it. In the same preface to *Les Précieuses* he speaks with some disdain of "Messieurs les auteurs, à present mes confrères"[9] and they appeared to him as a professional group to be satirized as much as the *marquis*. Dorante says in the *Critique* "La cour a quelques ridicules, j'en demeure d'accord, et je suis, comme on voit, le premier à les fronder. Mais, ma foi, il y en a un grand nombre parmi les beaux esprits de profession; et si l'on joue quelques marquis, je trouve qu'il y a bien plus de quoi jouer les auteurs."[10] And the *Femmes savantes* carried out the implied intention.

There was some defensiveness about this. He claimed that if he had had the time he would have written a "belle et docte préface" for *Les Précieuses*, "et je ne manque point de livres qui m'auroient fourni tout ce qu'on peut dire de savant sur la tragédie et la comédie."[11] And the *Avertissement* to *Les Fâcheux* says "Le temps viendra de faire imprimer mes remarques sur les pièces que j'aurais faites, et je ne désespère pas de faire voir un jour, en grand auteur, que je puis citer Aristote et Horace. En attendant cet examen, qui peut-être ne viendra point, je m'en remets assez aux décisions de la multitude, et je tiens aussi difficile de combattre un ouvrage que le public approuve, que d'en défendre un qu'il condamne."[12]

So we are back to the criterion of public approval. But Molière won't be caught on it. In the *Critique* Lysidas says to Dorante, "Enfin, Monsieur, toute votre raison, c'est que *l'Ecole des femmes* a plu; et vous ne vous souciez point qu'elle soit dans les règles, pourvu. . . ." Dorante interrupts, "Tout beau, Monsieur Lysidas, je ne vous accorde pas cela. Je dis bien que le grand art est de plaire, et que cette comédie ayant plu à ceux pour qui elle est faite, je trouve que c'est assez pour elle et qu'elle doit peu se soucier du reste. Mais avec cela, je soutiens qu'elle ne pèche contre aucune des règles dont vous parlez. Je les ai lues, Dieu merci, autant qu'un autre; et je ferais voir aisément que peut-être n'avons-nous point de pièce au théâtre plus régulière que celle-là."[13]

But, as we know, the *Critique* ends in good-natured confusion with no one convinced, and with the final word about Molière himself: "il ne se soucie pas qu'on fronde ses pièces, pourvu qu'il y vienne du monde."

I began this chapter by remarking on the explicit and balanced nature of Molière's critical position. The reader will I think easily agree that it *is* explicit, and I have quoted but a small part of Molière's expression of it. As to the balance, I hope it is apparent that it is a very delicate one, and depends upon mobility and adaptability. It is hard to fix, and this is as Molière would have it, for what is fixed is dead. This is the faith of humor and the life of comedy. Which brings us to the content of Molière's drama in its relation to our general theme.

Stated in broad terms this content seems as balanced and simple as the critical position. In the preface to *Les Précieuses* Molière says that if he had been allowed to do so he would have explained his attitude toward satire; he would have shown, he says, "que les plus excellentes choses sont sujettes à être copiées par de mauvais singes qui méritent d'être bernés; que ces vicieuses imitations de ce qu'il y a de plus parfait ont été de tout temps la matière de la comédie."[14] And he goes on to say that real scholars and really brave men never took offense at the Docteur or the Capitan. This statement furnishes an excellent *point de repère* for any discussion of Molière's morality, for it contains a principle and an historical justification of the principle in terms that remind us of the basically simple origins of his comedy. Molière's central characters from the Barbouillé to the hypochondriac are masks, and they have the single exaggerated trait of the mask. This trait is a fundamental human one, not necessarily bad to begin with, pushed to an extreme which makes it a distortion. It provides one side of the structure of Molière's plays. The other side of this structure derives just as easily from traditional comedy. It is the domestic situation. In the *Malade imaginaire* as in the *Précieuses* family relationships furnish the simple framework for the incident. Argan like Gorgibus is anxious to have a particular kind of son-in-law, and in both cases the choices are distasteful to the daughters. (It happens that in the two examples I have chosen, the satire is aimed in opposite directions. This is worth remembering.) The general structure is this, then: the distorted character is surrounded by members of the household whose desires are in conflict with his, and those desires are the desires of the audience, because they are normal, instinctive, reasonable human desires. The characters who represent the opposition to the central character do so out of instinct, because nature tells them to, like the lovers and the servants, out of bourgeois common sense, or out of reasonable experience with the world, as with the Cléantes and the Philintes. Because the central character is unyielding, the happy dénouement has to be managed by deception or by a *deus ex machina*. Sometimes even this is not possible. (*Dom Juan, Le Misanthrope*)

So excess is set up against instinct on the one hand and reason on the other. And the link between instinct and reason is *bon sens*, as it is between the enjoyment of the *parterre* and the appreciation of the Court. All very simple, this structure and this morality of good sense and moderation. Simple even the notion that the persons to be satirized are bad imitations of good qualities. How is it then that *Tartuffe* got Molière into trouble? This play is interesting not only for the fact that the satire is on the edge of seriousness, but that it is split between the characters of Orgon and Tartuffe. In fact the more one considers it the more it is apparent, as Rigal pointed out,[15] that the satire is really directed against Orgon and that if one makes him the central character, the play then falls into the regular Molière pattern with Tartuffe as the object of Orgon's distortion, as gold is for Harpagon and the medical profession for Argan. It is then possible to see a deeper content to Molière, expressed by Cléante's lines to Orgon in *Tartuffe*:

Hé quoi? vous ne ferez nulle distinction
Entre l'hypocrisie et la dévotion?
Vous les voulez traiter d'un semblable langage,
Et rendre même honneur au masque qu'au visage,
Egaler l'artifice à la sincerité,
Confondre l'apparence avec la vérité,
Estimer le fantôme autant que la personne,
Et la fausse monnaie à l'égal de la bonne?[16]

It is this fault of human beings that Molière is really criticizing. It is the capacity for confusing the symbols of desirable qualities or objects with the qualities or objects for which they stand. So in Harpagon money is confused with security and in Argan doctors with bodily well being. To put it another way, Molière's whole comedy is based on illusion, on the lack of distinction between the mask and the face. But there is more to it than that, for what makes the drama of the Molière play is the fact that the central characters reduce their whole existence to their particular illusion. They are monomaniacs. So it may be said that they are all victims of the same illusion, namely that it is possible to live according to a single principle.

And so *Le Misanthrope* and *Dom Juan* are allowed to fall into line, as it were, for otherwise it is hard to understand how they are representative of any Molière philosophy. But even so we need to stretch that philosophy in order to include them. That is one reason for their being, with *Tartuffe*, the outstanding and most serious comedies of Molière. And, when we stop to think of it, their central characters are not allowed to live, finally. Both Alceste and Dom Juan are true to their false principles to the extent that they both commit a sort of suicide rather than give them up. Granted that in the case of *Dom Juan* Molière was more or less guided by the legend as it existed, his characterization of the anti-hero still remains disturbing, and the simple morality with which we are able to endow the other Molière plays fails completely. All the values are reversed. It is Sganarelle who attempts to reason with the central character. But it is Dom Juan who is the intelligent man of the world. He is also the *jeune premier*, but instead of trying to marry a young girl destined by her eccentric father for someone she does not want, he is trying to avoid one to whom he is already married in order that he may continue to possess all women young or old, married or unmarried. With all this, what distaste we may feel for his character is continually alleviated by his moral and his physical courage, and what sympathy we may feel for Sganarelle is repeatedly assaulted by his ridiculous behavior and then by his cry for wages at the end. And finally if Dom Juan is a typical Molière character in that he attempts to live by one principle—that nothing outside himself is valid—it cannot be said that Molière makes him ridiculous. It is perhaps a great injustice to Molière to look at *Dom Juan* in terms of his other plays, but when we consider that this was the play he chose to produce right after *Tartuffe*, we may wonder whether he understood its implications, or for that matter the implications of *Tartuffe* itself.

The problem of *Le Misanthrope* is no easier. Here the reversal of values is not quite so sharp. But it is for this reason even harder to see precisely where Molière's morality is directed, and what, if anything, he was attempting to "say."

Alceste ends up by deciding to shun the world of men. But what is this world? It is made up mostly of sham, of pretentiousness, of injustice, of malice. It is a world of selfishness and of lies, in which bad poets are praised, in which influence and not equity controls the administration of justice (where was the king as in *Tartuffe*?), in which externals are taken as sure indications of true merit, and where characters as well as hearts may be used as matter for game regardless of the consequence. It is a world in which one says what one does not mean and in which nothing is worse than silence unless it be sincerity. Worst of all it is a world which pities a virtuous man. This is the world as seen not merely through the eyes of Alceste, but as seen by Molière, for all of what I have mentioned actually emerges in the play. And so in a sense the tables are turned. Instead of the usual ridiculous character attempting to operate in a sane and natural world, we have in Alceste a *simply logical* individual unable to operate in a world of completely distorted values. It is as though Molière had taken almost all the rest of his drama and put it in the background and had set against it one of his secondary characters. Yet this is not quite right, for Alceste is unlike any of the secondary characters of Molière. His is not any philosophy of *bon sens*. He is not practical. He fights (like Dom Juan) against overwhelming odds.

But he has a friend and counsellor who is practical. It is Philinte who preaches, like the *honnête homme* that he is, against excess. But excess of what? Alceste criticizes the presumptuousness of Oronte, the false prudery of Arsinoé, the unbearable insolence of Acaste and Clitandre, and the coquetry of Célimène. These are themselves excesses, of the kind that Molière himself satirizes, and for a moment it seems as though the playwright were denying himself. Yet of course this is not so. Alceste's view of life is humorless, and it is as exclusive in its judgment as it is inclusive in its range. Like Timon he hates those who are bad and he hates the rest for not hating as he does. He sees all men in only one light. Yet it is not Alceste's estimate of humanity which Philinte condemns. It is the manner in which Alceste reacts to the estimate. Philinte says,

Mon Dieu, des moeurs du temps mettons-nous moins
   en peine,
Et faisons un peu grâce à la nature humaine;
Ne l'examinons point dans la grande rigueur,
Et voyons ses défauts avec quelque douceur.
Il faut, parmi le monde, une vertu traitable;
A force de sagesse on peut être blâmable;
La parfaite raison fuit toute extrémité,
Et veut qu'on soit sage avec sobriété.[17]

And a little further on he continues,

> Oui, je vois ces défauts dont votre âme murmure
> Comme vices unis à l'humaine nature;
> Et mon esprit enfin n'est pas plus offensé
> De voir un homme fourbe, injuste, intéressé,
> Que de voir des vautours affamés de carnage,
> Des singes malfaisants, et des loups pleins de rage.[18]

Did Molière realize that there is no such thing as excessive virtue? Or did the words *vertu* and *sagesse* mean something other than virtue? Yet he must have been conscious of the paradox in "à force de sagesse on peut être blâmable." And surely the irony in the implied comparison of men to vultures, monkeys, and wolves uttered with such sangfroid must not have escaped him. I do not think he wanted Philinte to be right.

There are other reasons for thinking this. In the first place Alceste's attitude is largely theoretical. He makes a great effort not to be rude to Oronte and finally admits that "On peut être honnête homme et faire mal des vers."[19] More than this, he is in love with just the sort of person who represents what he detests. He does not attempt to justify himself, and admits its complete irrationality. Naturally the humanizing effect of such an inconsistency is tremendous. It is of course typical of Molière. Just as Alceste himself refused to include the complete Oronte in his condemnation (in which he seems to remove himself from his own inclusiveness) so Molière generally allows his characters to behave normally (i.e. sensibly or foolishly) somewhere in the play. In this connection it is useful to remember the passage from the *Critique* where Lysidas criticizes Arnolphe's having given money so freely to Horace: "Et puisque c'est le personnage ridicule de la pièce, fallait-il lui faire faire l'action d'un honnête homme?"[20] Dorante answers to this, "Quant à l'argent qu'il donne librement, outre que la lettre de son meilleur ami lui est une caution suffisante, il n'est pas incompatible qu'une personne soit ridicule en de certaines choses et honnête homme en d'autres."[21] This is the explanation of Orgon's "Allons, ferme, mon coeur, point de faiblesse humaine!" of Dom Juan's "Va, va, je te le donne pour l'amour de l'humanité." and of Argan's "Qu'ai-je fait, misérable?" when Louison pretends to be dead as a result of his blow. The door is always left open for sympathy in one way or another. Indeed, it is sometimes possible to laugh *with* the ridiculous character at the very height of his excess, as when Argan violently denies Toinette's assertion that he is naturally good. We should remember too that Molière himself played these parts. But in the case of Alceste it is left wide open, and the greatest reason for thinking that Molière did not want Philinte to be right is Eliante's speech to him about Alceste:

> Dans ses façons d'agir, il est fort singulier
> Mais, j'en fais, je l'avoue, un cas particulier,
> Et la sincérité dont son âme se pique
> A quelque chose, en soi, de noble et d'héroïque.
> C'est une vertu rare au siècle d'aujourd'hui,
> Et je la voudrais voir partout comme chez lui.[22]

It is Eliante who represents in the play what one might call Molière's ideal female. And Philinte does not attempt to contradict her, but passes to the subject of Alceste's unaccountable love for Célimène.

Who then represents Molière? Eliante, Alceste, or Philinte? I believe that it is impossible to say, unless they all do. And if that is so then we are faced with all sorts of contradictions. And it seems to me that these contradictions are there and are not removable. The world is as it is, Molière seems to say, with a great many objectionable features. One has to accept them. It is useless to attempt to correct them, and if one tries, one only makes one's self ridiculous, and yet. . . .

And so all the easy philosophy of moderation really breaks down and we are left with what is actually a rather heartless situation. Eliante, the sincere person who loves, or at least could love Alceste, too easily takes Philinte as second choice, while Alceste, who desperately wishes to love sincerely a sincere person, has to leave because he feels himself unworthy of the woman he ought to love, and because he feels that the woman he loves is unworthy of him. All of this is in the dénouement and the play has to be ended of course. But precisely, there could be no satisfactory end, because there is no humanly satisfactory general solution to the problem of human behavior. And in this play Molière put himself in a position where the morality was reduced to that problem. He could not let the mask alone.

With all the laughter and the simplicity and the balance then, Molière leaves us with a question mark, because he had himself the sense to see the satisfaction in excess, and the limitations of reasonableness.

3. THE FREEDOM OF RACINE

IF OVERT statements mean anything, Racine was much less concerned with theory than Corneille or Molière. We have only one or two declarations which could be looked upon as official clarifications of a critical position. But he had one peculiarity which reveals much. He was very sensitive to criticism, and this sensitivity showed itself in the sharpness with which he defended his plays against not so much the criticism as the critics. Generally speaking he felt that he was fighting a *cabale*, a minority. This was true, and the *cabale* was made up mostly of partisans of Corneille. Their criticism could never be very serious, for Racine's drama conformed easily to the dramatic ideals of the times. But it was this very fact that annoyed Racine, because he considered the criticism irresponsible.

The manner in which Racine defended himself suggests the presence in his mind of certain deeply felt if not consciously arranged principles. Whether or not he was stung into recognizing them is immaterial: what emerges is again the awareness of the latent conflict between analysis and instinctive enjoyment. And this awareness crystallized into a very keen sense of the need for defending the poet and his work against the critics, who mostly forgot to take into account the final effect of the play upon the audience or upon themselves. In insisting upon the effect of the play he was of course not different from Corneille or Molière. But since he took criticism so personally, and argued so pragmatically, his principles have to be dug out from his prefaces and put together. As in the case of the other two playwrights they are inseparable from his special genius, but what distinguishes them is that here they really have to do with the independence of the artist and the inviolability of his work.

It is an ironic fact that almost from the outset Racine wanted to produce a play with a minimum of subject matter, but that throughout his career he had to defend himself from the charge of having done exactly this. *Alexandre* (certainly not *La Thébaïde*) suffered this accusation. Racine in replying fell back upon the fact of enjoyment. Why, he asked, should the critics complain "si toutes mes scènes sont bien remplies, si elles sont liées nécessairement les unes avec les autres, si tous mes acteurs ne viennent point sur le théâtre, que l'on ne sache la raison qui les y fait venir, et si avec peu d'incidents j'ai été assez heureux pour faire une pièce qui les a peut-être attachés malgré eux depuis le commencement jusqu'à la fin?"[1]

Like Molière he seemed to think that critics missed the point more frequently than the public, and he seemed to feel that the public was on his side most of the time. Pyrrhus in *Andromaque* was accused by some of unbecoming brutality. Racine, who had also to stand the charge of softness in comparison with Corneille, maintained in the first preface that the only changes he had made in the characterization of his people was to "adoucir un peu la férocité de Pyrrhus." After all, the characters were all known persons. He was not at liberty to change them. It was not his fault if Pyrrhus was still too brutal. "Pyrrhus n'avait pas lu nos romans." But the public was with him: "Quoi qu'il en soit, le public m'a été trop favorable pour m'embarrasser du chagrin particulier de deux ou trois personnes qui voudraient qu'on réformât

tous les héros de l'antiquité pour en faire des héros par-
faits."[2]

There are two points to be noted in this statement.
First the independence of the subject matter with respect
to *him*. He was not responsible for the ferocity of Pyrrhus.
Secondly the importance of the final effect on the public, in other words the independence of the play with
respect to criticism. These two notions will continue to
assert themselves in Racine's work, the latter dominating
in his critical phase, the former in his creative phase.

The 1676 revision of this preface is amusing. The tone
is much less vehement, as it was in all the revised prefaces, and the question of Pyrrhus is not discussed. But
Racine finds something else to defend himself about and
another way to proclaim the freedom of the author. This
time, however, he is, so to speak, on the other side of the
fence, because he is now maintaining the right of the
author to alter the facts of history. In fairness to him it
should not be said that this involves a contradiction, for
in the first preface he was thinking about character, and
here he is talking about having made Astyanax live longer
than was actually true. Such an alteration is unimportant, he holds, and literary tradition justifies him amply,
but the point is (and he quotes a remark of Camerarius)
"qu'il ne faut point s'amuser à chicaner les poètes pour
quelques changements qu'ils ont pu faire dans la fable;
mais qu'il faut s'attacher à considérer l'excellent usage
qu'ils ont fait de ces changements, et la manière in-
génieuse dont ils ont su accommoder la fable à leur
sujet."[3]

It is bad enough to have critics pick at you. But they
have a way of misunderstanding completely, even when
it comes to the rules. Racine had no trouble with the
rules. He could even fall back on them as he did in his
defense of Pyrrhus. It is rather the critics, and sometimes
the public under the influence of the critics, who have the
trouble. In the *Avertissement* to *Les Plaideurs*, after explaining that his play was an experiment and that he
would really have preferred to imitate "la régularité de

Ménandre et de Térence," Racine complained "Cependant la plupart du monde ne se soucie point de l'intention ni de la diligence des auteurs. On examina d'abord mon amusement comme on aurait fait une tragédie. Ceux mêmes qui s'y étaient le plus divertis eurent peur de n'avoir pas ri dans les règles, et trouvèrent mauvais que je n'eusse pas songé plus sérieusement à leur faire rire."[4] The Paris reception of the play had been indifferent, but Versailles had laughed and eventually it was a success: Racine's public, like Aristophanes' public, had laughed. "Quoi qu'il en soit, je puis dire que notre siècle n'a pas été de plus mauvaise humeur que le sien, et que si le but de ma comédie était de faire rire, jamais comédie n'a mieux attrapé son but."[5] Again with his "quoi qu'il en soit" Racine rests his case.

But the attacks continued, trivial and contradictory, as it seemed to him, and with the *Britannicus* he became more violent. In the 1670 preface he listed the criticisms in all their variety and contradiction until he uttered the cry that introduced the allusion to Corneille, "Que faudrait-il faire pour contenter des juges si difficiles?"[6] One of these criticisms had been that the play was really over with the death of Britannicus, "et qu'on ne devrait point écouter le reste. On l'écoute pourtant, et avec autant d'attention qu'aucune fin de tragédie."[7] Once more the public's support, but even so, the lot of him who seeks to please it is a hard one. He lamented the fact that intelligent critics passed sympathetically over faults that ought to be pointed out, while only the stupid ones criticized aloud. By 1676, however, he could look back with tolerance upon these earlier troubles: "Mais enfin il est arrivé de cette pièce ce qui arrivera toujours des ouvrages qui auront quelque bonté. Les critiques se sont évanouies; la pièce est demeurée."[8] The work becomes independent.

The preface to *Bérénice* shows Racine himself moving toward a certain detachment, I think, though he still felt that he was misunderstood. Here an extended quotation seems fitting. It contains the best known of Racine's critical statements. As with *Alexandre*, the question of a play with a very simple plot was being argued. *Bérénice* had been a *tour de force* in this respect and Racine rightly thought he had brought it off. But he was criticized for having done just that. What can enrage an artist more than to be condemned for having done what he consciously sets out to do? And who is to say he has not the right to do it? Racine must have been thinking such thoughts when he wrote that certain critics "ont cru qu'une tragédie qui était si peu chargée d'intrigues ne pouvait être selon les règles du théâtre. Je m'informai s'ils se plaignaient qu'elle les eût ennuyés. On me dit qu'ils avouaient tous qu'elle n'ennuyait point, qu'elle les touchait même en plusiers endroits, et qu'ils la verraient encore avec plaisir. Que veulent-ils davantage? Je les conjure d'avoir assez bonne opinion d'eux-mêmes pour ne pas croire qu'une pièce qui les touche et qui leur donne du plaisir puisse être absolument contre les règles. La principale règle est de plaire et de toucher. Toutes les autres ne sont faites que pour parvenir à cette première. Mais toutes les règles sont d'un assez long détail, dont je ne leur conseille pas de s'embarrasser. Ils ont des occupations plus importantes. Qu'ils se reposent sur nous de la fatigue d'éclaircir les difficultés de la *Poétique* d'Aristote; qu'ils se réservent le plaisir de pleurer et d'être attendris; et qu'ils me permettent de leur dire ce qu'un musicien disait à Philippe, roi de Macédoine, qui prétendait qu'une chanson n'était pas selon les règles: 'A Dieu ne plaise, Seigneur, que vous soyez jamais si malheureux que de savoir ces choses-là mieux que moi.'"[9]

Racine was supposedly protecting the critics from themselves, but he was really saying that the artist is the judge. The criterion of pleasure is by now familiar.

The tone of this preface is gentle, perhaps only sarcastically so, but at least a certain restraint is apparent. He could not however resist at the end of it a sharp and not altogether fair retort to the Abbé de Villars who had expressed some reservations concerning the play with, as it appeared to Racine, insufficient critical apparatus and undue levity. What really hurt Racine probably was that

164

this was just another example of irresponsible and there-fore cruel criticism, with the added insulting proof of the critic's frivolous tone. But this is the last of his violent outbreaks, in public at least. *Bajazet* and *Mithridate* seem to have needed no defense. It may be that Racine felt at last secure from the rivalry of Corneille; it may be that his friendship with Boileau* was having some effect, or it might be that his increasing detachment foreshadows his retirement from the theater.

Still, there is one more assertion of the independence of the poet which I should like to point out by way of showing that the principle continued to function in Ra-cine's view. This is a statement made in the preface to *Iphigénie*. It was now in defense not of himself but of Euripides against certain critics who had failed to under-stand him. There was a lesson to be drawn from their misconstruction. "Je conseille à ces Messieurs de ne plus décider si légèrement sur les ouvrages des anciens. Un homme tel qu'Euripide méritait au moins qu'ils l'examin-assent, puisqu'ils avaient envie de le condamner. Ils devaient se souvenir de ces sages paroles de Quintilien, 'Il faut être extrêmement circonspect et très retenu à pro-noncer sur les ouvrages de ces grands hommes, de peur qu'il ne nous arrive comme à plusieurs de condamner ce que nous n'entendons pas. Et s'il faut tomber dans quel-que excès encore vaut-il mieux pécher en admirant tout dans leurs écrits, qu'en y blâmant beaucoup de choses.' "[10]

We may be permitted I think to suppose a degree of identification on Racine's part of himself with Euripides, for did not Euripides have to share some of the criticism leveled at Racine?

The independence and the wisdom of the artist, the demanding aloofness of the work of art, the humility of the critic. These seem to have been Racine's concern, and if he spent a good deal of time and ink attacking his critics and even his rival Corneille, his point of view is

* For the question of Boileau's influence upon Racine and others of the so-called "école classique," see R. Bray's *Boileau, l'homme et l'oeuvre*, Paris, Boivin, 1942, chap. III.

too consistent to have been the effect of mere vanity. Granted of course a generous share of touchiness in his character, I think these critical principles, if such they may be called, stem from his work, or from his conception of his work. If this can be said also of Corneille and Molière, it cannot be explained in the same way at all. Corneille's mature opinions were, as I have indicated, based on his experience with the public and a kind of innate resistance to external pressure, especially when it threatened his originality. Molière trusted the instinct of the public, but found in intelligent criticism a counteragent to pedantry and fadism and nonsense in general. Both of them were, intentionally or not, philosophically open and hard to pin down. But neither of them seems so deeply imbedded in unsympathetic misunderstanding as Racine. If he was so sensitive to criticism, was it not that he felt, like a parent for his child, only a partial responsibility for his plays? Did he not want them to be considered in their own terms, without his having to explain them or excuse them, beyond the ordinary statement of sources, which already, incidentally, relieved him of some responsibility? Corneille thought of his plays as constructed machines. He was proud of *Héraclius*. Racine, I think, despite his careful craftsmanship, felt his plays to be recreated or even remembered moments. Whether or not this is so, he remains infinitely inexplicable.

So Racine's drama exhibits a moral openness which is quite different from that of Corneille or Molière. We can still say of them with some degree of truth that they were stoic and naturalistic respectively. But what can we say of Racine? That he was a Jansenist, because he knew that the human heart is unpredictable, hopelessly complicated, and disastrously vulnerable? Let me in this connection quote a passage from Rapin's *Réflexions sur l'Eloquence*: "C'est un abîme d'une profondeur impénétrable que ce coeur: quelques découvertes qu'on y fasse, il y en a tous les jours de nouvelles à faire. Mais il ne suffit pas

pour en faire une peinture véritable de l'avoir assez péné-
tré: afin d'y reconnaître ses fourbes, ses tromperies, ses
dissimulations, ses faiblesses, ses soupçons, ses défiances,
ses jalousies, ses irrésolutions, ses contradictions, ses détours, ses inégalités, ses délicatesses sur son intérêt, son
orgueil, sa présomption, le mélange confus de toutes ses
affections, et enfin la pente naturelle et presque incon-
cevable qu'il a à la malice et au déguisement. Il faut encore
lui ôter le masque de vertu, de candeur et de sincérité
dont il se sert pour exercer d'ordinaire avec plus d'artifice les raffinements de la dissimulation . . . il faut lui
dépeindre ses fausses modesties dans les choses qu'il
recherche; ses excuses artificieuses dans celles qu'il fuit;
la perversité de ses jugements dans celles qu'il estime; la
faiblesse de ses résolutions, et l'agitation continuelle de
ses inquiétudes dans le bien qu'il poursuit. Je ne finirais
point si je voulais en découvrir tous les détours, et en
déployer tous les replis."[11] This passage, which I have
shortened, and which reminds one of La Rochefoucauld's
much more artistic maxim number 563, was written by a
Jesuit. If Racine had been educated by that order would
his conception of the human heart have been different
from what it was?

Certainly Racine had a conception of personality and
of reality. But from *Andromaque* to *Phèdre* they are nowhere stated explicitly. They are everywhere implied but
they cannot be analyzed in any sort of systematic fashion.
There is in Racine a notion of energy. His plays are
loaded with it, are pushed along by it. But this energy is
not directed as in Corneille; it is blind, uncontrolled, ex-
plosive. So Racine's plays proceed by interruptions, shat-
tering dissonances, relentless mutilations of harmony and
continuity within the smooth shell of the skillfully
blocked scenes and the seemingly effortless couplets.

Are we prepared then to say that inability to control
the passions is the essentially human element in Racine's
psychology? If so, what do we do with the characters of
Andromaque, Bérénice, Monime, Iphigénie? The answer
is that Racine's conception of the human heart and his

notion of energy allow for wild instability but do not necessitate it. Yet there is no principle of determination or discrimination, and there is no knowing who shall be the victim or the vessel of the forces of moral or physical destruction. This is perhaps a Jansenistic tendency, but as we know, it is also a Greek one. The emphasis upon moral confusion is Christian and peculiarly modern, but not especially Jansenist. As in the lines from *Measure for Measure*:

> . . . man, proud man,
> Dressed in a little brief authority,
> Most ignorant of what he's most assured,
> His glassy essence like an angry ape
> Plays such fantastic tricks before high Heaven
> As make the angels weep. . . .[12]

But Racine's people are not angry apes. They possess all the sense of dignity their creator can give them, which however does not save them. Nor does it help to explain them. They stand, as in *Andromaque*, balancing their dignity, their love, their minds and their feelings against the encircling and concentric forces of mythological, historical, political, and personal hatred, on the thin line between total celebration and total loss, between all and nothing. They are, like the plays, as Racine wished them to be, open and free; they are free to ravin down their proper bane. Like Oreste, they accept their destiny as they fight it: to fight it *is* to accept it. But though Oreste is explicit in this acceptance, in general we can only infer it, for Racine's openness is helped by the lack of generalities of the kind to be found in Shakespeare and even in Corneille and Molière. Racine's people, in the last hours of their lives, have little time for meditation and comment.

One comes always finally to *Phèdre*. I believe that from *La Thébaïde* forward Racine was preparing to write it, and though he did not want to say so outright it is everywhere evident in the preface that he considered it his best play. And so, if we look at it in this light, it seems to bring to fulfillment much of what is only tendential in the earlier plays.

What I have been saying up to now has had to do with the openness of Racine's *morale*, the difficulty of attaching it to any positive point of view which he might be said to represent, and the consequent autonomy of his drama in the creative and critical domain. If any part of this is true it is true at the human level. But how much more so and more noticeably so it is when the entire Universe is involved. We become aware that the convolutions of responsibility really extend to infinity. This was from the beginning, as I see it, a principle in Racine's whole approach to his work, informing both his attitude toward criticism and his plays. Jocaste's second speech in *La Thébaïde* contains the lines,

> O toi, Soleil, ô toi qui rends le jour au monde,
> Que ne l'as-tu laissé dans une nuit profonde!

And Etéocle in the first scene of the fourth act of this same first play seems to foreshadow almost all of Racine when he says,

> On dirait que le Ciel, par un arrêt funeste,
> Voulut de nos parents punir ainsi l'inceste,
> Et que dans notre sang il voulut mettre au jour
> Tout ce qu'ont de plus noir et la haine et l'amour.

In both of these speeches the Manichean opposition of darkness to light is evident. It can be found all through *La Thébaïde* as it is all through Racine. *La Thébaïde*, incidentally, ought to be more frequently read, with all its shortcomings.

But of course no play of Racine expressed this extended responsibility so fully as *Phèdre*. And yet no character created by Racine was ever so completely inhabited by a sense of guilt as Phèdre. Far from being mitigated by the involvement of the Universe, this guilt is instead heightened to universal proportions.

> Et moi, triste rebut de la nature entière,
> Je me cachais au jour, je fuyais la lumière;
> La mort est le seul dieu que j'osais implorer.[13]

But the effect of this is to make of Phèdre's suicide (itself a sin) a sacrifice, since only her death can set the dislocated Universe to rights again.* Her last words are, we remember:

> Déjà je ne vois plus qu'à travers un nuage
> Et le ciel et l'époux que ma présence outrage;
> Et la mort, à mes yeux dérobant la clarté,
> Rend au jour qu'ils souillaient, toute sa pureté.[14]

These lines conclude Phèdre's confession, and with them one ought to be able to sum up, as she seems to, her part in the tragedy. But it is hard to say what should be made of that confession. It is not unequivocal. She places the major portion of blame on the "détestable" and "perfide" Oenone. This is the closest Racine allowed himself to come to any direct assessment of Phèdre's guilt. But we must remember that she was speaking only of the catastrophe. Her real guilt was in being, and not in the events resulting from that being, and she has after all taken poison. Since this is so, however, we might have expected her to excuse Oenone, who acted only from devotion to her, and to assume full responsibility for everything. But she does not do this and so the effect of the confession is to maintain her impurity up to the very last, and only her death by purifying the Universe can purify her.

Thus, in spite of the reminder to the audience that Oenone was largely responsible for the catastrophe, Racine seems to stand away from Phèdre in the end even more than in the beginning. We know from the preface that he pitied her as a princess with noble and virtuous feelings, and as one who was horrified "toute la première"

---

* It is curious to note how frequently in Racine appears the theme of the fateful stranger who brings trouble and who represents the forces of nature. It is of course a Greek theme and will be taken up again by Ibsen.

170

at her passion. But of this pity not a word in the play. If
Phèdre's death in any way expiated her guilt there was
no one to say so. Compare the elaborate tribute to Hippolyte[15] (merely the victim of the catastrophe) with
Panope's "Elle expire, Seigneur," and Thésée's absolutely
ununderstanding but understandable

> D'une action si noire
> Que ne peut avec elle expirer la mémoire![16]

After which he goes to mourn his son and to look after
Aricie, while Phèdre and her confession and her death
are forgotten.

The trick then has been to spare Phèdre not at all, to
ask no sympathy directly in the play, yet to cause her
to be pitied even while her guilt is made more and more
her own, so that the very degree of blameworthiness is
the degree to which she is pitied.

One would not expect Thésée to understand this. He
would not distinguish between the catastrophe, which is
only the destruction of Hippolyte, and the tragedy, which
is the creation of Phèdre. Yet this distinction must be
made even though in the play the tragedy and the catastrophe are inseparable. And this fact perhaps gives us a
key to the final believability and incomprehensibility of
Phèdre. For the catastrophe I believe is reducible, analyz-
able: it is a series of events, ironic, pathetic, and from
some points of view maybe tragic. But the responsibility
is clearly shared by man, god, and nature, or I should say
men, gods, and animals, or to put it even more specifically,
Phèdre, Oenone, Thésée, Neptune, the monster and the
horses. In the end it passes out of human hands. But the
tragedy, which is an abominably rapid multiplication of
evil, is ultimately inexplicable (and who shall be held
responsible for it?), even though at the last it is mostly
Phèdre's work. This irreducibility could perhaps be expressed by saying that the noble and virtuous Phèdre
knowingly infected the Universe because she was knowingly its horrified victim, and this because she was
knowingly its cooperating creation. It had been her wish

to die before this creation occurred, but this she was not vouchsafed even in her own will. Before she could die her creation had to be consecrated in catastrophe. This is why for the purposes of the play the tragedy and the catastrophe are inseparable, for had her poisonous being not manifested itself in poisonous acts, we should blame her less and pity her less.

I have attempted to convey the paradoxical and inconclusive nature of *Phèdre* by insisting upon its moral openness.* But there is more to be said, for after all *Phèdre* is not a moral treatise or an *exemplum*, but a play and a poem, and as such it frees itself still further from its author and from us. This fact is made only more salient by Racine's insistence in the preface on the moral aspects of the play. But we do not nowadays consider that its greatest value lies in its warning to young ladies of the disorder caused by the passions. The Seventeenth Century was not unanimously of this opinion either.

To begin with, the subject matter and the story belong to legend. Euripides and Seneca made them literature. Time has twisted them and molded them. Between Seneca and Racine stand Christianity, the Reformation and the Counter-Reformation, and the Renaissance with a whole modern conception of Greek and Roman art. Besides the two dramatists of antiquity, Plutarch, Virgil, Ovid and even Sappho had a hand in the composition of Racine's play. Just as the responsibility for the tragic fate of the Cretan princess is lost in universality, so Racine's play was a thing which came to be and which in some important respects could not be other than it was, and its creation was as complicated as that of its central character. Racine said that he owed the idea of Phèdre to Euripides.[17] What he means is obvious. But is it true? He also said that he made her less "odieuse" than the ancients had.[18] Did he? The play has so freed itself from the au-

* Cf. Marcel Chicoteau, *Studies in the Ephectic Attitude*, No. 3, "Les attributs de l'ephectisme grec et leur survivance dans une cosmologie racinienne," Cardiff, Priory Press Ltd., 1943.

thor that almost everything he says about it in the preface is at best only half true.

What is certain is that Racine was able to see in Euripides, Seneca, and Plutarch the possibility of a domestic tragedy which would be an evocation of everything terrifying and fascinating in the upheaval of nature, and everything furious, bloody, and monstrous in the basest actions of the most favored mortals; that in the year 1677 under the reign of the most courtly of monarchs a woman whose grandfather was the sun, whose brother was half man, half bull, and whose stepson was destroyed by a monster out of the sea, could be the subject of such a play; that finally a writer reared in the most pious of Christian atmospheres should find the words with which to make it. For in the last analysis what welds this drama of the elements and of monstrosity together and finally sets it free is the expression of passionate human utterance in a world without rational or physical limits, by means most inexplicable of all, the music of Racine.

V: The Secret of the Critics

RAPIN, BOUHOURS, BOILEAU, LA BRUYÈRE AND FÉNELON

WITH le P. Rapin and Nicolas Boileau we are in the very center of high classic criticism. Boileau particularly stands for French Classicism, and Rapin seems to second him with less *éclat* and more responsibility for the frightening side of judicial criticism. Just what their responsibility was from an academic or an official point of view need not interest us here. What made them effective is more important. It is my belief that they, like the artists, had their secret, and that this secret was the knowledge of what is hidden and what is mysterious about art. The others had it too: Bouhours tried to express it and was more articulate as well as more explicit than Rapin, who also tried. Boileau and La Bruyère saw it at the level of the sublime, the latter more disturbed by it than the former. Boileau and Fénelon carried the knowledge of it past the high moment of Classicism and past the end of the century.

All of these critics, it will be seen, inherit a good deal of their literary sensibility from those who went before them. Just how much of it was passed on into the Eighteenth Century, through Du Bos, through Diderot to Baudelaire and modern criticism can be for the reader to decide. But their knowledge, like that of the practitioners, is significant here as the cause, the result, and the proof of the complexity underlying the apparently so well regulated Seventeenth Century.

1. "GRÂCES SECRÈTES ET BEAUTÉS CACHÉES: LE P. RAPIN

RAPIN comes curiously into this study. From one standpoint he represents all that is tiresome and naively arrogant in Seventeenth Century French classicism. One gains this impression from Saintsbury.[1] Rapin does not dazzle surely, nor are his literary judgments very perceptive in any modern sense. Bouhours possessed this quality more. Rapin is balanced, considered, even cautious, always warning against extremes as he himself avoids them. His constant point of reference is the familiar faith in the study of the ancients and in the precepts to be derived therefrom. Yet through this caution and this conventionality I can detect a persistent note sounding a kind of humility or delicacy in the presence of art which is deeply characteristic of the century as I see it. The note comes in large part from Cicero and Quintilian, and if this fact detracts from Rapin's originality, it helps us nonetheless to understand how the effect of the Ancients, associated naturally with the traditional conception of Classicism, really contributed elements seemingly in conflict with that conception. Still, what originality Rapin does have lies in the fact that in him these elements ultimately dominate, almost against his will. It is because of this peculiar turn to his otherwise mostly uninspired criticism that I find him interesting and useful.*

Rapin's reputation was high during his lifetime in and out of France. Biographically and bibliographically however he has not fared well. His friend le P. Bouhours did a biographical piece on him in 1687. This may be found in the second volume of the 1723 edition of Rapin's *Carmina*, but, except for Ch. Dejob's Latin dissertation *De Renato Rapino* (Paris, 1881) scarcely anyone in modern times has given him any special attention. His memoirs were published by Domenech in 1861 and by Aubineau in 1865. His bibliography can be found in Sommervogel's *Bibliothèque de la Compagnie de Jésus* (Paris, 1895, VI, 1443). Saintsbury devotes some space to him in his history of criticism, and he appears on numerous occasions in the pages of Sainte-Beuve's *Port-Royal*. Neither of

* Concerning his character see the correspondence of Mme de Sévigné, Monmerqué ed., Vol. v, p. 531, letter of 29 May, 1679, to Bussy-Rabutin.

these critics is very friendly to him. Bourgoin and Brunetière omit him altogether. An article by M. Bouchard
on him as a precursor of La Bruyère appeared in the
Revue d'histoire littéraire in 1931. I suspect he deserves
better, for he was honest and no fool. His critical work,
done principally in the 70's, was not voluminous, but it
was not trivial. It consisted mainly of observations on
secular and religious eloquence, on history, poetry and
philosophy. These observations were presented sometimes as comparisons of Greek with Latin authors,
sometimes as brief historical surveys, sometimes simply
as *réflexions*. In the historical surveys he paid more attention to the moderns, French and foreign, than was usual
for the time, and his acquaintance with European literary
history was wide if not deep. As was the custom, however, he omitted judgments on living contemporaries,
preferring, as he once said, to leave this task to time.

His main position as an historically-minded judicial
critic was about what one might expect. He admired
what was finished, polished, and delicate, sometimes at
the expense of vitality and boldness, to which nevertheless he always gave due credit. So naturally the Romans
come off better than the Greeks in the long run, and I
need hardly add, the Ancients better than the Moderns.

This preference is evident when he considers the major
literary forms, although he is not blind to modern merits.
The epic of course ended with Virgil and tragedy with
the Greeks. He thought the French lacked a real sense of
tragedy because they were too civilized, and it seemed to
him that the introduction of love as the main theme of
serious drama actually constituted the formation of a new
genre. This is not at all a stupid observation.

It was in connection with the discussion of modern
serious drama that he made his interesting remark about
the English, "Les peuples, qui paraissent avoir le plus de
génie pour la Tragédie de tous nos voisins sont les An-
glais; et par l'esprit de leur Nation qui se plaît aux choses
atroces, et par le caractère de leur langue qui est propre
aux grandes expressions."[2]

However, he was not despairing of the situation in France. He thought the French were really better writers than the English, and especially since 1635, "Nous avons parmi nous des génies heureux qui se sont déjà signalés sur le théâtre et qui promettent encore de s'y signaler davantage."[3] This, if the "fantaisie des Opéras de Musique" did not turn writers away from tragedy.

Far from being lost in antiquity, Rapin saw in Molière a definite improvement on the Ancients, because the field of satire had been broadened to include "tout Paris et la cour" and consequently had a more nearly universal appeal. That is, it was understandable to more people. "Les beautés des portraits qu'il fait sont si naturelles qu'elles se font sentir aux personnes les plus grossières, et le talent qu'il avait à plaisanter s'était renforcé de la moitié par celui qu'il avait de contrefaire. Son Misanthrope est à mon sens le caractère le plus achevé et ensemble le plus singulier qui ait jamais paru sur le théâtre."[4] In spite of his admiration for Molière however, Rapin could not resist pointing out that his dénouements were defective. This is a fact which we are today very happy to neglect. Rapin could not do so. But, as we shall see, for him there is always a worm in the apple.

In lyric poetry Virgil and Horace remained unequaled. Rapin's opinion of French lyric poetry of his day was not very high. Like his fellow critics he thought that French *bel esprit* and the influence of Italian and Spanish mannerism were responsible for its low state. His estimates of Ronsard and Malherbe were about those of Chapelain though less vigorously set forth. There is therefore nothing very extraordinary about Rapin's opinions in the field of lyric poetry.

However he did make one remark about Horace which is revealing and typical: "il faut être bien éclairé pour voir tout son esprit car il se trouve dans ses vers de certaines grâces secrètes et des beautés cachées qui sont connues de peu de monde."[5] This sense of hidden values is the key to Rapin, and it applies to the making of literature as well as to the appreciation of it.

If Rapin's judgments of particular authors are fairly conventional, his ideas on poetry and eloquence in general seem at first glance equally so. Genius must modestly seek the aid of technique, imagination and good sense. Brilliance is worth little without solidity. Grandeur must be expressed simply and naturally but not coldly, while purity must not degenerate into preciousness nor figured speech into nonsense. The ultimate aim of art is moral, but its intention and its means are to please and to go straight to the heart. The orator must be himself a man of integrity, must fit his diction to the needs of the subject and to the character of the audience. He must avoid affectation, but must appeal to the passions as well as to the reason and must therefore be himself impassioned and must understand human nature. And so on and so forth according to Aristotle, Horace, Cicero, and Quintilian. Rapin is a "safe" critic.

But I insist that this conventionality has its reverse side, which is evident throughout all these general considerations. And that is a sense of the inexplicable more positive than mere bewilderment. It is especially noticeable when he comes to discuss the rules. He allowed that they exist to help the poet and the orator achieve perfection, but he never seemed completely convinced of their real usefulness (although he kept insisting upon it), and the question of genius shook his confidence all the time so that he was never really comfortable with them. His statement with regard to Molière is an entertaining example of his distress. Among certain difficult problems confronting the writer of modern poetry he listed as the most important, "de savoir si l'on peut plaire en Poésie contre les règles: j'applique cette question à notre Poésie en particulier, quoi qu'elle soit commune à la Poésie en général: parce que la plupart de nos Poètes se font une fausse liberté de ce méchant principe. Ce n'est que par là que Molière voulait sauver l'irrégularité ordinaire de ses comédies. Il est vrai que sa témérité a été heureuse, et qu'il a plu dans ses pièces contre l'art. Mais je prétends que ni lui, ni les autres ne plaisent jamais, que par les règles: ils ont des traits naturels par où ils réussissent et ces traits sont des coups de l'art: car l'art n'est autre chose, comme j'ai dit, que le bon sens réduit en méthode. Ce ne sont que ces traits qui plaisent dans les pièces irrégulières, où ce qui est irrégulier ne plaît jamais, parce qu'il n'est jamais naturel."⁶ Unless I misread the passage, here is a good example of a cornered critic.

Now if this were all Rapin had to say we should be justified in dismissing him as a confused and self-contradictory dogmatist. There is no denying the confusion and the contradiction. It increases the more we read in him. But I believe this is precisely because he moved, or tried to move, more and more close to the secret of poetry and of eloquence, as he sought the answer to those "grâces secrètes et beautés cachées" which constantly haunted him and disturbed his faith in the utility of example and precept. He made an honest and a brave attempt without sufficient equipment, historical or personal. Because of this I find him sympathetic.

It was his concern for eloquence which led him on, for of all the problems which occupied his thoughts I imagine this one was closest to his heart. The obvious necessity of persuasion and attractiveness in a realm where demonstration alone ought to suffice must have appeared to him as a very special and practical difficulty. He was a Jesuit. So his collected critical works begin with a comparison of Demosthenes and Cicero, contain a *Réflexions sur l'Eloquence* and end with a sort of rhetoric of his own which he called *l'Eloquence des Bien-séances*. This last work is probably his least impressive, but it interests me the most because it pushed to the bitter and inconclusive end his preoccupation with hidden charms. But the preoccupation is noticeable in all his work, and it forms a kind of antiphony to his dogmatism. I should like to show how this is so.

In the piece on Demosthenes and Cicero he made this basic confession, "La persuasion en général est cet art admirable dont retentissent toutes les écoles des Rhéteurs, et que tous les Déclamateurs promettent avec tant de faste d'apprendre à leurs disciples quoi qu'ils ne le sachent pas eux-mêmes. C'est le secret merveilleux de toucher le coeur, que la Rhétorique recherche depuis si longtemps par ce grand attirail des préceptes sans l'avoir encore pu trouver. En effet il est bien plus aisé de le sentir que de l'exprimer."[7]

The problem was certainly complicated by the fact that Rapin was naturally especially interested in pulpit oratory, for which no Ancient precedent exists. Paradoxically this should have made matters easier, for he saw the sublimity of Christianity as Balzac, Pascal, and Boileau (to name lay critics only) saw it: "Il y a je ne sais quoi de si grand, et de si relevé dans nos mystères qu'il suffirait de les exposer simplement et sans art au peuple pour mériter toute la gloire qu'on peut espérer de l'Eloquence, s'il était honnête de prêcher pour sa réputation."[8]

But the problem unfortunately is not so simple. There are techniques, there are things to be learned, and yet at the end of his introduction to the *Réflexions sur l'Eloquence*, he complained, "Mais après tout, il faut avouer la vérité, quelque avantage qu'on ait en l'Eloquence, par les instructions de si grands maîtres [Aristotle, Cicero and Quintilian], l'art y fait moins que le génie: et la plus grande partie des sujets que traite l'Orateur sont de telle nature que l'opinion y a plus de part, et a beaucoup plus d'effet que la science. Car on parle souvent en des Assemblées qui sont pleines d'ignorants: c'est presque toujours le peuple qui juge du discours: et il se trouve des gens dans toutes les professions qui ont de l'éloquence et qui parlent bien sans en avoir appris aucunes règles."[9]

And in the *Réflexions* themselves we read this equally discouraged observation: "Il faut moins de génie dans l'Eloquence pour inventer les choses que pour les arranger: ce tour qu'il faut leur donner pour les mettre dans la place où elles doivent être coûte bien plus que la peine qu'on se donne de les penser. Car tout esprit raisonnable peut penser raisonnablement: mais il n'est pas aisé de donner à ce qu'on pense cette grâce qui rend les choses agréables, et qui les fait admirer. C'est en quoi consiste l'Eloquence: non pas cette Eloquence des paroles, que l'on ne sait ordinairement que trop, mais l'Eloquence des choses, qu'on ne sait presque point du tout, qu'on apprend rarement, et qu'on ne peut espérer que d'un naturel heureux."[10]

But of course this talent *can* be acquired, by proper study and association. So the counterplay runs, between natural genius and acquired skill, between the attractive and the reasonable. It is only to be expected that we should note it in the remarks on poetry as well. Indeed for Rapin the mystery of poetry was so profound that for a moment eloquence seemed relatively simple. "On peut devenir Orateur, sans avoir de naturel à l'Eloquence: parce que l'art peut suppléer au défaut de la nature. Mais on ne peut être Poète sans génie dont rien ne peut tenir la place et au défaut duquel tout l'art n'est pas capable de suppléer."[11]

This statement is from the *Réflexions sur la poétique*. We shall pass over the inconsistency of it. It led to the conclusion that, all things considered, "l'avantage du génie est toujours préférable à celui de l'art."[12] But these *Réflexions* suggest constantly that poetic virtues have their own defects and that genius is therefore subject to restraint. It is the common sense view.

Still the sense of mystery prevails. "La partie la plus importante et la plus nécessaire au Poète pour réussir dans les grands sujets est de savoir bien distinguer ce qu'il y a de beau et d'agréable dans la nature pour en faire de fréquentes images. Car la Poésie est un art où tout doit plaire. Et ce n'est pas assez de s'attacher à la nature qui est rude et désagréable en certains endroits: il faut choisir ce qu'elle a de beau avec ce qui ne l'est pas: elle a des grâces cachées en des sujets qu'il faut découvrir."[13] Only the genius knows how to do this.

And then this quality is carried into poetry itself, and all art: "Il y a encore dans la poésie comme dans les autres arts de certaines choses ineffables, et qu'on ne peut expliquer: ces choses sont comme des mystères. Il n'y a point de préceptes pour enseigner ces grâces secrètes, ces charmes imperceptibles et tous ces agréments cachés de la Poésie qui vont au coeur. Comme il n'y a point de méthode pour enseigner à plaire c'est un pur effet du naturel."[14]

By now it is unnecessary to say that Rapin immediately urges that this quality needs the aid of technique to succeed in any ambitious work of art. However when the choice of subject matter has been successfully made and its disposition happily effected all is not yet done, for "outre ces grâces que la Poésie trouve dans l'expression des moeurs et des passions, il y a je ne sais quoi dans le nombre, qui est connu de peu de gens, et qui toutefois est d'un grand agrément dans la Poésie." Homer possessed this *agrément*, and so did Virgil, as far as Latin allowed him to inherit it from Homer. But French does not permit it as the Greek did, and this is very unfortunate, for "c'est une des plus grandes beautés de la Poésie."[15]

The situation then seems almost hopeless as far as poetry is concerned, and it is understandable that Rapin did not attempt to do for it what he tried to do for eloquence. On the other hand, if it had been at all possible for him to construct a successful rhetoric on the foundation which he chose to lay, he might have been able to go on and accomplish a poetic. But the rhetoric was difficult enough.

The basic principle of *De l'Eloquence des Bien-séances* is suggested by the title. The notion of *bienséance* is of course central to the whole Classic system. Rapin realized its importance and had commented upon it in his essay on poetry where he had said "Outre toutes ces règles prises de la Poétique d'Aristote, il y en a encore une dont Horace fait mention à laquelle toutes les autres règles doivent s'assujettir, comme la plus essentielle, qui est la bien-séance." After listing as offenders against it Pulci, Guarini, Ronsard, Ariosto, Tasso, Théophile, Lope, Dante, Boccaccio, and Marino (quite a distinguished lot on the whole) he had concluded, "Enfin tout ce qui est contre les règles du temps, des moeurs, des sentiments, de l'expression est contraire à la bien-séance qui est la plus universelle de toutes les règles."[16]

Naturally a "rule" of such wide application would be hard to define. In thinking about it one begins to be less sure of the meaning of the term "règle" itself. I suspect that even for Rapin "les règles" represented a much less limited and well-ordered set of principles than we are apt to imagine. However this may be, Rapin based his rhetoric upon the *règle* of *bien-séance*, or rather upon the principle of *les bien-séances*, with what success we shall see.

The full and official title of the rhetoric is *Observations sur l'Eloquence des Bien-séances*. Rapin wished it to be considered an entirely new sort of thing, though here only briefly sketched: he would leave the elaboration of it to someone with more leisure than was his. He explained his purpose in the *Avertissement*: "L'art de parler ne peut comme il faut parvenir à sa fin, qui est de persuader, que par l'art des Bien-séances, et cet art des Bien-séances, que j'entreprends d'expliquer, ne consiste que dans une convenance parfaite de ce que dit l'Orateur, avec la manière dont il faut le dire. . . . Tout consiste enfin en cet art, à se bien mettre dans l'esprit que pour y réussir, il faut moins prendre garde aux règles de l'Eloquence ordinaire, qu'au temps et aux autres circonstances qui sont essentielles au sujet. En quoi on ne se trompe point, quand on a toute la lumière qu'il faut pour connaître ce qui sied bien, et qu'on a assez de génie pour le pratiquer. Mais quelle délicatesse d'esprit, et quelle pénétration ne faut-il pas pour sentir les Bien-séances dans chaque sujet sans s'y méprendre? Et c'est à mon sens dans cette pratique exacte des Bien-séances, et dans l'idée qu'on s'en fait, que consiste le bon goût en toutes choses."[17]

I think we shall agree that Rapin did well to leave the elaboration of his treatise to someone with plenty of time, for it took two centuries or so before the implications of his thesis began to be understood.

The treatise is limited to twenty-five short sections. Twenty-one of these are taken up with the effort to explain the nature of the *art des Bien-séances*, in other words to explain the basic principle of the rhetoric. At that, not much progress is made beyond saying that proportion, delicacy, naturalness, and simplicity are all related to it and that the surest way to achieve it is through the study of the Ancients. One must have genius to begin with of course, but that is not enough: "Outre le génie, qui doit être le premier fonds de cet art, il y a des secrets cachés, qui en font la perfection, qu'il faut tâcher de pénétrer, en les méditant."[18]

By about the fourteenth or fifteenth section of the treatise the initial momentum has died down and it begins to seem as though things were not going too well. It becomes more and more apparent that Rapin had got himself into an extremely difficult problem. And he knew that he was not having an easy time of it. But he was in it honestly and he persisted. "Mais il arrive souvent que cette perfection n'est ni bien connue de ceux qui l'ont acquise ni bien enseignée par ceux qui y sont les plus grands maîtres, lesquels n'ayant point d'autre règle ni d'autre guide, que leur génie, plaisent sans savoir pourquoi: si ce n'est qu'ils ont un goût plus exquis pour ce qui sied, que n'ont les autres: sans savoir toutefois que c'est par ce goût qu'ils plaisent. Demandez par exemple à Cicéron si habile en cet art ce que c'est que ce *decorum* qu'il a si bien observé dans tout ce qu'il a écrit: il vous dira qu'il n'y a rien de si difficile que de le sentir et de le dire. C'est une convenance, ou plutôt une proportion secrète et en quelque façon imperceptible de tous les traits du discours avec le sujet."[19]

Then comes a curious passage: "Après tout, dès qu'on a pu découvrir quelque rayon de cette beauté cachée, et de cet art inconnu, qui sait plaire par les Bien-séances, et par l'usage qu'on en fait: on pourrait faire des démonstrations dans l'Eloquence aussi certaines pour toucher l'esprit, qu'on en a trouvé dans la Musique pour toucher l'oreille par les proportions secrètes de cette harmonie qui plaît à coup sûr."[20] I find it curious because it expresses a very precise aspiration in a manner which somehow suggests that the possibility of fulfillment is slight. Pascal wrote a similar passage* using geometry instead of music as the comparison, but definitely doubting that the secret could be found. Thucydides, Demosthenes, Cicero, and Livy had the secret, Rapin continues, "C'était aussi bien plus leur coeur que leur esprit qui parlait."[21]

Now Rapin suddenly becomes acutely conscious of the difficulty of his subject, so that the twenty-second section begins, "Mais enfin pour ne pas parler en l'air d'un sujet que je veux rendre solide, en l'approfondissant, et en cherchant à l'éclaircir, faisons un dernier effort pour tâcher d'expliquer ce que c'est qu'un art si inexplicable." It is, he says, the purest flower of reason, "le seul bon sens de l'Eloquence," the most direct route to the heart, and all that is most exquisite in the art of speech. "Sur quoi, après tout, il n'y a rien à dire qu'en général." It consists in conformity to one another of the character of the speaker, of the subject, of the audience and of the manner of speech, according to Quintilian. Rapin, one feels, is beginning to give up. "C'est cette harmonie secrète et ce rapport parfait de toutes les parties, qui fait cette Bien-séance que nous cherchons, dont le détail serait infini: et on se tromperait de prétendre réduire en art et en méthode cette science dont on pourrait faire des livres si on l'avait bien comprise. Mais rien n'est plus difficile: car ce qui convient à l'un ne convient pas à l'autre, et ce qui plairait aujourd'hui choquerait demain: rien enfin n'est plus dépendant des circonstances, le temps, le lieu, le sujet, la personne, tout en est."[22]

So overwhelmed by the complexity of the matter does Rapin seem that he has fallen into complete relativism. But he does not abandon his criterion of good taste derived from a knowledge of the Ancients, whose "grâces les plus cachées" and whose "beautés les plus secrètes" are merely *Bien-séances*. "Ce n'est qu'en les connaissant

* See above, p. 125.

qu'on parvient à ce bon goût dont on dispute tant aujourd'hui."[23]

The treatise ends with a sudden expansion of the whole
idea. Rapin proclaims that "les curieux habiles ne connaissent de beauté dans l'ordonnance d'un tableau, ou
dans les proportions d'une statue, que par les Bien-
séances. Il en est ainsi de tous les autres arts; comme de
l'Architecture, et de tous ces admirables ouvrages qu'on
admire le plus en ce siècle."[24]

If I did not have a point to make I should have to apol-
ogize to the reader for taking him on such a merry-go-
round. But we are not occupied here with a mere literary
curio. The *Observations sur l'Eloquence des Bien-séances,*
inconclusive as they are, represent the creed of a critic.
They come as close as anything in the century to a general theory of literature, or even of art. Given the times
they had to be inconclusive and circular, and a circle
looks very much like a zero. But they reveal a real sense
of the singularity of the artistic act, and an acceptance of
that act as valuable in its singularity as well as in its
mystery. When we ask ourselves how dogmatic or how
closed the Classic system was, we should remember
Rapin's difficulties sympathetically. If he put his faith in
models, and if he had pretensions to method, it was because he needed their help in the presence of a great
secret. And yet he knew that, with all his critical apparatus, he did not possess that secret.

2. "LE JE NE SAIS QUOI": LE P. BOUHOURS

THE Jesuit Dominique Bouhours, constant companion of
le P. Rapin and friendly adviser of Racine and Boileau,
published in 1671 a collection of essays in dialogue form
entitled *Entretiens d'Ariste et d'Eugène.* One of these
dialogues was called *Le Je ne sais quoi.* It was the first
time, with one possible exception, that anyone had attempted anything like a detailed analysis of this notion,
which, expressed in varying degrees of substantiveness

("je ne sais quoi," "un je ne sais quoi," "ce je ne sais quoi," "le je ne sais quoi") has appeared rather frequently in the pages of this study. The possible exception is a discourse on the subject reportedly delivered to the Academy in its early days by Gombauld, but never published and, so far as is known, never recorded.[1] What was the significance of the Abbé Bouhours' desire to write of "le je ne sais quoi"?

The phrase "je ne sais quoi" is commonly used, in our day, not only in French but in other languages including English, to express a quality which is recognized only by one's affective reaction to it. It has achieved such wide usage because it describes at once the thing referred to and one's inability to define it. Current already in the Latin *nescio quid*, it is a compact way of saying, "a certain quality which may or may not be definable but which I at least cannot define, though I am aware of its existence because of the effect which it has upon me." Today the phrase has little more than a negative value, but in French literary circles of the Seventeenth Century, when its use seems to have become fairly widespread, its implications were more positive, so much more so indeed, that it attained a sort of independent category and became thus a quality in itself and was no longer merely a phrase designed to express indefinability. In other words it was not only "je ne sais quoi," or "un je ne sais quoi," but it was "*ce* je ne sais quoi" and "*le* je ne sais quoi."

The concept and the phrase are important to us principally as terms of literary criticism, of course, but they had nonetheless a wider application. Pascal was probably the most famous man of the century to make use of them, though he did so not in connection with literature, but in connection with human nature, love, and human affairs: "Qui voudra connaître à plein la vanité de l'homme n'a qu'à considérer les causes et les effets de l'amour. La cause en est *un je ne sais quoi* [CORNEILLE], et les effets en sont effroyables. Ce *je ne sais quoi*, si peu de chose qu'on ne peut le reconnaître, remue toute la terre, les princes, les armes, le monde entier."[2]

We shall see presently how Pascal's reference to Corneille applied. For Corneille, the *je ne sais quoi* meant the mysterious attraction of lovers to each other. For the Cardinal de Retz, it meant a personal quality which could certainly be interpreted ambiguously, as when he said of La Rochefoucauld, "Il y a toujours eu du je ne sais quoi en tout M. de la Rochefoucauld," and went on to explain, in that masterpiece of polite destruction, how difficult it was to fix the real point of his adversary's (unfortunate) character.[3]

Neither Pascal's nor Corneille's nor Retz's use of the phrase in question had anything to do with literature, but the literary connection is clear in the *Femmes savantes*, where Molière, with satirical intent, of course, has Philaminte say of Trissotin's verses,

> On sent à ces vers jusques au fond de l'âme
> Couler je ne sais quoi qui fait que l'on se pâme.
>
> (Act III, sc. 2)

I have mentioned these few examples of the use of the phrase to show the variety of its application, and to show, as in the case of the Molière quotation, how it could become involved in the analysis of literary qualities and of critical reactions. I now wish to examine the "je ne sais quoi" more specifically as a term of literary criticism.

Students of criticism and of critics have noticed the existence of the phrase. Doncieux, in his biography of the Abbé Bouhours,[4] noted that it had been used as early as 1589 by Mlle de Gournay, but gave no reference for his statement. He also remarked incidentally that Marivaux and Montesquieu had made use of it. Livet, in his *Précieux et précieuses*[5] mentioned Mlle de Gournay, this time referring to her *Promenoir de Montaigne*, where she had said, "l'amour, qui est je ne sais quoi, doit sourdre aussi de je ne sais quoi."

Joel Spingarn quoted Doncieux in his *Literary Criticism in the Renaissance*,[6] and he quoted Livet in the introduction to his *Critical Essays of the Seventeenth Cen-*

tury,[7] where he also remarked on Feijóo's use of the expression in Spain.* In this introduction Spingarn discusses the concept of the "je ne sais quoi" in its relation to what he calls "the School of Taste" and the place of this school in the history of Seventeenth Century literary criticism. This is the most extended modern treatment of the subject so far as I know, and the one which most suggests what I am trying to do here. It is so broad and its background is such that, though the topic is English criticism,† no student of Seventeenth Century French literature can afford to ignore it.

Others who have taken note of the use of the "je ne sais quoi" in the history of literary criticism are Croce in his *Aesthetic*,[8] Irving Babbitt in his *The New Laokoon*,[9] and Lanson in his history of French literature. Lanson mentioned Gombauld's never published discourse to which I have referred, but he refused to attach any importance to it whatsoever, saying, "Cela ne menait à rien," and using it as an example of the gropings of the youthful Academy.[10]

However, Henri Jacoubet in 1928 published an article, "A propos de Je-ne-sais-quoi," in the *Revue d'Histoire littéraire*,[11] where he observed connections between the French conception of the "je ne sais quoi" and allusions to it in Spanish and Italian literature and criticism, notably in the writings of Gracián. He also suggested that the use of the phrase and the notion behind it had more serious implications than was commonly supposed.

There is no question about the wide use of the phrase in and out of France before the Seventeenth Century, but there are two restrictions which must be kept in mind.

* In this connection one may consult Menéndez y Pelayo's *Historia de las ideas estéticas en España*, Obras completas, Edición Nacional, Vol. III, pp. 104ff. Prof. Américo Castro, to whom I am indebted for this reference, points out also the use of the *yo no sé qué* in the poetry of Juan de la Cruz; the connection is religious, but we have surely seen how the terms of the literary experience and those of the religious experience are closely related.

† Cf. also an article on the same theme in English criticism, "Grace Beyond the Reach of Art," by S. H. Monk, in the *Journal of the History of Ideas* for April, 1944.

First, in these earlier uses the form generally was simply "je ne sais quoi" or at the most "un je ne sais quoi."* Secondly, such uses did not apply to literary but rather to other personal emotional experiences, religious or amatory.

This at least is the present state of my information. Now the earliest use which I have found of the phrase as applied to literature happens also to be the earliest example which I have seen of its extension to substantive independence. It is also italicized. François Ogier in his *Apologie pour Monsieur de Balzac*, which was published in 1628,[12] wrote as follows: "La plupart des livres vieux et nouveaux sont semblables à ces pays déserts, où il faut faire plus de vingt-cinq lieues pour voir un clocher: c'est à dire que les bonnes choses y sont aussi rares qu'elles sont épaisses dans les écrits de M. de Balzac, où il n'y a pas une seule ligne qui n'arrête les yeux, et n'ait sa beauté particulière. Car soit que l'on considère les richesses de l'élocution, soit qu'on ait égard à la nouveauté des inventions, ou à la force des pensées, soit qu'on cherche cette Grâce, et cette Vénus, qu'Apelles inspirait en ses tableaux, et que les Italiens nomment *le je ne sais quoi*, qui est l'aveugle qui ne remarque tout cela dans la plus courte de nos périodes?"

Balzac himself, incidentally, was later to use the same comparison of the wilderness in describing a certain kind of literature.† It is also interesting to note the relation in this passage of *taste* to *sight*, the comparison of the insensitive man to the blind man which is so frequently made in the century. It was used also by Racan in an ode to Balzac which was part of the collection of laudatory verse introducing Ogier's piece. Racan wrote in the eighth stanza of this poem,

* As in the quotation from Mlle de Gournay mentioned above. See also in *L'Ombre de la Damoiselle de Gournay*, Paris, 1626, p. 379, where, in a statement of how much closer the superior man is to God than to "la tourbe vulgaire," she says, "Conformément à quoi les Gymnosophistes appelaient Dieux les gens d'excellente vertu, comme tenant je ne sais quoi de céleste."

† See above, p. 20.

> Les choses les plus ordinaires
> Sont rares quand il les écrit
> Et la clarté de son esprit
> Rend les mystères populaires.
> La douceur et la majesté
> Y disputent de la beauté,
> Son éloquence est la première
> Qui joint l'élégance au savoir,
> Et qui n'a point d'yeux pour la voir
> N'en a point pour voir la lumière.[13]

One ought to remark here the juxtaposition of *clarté* and *mystère* as well as *douceur* and *majesté*, which resembles the union of elocution, novelty and forceful thought with *Grâce* and "Vénus" in the quotation from Ogier himself. It is possible of course that Racan read Ogier before composing his own piece.

Ogier's use of the "je ne sais quoi" in a literary sense is not the only early one. Three years later Mairet in the "Préface en forme de discours poétique" to his pastoral *Silvanire* wrote, in the first section called "Du poème et de ses parties," "Et finalement l'art de faire des vers non seulement dans la rigueur des règles mais encore avec cette élégance et cette douceur qui s'admire plutôt qu'elle ne se laisse imiter, telle qu'on la remarque en ceux de Monsieur Malherbe et qu'on ne peut mieux exprimer que par ce je ne sais quoi, qui fait que de deux parfaitement belles femmes, l'une sera plus agréable que l'autre, sans que l'oeil qui reconnaît cette grâce en puisse deviner la raison."[14]

Here one should note the comparison to feminine attractiveness, again so frequent in the century, and once more the relation of taste to sight which is carried with it. The mention of Malherbe is amusing in this connection. Thirty years later he would not have been used as an example.

Yet another forty years were to pass before anyone took the notion of the "je ne sais quoi" seriously enough to write and publish an essay on it. This, as I have said, was done by the Abbé Bouhours. His *Entretiens d'Ariste* *et d'Eugène* appeared in the full flush of the Age of Louis XIV. The work was immediately and widely successful. It consisted of six essays in dialogue form: *La Mer, La Langue française, Le Secret, Le Bel esprit, Le Je ne sais quoi,* and *Des Devises.* All these were pleasantly presented, showing much learning and a good deal of wit. Bouhours had the background but not the proverbial lack of proportion of the *docte,*[*] and he appealed to a society still largely made up of *précieux.* His biographer Doncieux[15] puts him between the "partisans de la raison classique" and the "famille de beaux esprits" (who in Doncieux's opinion had escaped the influence of Boileau) and describes him thus: "C'est un esprit mitoyen, éclectique, docile aux diverses influences ambiantes, et ses écrits nous donnent, à le bien prendre, comme l'élixir et la fleur des opinions littéraires de la bonne compagnie de son temps." It is on the whole a fair description, except that Doncieux made a mistake in splitting so definitely the précieux from "la raison classique" which he of course identifies with Boileau.

Bouhours' later reputation at home and abroad, and especially in England,[†] did not depend only on the *Entretiens.* He continued to interest himself in questions of language and style. *La manière de bien penser dans les ouvrages de l'esprit* was really a more serious work of literary criticism than anything in the *Entretiens,* except perhaps for the essay on the French language. But alas, the *Manière* was published only in 1687 when its author had reached the age of fifty-nine, and it seems when one reads it, as though a certain stiffness had set in. It was again a series of dialogues, where Eudoxe represents the true French taste and Philanthe the misguided lover of Italian and Spanish *clinquant.* It is Eudoxe's mission to

[*] Cf. the introduction of René Radouant to his edition of the *Entretiens* for the "Collection des chefs-d'oeuvres méconnus," Paris, 1920. In this edition only three of the original six dialogues are included. Of these *Le Je ne sais quoi* is one. When discussing that dialogue I shall refer to this edition.

[†] Addison, in his sixty-second *Spectator,* called him "the most penetrating of all the French critics."

convert his friend to the proper way of looking at things, and needless to say the mission succeeds, to the greater glory of everything French. Much of the terminology is of the sort which interests us, but it is evident that Bouhours' ideas have become fixed, that qualities are ordered categorically, and that the "je ne sais quoi" has become more a substitute for other really substantial qualities than anything else.[16] One feels that the abbé has fallen into the ways of so many of his fellow critics and that his purism and his chauvinism (already evident in the dialogue of the *Entretiens* on the French language which I have just mentioned) have extended themselves into a whole system of rhetoric.

So it is that the *Entretiens d'Ariste et d'Eugène* remain for us the most interesting of his works. Here, not only in *Le Je ne sais quoi*, but in others of the dialogues, one notes a preoccupation with the mysterious and the inexplicable which seems almost to determine his choice of titles. The first dialogue, for instance, treats of the sea, in all its variety of moods and enigmatic behavior. And in speaking of the tide, Eugène says, "Il y a des mystères dans la nature comme dans la grâce, incompréhensibles à l'esprit humain: la sagesse ne consiste pas à en avoir l'intelligence; mais à savoir que les plus intelligents ne sont pas capables de les comprendre. Ainsi le meilleur parti pour nous est de confesser notre ignorance et d'adorer humblement la sagesse de Dieu, qui a voulu que ce secret fût caché aux hommes."[17]

This unscientific, or at least unprogressive link between adoration and secrecy is further stated when in discussing the origin of salt in the sea Eugène says, "Ce sont des secrets, qu'il faut adorer, et qu'il ne faut point approfondir. Disons-le encore une fois, c'est proprement dans la mer que Dieu est admirable et incompréhensible."[18]

There is nothing revolutionary in either of these two statements. But then we note that the title of the third dialogue is *Le Secret* and that its theme is the great power given the statesman by the impenetrability of his designs, and the conclusion is that the ability to retain a secret is an admirable quality and a great strength in the world.

Moreover, the dialogue *Le Bel esprit* allows to Fortune, chance, and fatality an important role in human affairs, and the last dialogue on *Les Devises*, a subject which seemed especially fascinating to Bouhours, contains more observations which contribute to one's impression that the abbé did indeed adore mystery. In speaking of the symbolism of emblems,* the dialogue takes this turn: "Il y a des métaphores de deux sortes: les unes sont superficielles, et ont un sens si facile, que tout le monde les comprend d'abord; les autres renferment un sens profond et caché; on ne les conçoit qu'en les pénétrant: mais aussi dès qu'elles sont conçues, elles donnent de l'admiration et du plaisir."[19] The virtue of mystery is then not necessarily to remain mysterious. Mystery is a relative virtue, it might be said. "Les métaphores tiennent un peu de l'énigme, selon le sentiment d'Aristote; mais selon celui de Cicéron, elles ne doivent point être obscures. Il faut joindre les pensées de ces deux grands hommes pour former une idée parfaite de la Devise; c'est à dire, qu'il faut concevoir en même temps je ne sais quoi de mystérieux, et de clair; ou plutôt quelque chose qui ne soit ni trop clair ni trop obscur."[20]

If one adds these various observations to those in the dialogue on the "je ne sais quoi," there does seem to exist in Bouhours' mind a consciousness of the value of the half-understood which does not operate only in the field of religion, and which, while it certainly does not make of him a willful obscurantist, is not altogether compatible with the usual conception of classic standards.

As I have suggested, all these thoughts are not very profound. Neither is the dialogue on the "je ne sais quoi." But it is broad in its application, and in its light-hearted way it raises a number of difficult and related issues. René

* In connection with the history of emblems and emblematic books, see Mario Praz, *Studies in Seventeenth Century Imagery*, London, The Warburg Institute, 1939-1947, 2 vols. and especially with reference to Bouhours, I, 53.

Radouant, who edited the *Entretiens*, calls it "une chose
très légère, mince d'étoffe, qui vaut surtout par l'aisance
du tour, la délicatesse du style."[21] I think it merits more
consideration than that, because Bouhours was perfectly
well aware of the implications of his subject even if he
was afraid of seeming ponderous in insisting too much
upon them.

The dialogue takes its direction from some remarks exchanged by Ariste and Eugène upon the subject of friendship. What is it that draws people together? What precisely creates the bond? It is a mystery, and the two
friends agree that the best description of this indescribable something is to be found in the lines from Corneille's
Rodogune:

> Il est des noeuds secrets, il est des sympathies
> Dont par le doux rapport les âmes assorties
> S'attachent l'une à l'autre & se laissent piquer
> Par ces je ne sais quoi qu'on ne peut expliquer.[22]

But it is not only in the secret breeding of fancy that
the "je ne sais quoi" has its effect: or perhaps I should say
that the effect is not limited to the spiritual aspects of
human relationships. For it enters into the external, physical aspect: "Ce n'est précisément ni la beauté, ni la
bonne mine, ni la bonne grâce, ni l'enjouement de l'humeur, ni le brillant de l'esprit puisque l'on voit tous les
jours des personnes qui ont toutes ces qualités sans avoir
ce qui plaît et que l'on voit d'autres au contraire qui
plaisent beaucoup, sans avoir rien d'agréable que le je ne
sais quoi."[23]

This quality then is beyond natural beauty because
though it animates it, at the same time it can substitute
for it and correct natural defects. Yet it is experienced
everywhere, but remains of course indefinable. It can be
compared to light, or to actions the speeds of which are
so great that we know of them only by their results, or to
magnetism, or to the wind. But (or consequently) it is
adored, like the undiscovered river of Egypt, or the Unknown God.[24]

Eugène remarks upon the prevalence of the concept in Italian and Spanish literature, and he quotes from these. Ariste replies, "Si vous vouliez vous donner la peine de lire nos livres avec autant de réflexion que vous avez lu les Italiens et les Espagnols, vous trouveriez que le je ne sais quoi a beaucoup de vogue parmi nous, et que nous sommes en cela aussi mystérieux que nos voisins."[25]

There is a negative aspect, too, to the "je ne sais quoi," for every day one sees people who "dans les règles, devraient plaire infiniment et qui néanmoins déplaisent fort."[26] Not only is this true, but the same person may be agreeable to one individual and not to another. If this is so, says Eugène, then we are led into an individualistic position with respect to standards of judgment (they are still speaking of personality) and we are wrong in condemning anyone's taste no matter how bizarre we may find it. We should therefore hold nature responsible and not ourselves, for we are powerless to control nature.[27] Ariste answers, "En effet ces je ne sais quoi en beau et en laid, pour parler de la sorte, excitent en nous des je ne sais quoi d'inclination et d'aversion où la raison ne voit goutte et dont la volonté n'est pas maîtresse. Ce sont des premiers mouvements qui préviennent la réflexion et la liberté."[28]

These "je ne sais quoi," continues Ariste, are all around us, in nature and in our feelings about nature. Eugène, however, suggests that this can be true *only* of nature (he had said we were powerless to control her), "car pour les ouvrages de l'art, toutes les beautés y sont marquées, et l'on sait bien pourquoi ils plaisent."[29] And here, as though he had been waiting for Eugène to attempt just such a distinction, Ariste disagrees. No, what really charms us in painting and in sculpture is again the "je ne sais quoi." This is why artists try so hard to conceal their art, as though to know why an object is pleasing were to find it less so. As for literature, "Les pièces délicates en prose et en vers ont je ne sais quoi de poli et d'honnête qui en fait presque tout le prix et qui consiste dans cet air du monde, dans cette teinture d'*urbanité* que Cicéron ne sait comment définir." Ariste's illustration of his assertion shows how the years have passed: "Il y a de grandes beautés dans les livres de Balzac; ce sont des beautés régulières qui plaisent beaucoup, mais il faut avouer que les ouvrages de Voiture, qui ont ces charmes secrets, ces grâces fines et cachées dont nous parlons, plaisent infiniment davantage."[30]

One may not agree with Bouhours' estimate of Balzac and Voiture, but it is of course his condescension towards regular beauty and his preference for the secret and the hidden which are worth noting.

Bouhours so far reads like a synthesis of the opinions which we have encountered up to now in this study. But since he was in a mood for philosophy, and since this was an essay on the "je ne sais quoi" and not a discussion of literature or love, the abbé went far beyond these topics and expanded his subject into what became practically a principle of human behavior. For, according to him, the "je ne sais quoi" is the object of most of our passions. It is the foundation of love and hate, but also of desire and hope: it is what lies beyond even the goals which human beings set for themselves. It is what we really aspire to, as it were without knowing it, and what we never attain, and that is why we never enjoy a sense of total achievement.

One may imagine what a Kierkegaard or a Freud might do with a notion of this sort, but it was not for Bouhours to probe or to turn inside out or to examine minutely its countless implications. La Rochefoucauld might have done so, at least in more detail than Bouhours, but even he as we know would leave philosophy to the philosophers and theology to the theologians; and so Bouhours, who was composing a dialogue to be read with enjoyment and without effort, preferred to pass on to the larger and more obvious conclusions.

From the point he had now reached (where we may see, incidentally, a reflection of the *beau idéal*) it was but a step to religion. Bouhours, to the disgust of some of his more austere contemporaries,[31] made that step. The sense of the immortality of the soul, a soul unsatisfied by earthly grandeur, the sense of another order which is the terminus of our desires and the center of felicity, an order promised by God but unattainable and inconceivable in human terms, is the sense of the "je ne sais quoi."

"Ainsi donc," says Eugène, "le je ne sais quoi est de la grâce, aussi bien que de la nature et de l'art." And Ariste replies, "Oui. La grâce elle-même, cette divine grâce qui a fait tant de bruit dans les écoles* et qui fait des effets si admirables dans les âmes, cette grâce si forte et si douce tout ensemble, qui triomphe de la dureté du coeur sans blesser la liberté du franc arbitre, qui s'assujettit la nature en s'y accommodant, qui se rend maîtresse de la volonté en la laissant maîtresse d'elle-même, cette grâce dis-je, qu'est-ce autre qu'un je ne sais quoi surnaturel qu'on ne peut ni expliquer ni comprendre?"[32]

We have seen the link between the "je ne sais quoi" and the heavenly expressed more than once, but never so fully as here. It is surely a natural link to imagine. The use of the phrase coupled with the idea of grace must have been frequent among preachers of the period. Bossuet in the *Traité de la connaissance de Dieu et de soi-même* said, "Je ne sais quoi est imprimé dans le coeur de l'homme pour lui faire reconnaître une justice qui punit les pères sur leurs enfants comme étant une portion de leur être. . . . Ainsi nous portons au fond du coeur une impression de cette justice qui punit les pères dans les enfants. . . ."†

As Bouhours said, inexplicable impressions correspond to mysterious qualities, and all partake of the "je ne sais quoi." Méré, Pascal, and La Rochefoucauld had seen this correspondence too, but a much more thorough account of the whole process is to be found in a document of the highest interest written by Nicole concerning *les pensées*

---

* This somewhat offhand reference is undoubtedly to the Jansenist controversy.

† I am indebted to Prof. Gilbert Chinard for this quotation. Cf. a more special and better known use of the phrase, based on Tertullian, in Bossuet's *Sermon sur la mort*: "un je ne sais quoi qui n'a plus de nom en aucune langue."

imperceptibles. It has been recently reproduced in G. Chinard's *En lisant Pascal,*[33] and it gives further proof of the close relationship of religious thought to the sort of criticism with which we are dealing. To understand how much of the Seventeenth Century was the extension of Scholasticism and how much of it was an Augustinian reaction against that Scholasticism is perhaps to understand the true nature of its Classicism.

To return to the dialogue on the "je ne sais quoi," it is interesting to note how well Bouhours' description of the operation of grace fits the essential irony of the artistic act. Even more, the transition from the consideration of personal relationships through personality itself to all nature, thence to art and finally to divine grace has been so gentle that one scarcely realizes at first that Bouhours was assigning a positive value to all experience which lies outside the order of the reason and the order of the senses. And it is very hard not to feel that, if only by implication, this experience was in his mind a truer one.

The conclusion of the dialogue follows quickly. There is very naturally little left to say. But Eugène remarks that though the "je ne sais quoi" seems to be "l'asile de l'ignorance, car il me semble qu'on se sauve toujours par là quand on ne sait plus que dire," still the discussion of it has brought them a long way, proving thereby the usefulness of speaking about incomprehensible subjects and matters which are not to be found in books. Ariste answers, "Il est vrai que le je ne sais quoi est peut-être la seule matière sur laquelle on n'a point fait de livres et que les doctes n'ont pas pris la peine d'éclaircir. Il s'est fait des discours, des dissertations et des traités sur les sujets les plus bizarres; mais aucun auteur, que je sache, n'a travaillé sur celui-ci." But Eugène reminds him of the speech which Gombauld had made at the Academy some thirty years before. However, he says he is ignorant of its contents since it has never been published, though, he concludes, the world is probably no worse off for the fact, the subject being in the nature of those things which can never be understood and can only be admired.

Ariste ends the dialogue with a laugh, saying, "Je suis bien aise que vous preniez enfin le bon parti et que vous vous contentiez d'admirer ce que d'abord vous vouliez comprendre."

No matter how rationalistic the Seventeenth Century was, it nourished from Balzac to Fénelon a suspicion of the pat formula and the easy explanation, especially when things which have to do with the spirit and the imagination were concerned. It has always been correct to hold this suspicion, and the men of imagination in the century were no different from their ancestors or their descendants in this respect. By the time of Bouhours this suspicion was sufficiently crystallized to be given a label and to merit at least an essay under that label.

Actually, however, the real expression of that suspicion in terms of the whole century demanded a more profound spirit than Bouhours. In the *Pensées*, published only the year before the *Entretiens*, Pascal had taken magnificently full account of the "je ne sais quoi."

One would not of course say that this suspicion was the distinguishing mark of the century. This would be simple distortion. But I believe that it is a distinctive and necessary element of the complex which we now call Classicism. We shall see that even Boileau and certainly La Bruyère continue to reflect this complexity, and to contribute to it.

3. "QU'EST-CE QUE LE SUBLIME? OÙ ENTRE LE SUBLIME?": BOILEAU AND LA BRUYÈRE

BOILEAU

WITHIN the framework of the complex which we are trying to recover, the sublime might be described as the "agrément inexplicable" or the "je ne sais quoi" considered on a higher plane. Offhand it connotes a more lasting, a deeper, and a solider excellence. "Sublime" is after all a more positive term than the other two, and it suggests less directly the limitations of the human mind and more reverently the aspect of art which partakes of the divine. But all three terms are certainly related.

In the last quarter of the century two outstanding literary figures found themselves preoccupied with this problem of the sublime. These were Boileau and La Bruyère. Whether it was that the *précieux* tradition was not so strong in them, or that simply in time the deeper implications of the problem were becoming more evident, I do not know, but with them a more serious note begins to sound. Yet at the same time where Boileau seems to gain confidence from the notion, La Bruyère is less sure of himself, and it is he who asks the question as Boileau thinks to give at least a partial answer. But neither believes himself to have the final one.

There are several ways of looking at Boileau. There is first of all, of course, the author of the *Art poétique*, the great lawgiver. But there is also the poet, the artist who worked so hard to make his verses behave, and who seemed at times to be the reincarnation of Horace. And there is the satirist, possessed by a demon of corrective ridicule whom the poet and artist could not always keep in check. And finally there is the man of taste whose honesty sometimes embarrassed his friends, but who supplemented his sharply expressed opinions with the study, translation, and commentary of Longinus. It is this last Boileau who interests me here. He is, I believe, less understood than the legislator or the poet or the satirist. In any case to understand the man of taste is to understand the others better.

Boileau himself in his later days wished to be remembered as other than he was commonly thought to be. I am not sure that he achieved this hope. The *Art poétique* remains his principal monument. But in his tenth epistle, which, like Horace, he addressed to his own verses, he asked that he be rescued from his detractors, and said,

Déposez hardiment qu'au fond cet homme horrible,
Ce censeur qu'ils ont peint si noir et si terrible,
Fut un esprit doux, simple, ami de l'équité,

Qui, cherchant dans ses vers la seule vérité,
Fit, sans être malin, ses plus grandes malices:
Et qu'enfin sa candeur seule a fait tous ses vices.[1]

This was written in 1695, when Boileau was fifty-nine years old, and when, as he said in this same epistle, his white hair was covered by a blond peruke.[2] To be sure he had made his peace with many of his enemies. The quarrel with Perrault had been patched up the year before (though Boileau was not to explain himself fully for another five years), Quinault had been pardoned, Boursault had been pardoned. A letter from Racine in 1687 had commented amusedly upon this amnesty. In speaking of the *comédiens* who had lost their theater in the rue Guénégaud and could find no place to go unless it was near the Paris dump, he remarked, "Ce serait un digne théâtre pour les oeuvres de M. Pradon: j'allais ajouter de M. Boursault; mais je suis trop touché des honnêtetés que vous avez tout nouvellement reçues de lui. Je ferai tantôt à M. Quinault celles que vous me mandez de lui faire. Il me semble que vous avancez furieusement dans le chemin de la perfection. Voilà bien des gens à qui vous avez pardonné."[3]

Boileau's reply to this was, "J'ai fort ri de la raillerie que vous me faites sur les gens à qui j'ai pardonné. Cependant savez-vous bien qu'il y a à cela plus de mérite que vous ne croyez, si le proverbe italien est véritable, que, *Chi offende non perdona.*"[4]

Even before this in the preface to the 1683 edition of his works Boileau had given some (grudging) credit to Chapelain, and granted some genius to Saint-Amant, Bréboeuf, and Scudéry. It took him until 1701 before he could add "Cotin même," in a reiteration of his magnanimity.[5] And of Quinault he had said in the 1683 preface, "J'ajouterai même . . . que dans le temps où j'écrivis contre lui, nous étions tous deux fort jeunes, et qu'il n'avait pas fait alors beaucoup d'ouvrages qui lui ont dans la suite acquis une juste réputation."[6]

My point is that he was trying to avoid the accusation

of blind dogmatism born of jealousy or ill-will. In the first preface of all to his collected works he had tried to protect himself by saying that "le Parnasse fut de tout temps un pays de liberté; . . . le plus habile y est toujours exposé à la censure du plus ignorant . . . le sentiment d'un seul homme ne fait point la loi."[7]

In other words his opinions about the writers of his day were purely personal, if that was any comfort to those whom he criticized adversely. But what aroused so much antagonism was not that he was laying down the law, but that in a time when adverse criticism was seldom directed by respectable men of letters against their contemporaries, and when indeed living writers were scarcely ever mentioned by name, Boileau was bold enough to say outright who in his opinion was bad and who was good. It is understandable of course that the bad said of his colleagues far outweighed the good, since there are always more bad writers than good, and since his nature was essentially corrective. The constructive side of his criticism was mostly reserved for those with whom he associated personally and it was applied in conversation with them.

Not that he thought himself without a mission. It was the mission of the satirist: to castigate the weakness of the age. This included the weakness of bad writing. But how much real criticism is one going to find in a satire or an epistle? If one reads through Boileau one finds that the greater part of it consists in simple judgments. This or that poet is trivial, heavy, or dull. If the criticism is favorable, as in the case of the epistle to Racine or the *stances* to Molière, it consists correspondingly in simple praise and encouragement. I am referring to Boileau's verse now. This does not apply to his prose.

Thus Boileau's real position as a critic is apt to be obscured by his verve as a satirist, or in rare cases as an apologist. If he was the "régent du Parnasse" through his satire, it was only by means of intimidation and positiveness, and not through any careful analysis. He depended upon nothing more complicated than taste and good sense, and he appealed to these qualities in his readers.

There is, of course, the *Art poétique*. Here the taste and good sense are set down in more general terms. This is the Boileau whom most people know. If the poem is examined without regard to its place in the history of criticism it will be found to embody and set forth a number of perfectly sound general precepts which any young writer at any time ought to know, plus a statement of the then accepted literary formalities and practices (and what age is without them?) with some historical background. The same could be said for its Horatian and Aristotelian prototypes. But it is at the same time, like Horace's poem, a rather remarkable *tour de force*. It is amusing, epigrammatical, and piquant. It is the work of a satirist and a virtuoso possibly more than it is the credo of a critic. Yet ironically it stands as the great expression of French classic *raison* and seems to place Boileau firmly in the ranks of the "rule critics." However, setting aside the now familiar argument that he *established* nothing, we may still ask the question: what did this sort of criticism really mean to him, and how much did he live by it?

It seems to me that Boileau set his standards beyond rules. He was in search of the sublime. In the second of his satires, composed in 1664 and addressed to Molière, he complained that he lacked the playwright's facility in rhyming. Had he no conscience, he said, it would be easy enough, and,

> Un sot, en écrivant, fait tout avec plaisir:
> Il n'a point en ses vers l'embarras de choisir;
> Et, toujours amoureux de ce qu'il vient d'écrire,
> Ravi d'étonnement, en soi-même il s'admire.
> Mais un esprit sublime en vain veut s'élever
> A ce degré parfait qu'il tâche de trouver;
> Et, toujours mécontent de ce qu'il vient de faire,
> Il plaît à tout le monde, et ne saurait se plaire.[8]

Nevertheless the urge had hold of him. Surely the fact that Boileau was a practicing poet and an extremely care-

ful craftsman had something to do with his understanding of literature and of those who make it. It gave him
his extraordinary sense of rightness and it gave him also
his lack of respect for those of the trade in general. Of
those few whom he singled out for greatness almost every
one remains today in high esteem. He was not the only
one to perceive their merit of course, but he refused to be
taken in by the momentary vogue for a great many others
who have since sunk to the lesser ranks. He knew how
much of mystery there is in poetry and how much there
is of sham.

In the *Art poétique* there are hints of this knowledge.
It begins with the mention of the "influence secrète" of
Heaven.[9] But this is no more than the traditional recognition of genius. The most dogmatic and narrow rule
critic could admit that much. The passage where the
"esprit vigoureux" is allowed to go beyond the limits set
by the rules[10] is more significant, but taken by itself it
is still not much of a contribution to literary theory.
There are, however, a certain number of lines such as

> Soyez simple avec art,
> Sublime sans orgueil, agréable sans fard.[11]

which suggest the presence of a paradox, even though it
is, as we know, standard classic doctrine. The paradox
emerges even more clearly in the lines which have to do
with the ode,

> Son style impétueux souvent marche au hasard:
> Chez elle un beau désordre est un effet de l'art.[12]

Boileau was quite conscious of the particular paradox
involved here, for he was to return to this precept many
years later at the height of his quarrel with Perrault,
when the whole problem became part of the Ancient-
Modern argument. But even before the *Art poétique* he
had shown his acceptance of it in the *Dissertation sur la
Joconde* where he analyzed the superiority of La Fontaine's *conte*. I have already quoted in the chapter on
La Fontaine a passage from it where he praised the sim-

plicity, the directness, and the "naïveté" or naturalness of the poet and concluded that it was impossible to demonstrate the effectiveness of these qualities to one who lacked the capacity for feeling it, and that it was after all a "je ne sais quoi." The *Dissertation* was probably written about 1665.* It is an interesting document in many ways. It is one of the best examples of applied literary criticism in the century and it shows that Boileau was not limited either to the generalities of the *Art poétique*, or to the bare emotional expressions of the satires and epistles, or to the burlesque of the *Héros de roman*. But it interests me particularly here for it indicates that early in his career Boileau was dependent upon a criterion of taste and of non-rational judgment along with all his talk of *raison* and *bon sens*.

He returned as I have said to the question of the "beau désordre" in his argument with Perrault. This was in the *Discours sur l'ode* where he defended Pindar, the Ancients, poetry and himself against the prosaic Modern attack. Accompanying the essay was an ode of his own composition on the taking of Namur. It was to serve as an example in the style of Pindar. It is not a successful poem, and of its many faults the lapse into satire at the very end is surely the worst and most inexplicable. The ode begins,

> Quelle docte et sainte ivresse
> Aujourd'hui me fait la loi?[13]

and the tone is maintained until in the last stanza Boileau writes,

> Pour moi, que Phébus anime
> De ses transports les plus doux
> Rempli de ce dieu sublime,
> Je vais, plus hardi que vous,
> Montrer que, sur le Parnasse,
> Des bois fréquentés d'Horace

* See R. Bray's very informative article on the question of the authorship of the *Dissertation*, in the *Revue d'histoire littéraire* for 1931; also Ch. H. Boudhors, *Oeuvres complètes de Boileau*, ed. cit. *Dissertation*, pp. 127ff., and P. Clarac, *Contes et Nouvelles de La Fontaine*, Paris, Belles Lettres, 1934, I, viii.

Ma muse dans son déclin
Sait encore les avenues
Et des sources inconnues
A l'auteur du Saint-Paulin.[14]

The author mentioned is of course Perrault. Boileau had also composed a stanza which was to be the second one of the ode. But he did not publish it. It was equally out of keeping with the whole poem. It ran,

Un torrent dans les prairies
Roule à flots précipités;
Malherbe dans ses furies
Marche à pas trop concertés.
J'aime mieux, nouvel Icare,
Dans les airs suivant Pindare,
Tomber du ciel le plus haut,
Que, loué de Fontenelle,
Raser, timide hirondelle,
La terre comme Perrault.[15]

Boileau's demon was the demon of satire. No true lyric poet would have so brutally thrown away the whole effect of his poem, unless the general intention happened to be satirical as is the case sometimes with Horace, who obviously came between Boileau and Pindar here.* But it is still very hard to understand how Boileau the critic would not have seen that his entire argument was spoiled. He should have been especially careful, for he realized and often admitted his limitations as a lyric poet.

Be that as it may, the argument in the essay runs as follows: Perrault "a surtout traité de ridicules ces endroits merveilleux où le poète [Pindar], pour marquer un esprit entièrement hors de soi, rompt quelquefois de dessein formé la suite de son discours; et afin de mieux entrer dans la raison, sort, s'il faut ainsi parler, de la raison même, évitant avec grand soin cet ordre méthodique et ces exactes liaisons de sens qui ôteraient l'âme à la poésie lyrique. Le censeur dont je parle n'a pris garde qu'en at-

* I am indebted to my friend S. D. Atkins for this suggestion.

taquant ces nobles hardiesses de Pindare, il donnait lieu
de croire qu'il n'a jamais conçu le sublime des Psaumes
de David, où, s'il est permis de parler de ces saints can-
tiques à propos de choses si profanes, il y a beaucoup de
ces sens rompus, qui servent même quelquefois à en faire
sentir la divinité. Ce critique, selon toutes les apparences,
n'est pas fort convaincu du précepte que j'ai avancé dans
mon Art poétique, à propos de l'ode." Boileau then
quoted the lines I referred to above, and continued, "Ce
précepte effectivement, qui donne pour règle de ne point
garder quelquefois les règles, est un mystère de l'art,
qu'il n'est point aisé de faire entendre à un homme sans
aucun goût, qui croit que la *Clélie* et nos opéra sont les
modèles du genre sublime. . . ."[16]

He went on to explain how the ode to follow was to
be in the manner of Pindar, "C'est-à-dire pleine de
mouvements et de transports, où l'esprit parut plutôt en-
traîné du démon de la poésie que guidé par la raison."
But he was not certain that the public would like it, accustomed as they had become to the "sages emporte-
ments de Malherbe."[17]

In this short *Discours* then one may find united for discussion many of the questions which have been occupy-
ing us throughout this study: the relation of reasonableness to poetry in the creation of it and in the judgment of
it; the question of lyric poetry in the century and the effect of Malherbe; the irregular sublimity of the Biblical
style. In short the mystery of art, and of taste, and of the
sublime. The piece was composed in 1693, but the questions and the answers are old ones.

The year following, Boileau published the first nine of
his *Réflexions sur Longin.* But he had translated Longinus
first in 1674 and published it with a preface. To this preface we must now return, for a closer understanding of
what the sublime meant for Boileau. Here is his definition
of it: "Longin n'entend pas ce que les orateurs appellent
le style sublime, mais cet extraordinaire qui frappe dans
le discours, et qui fait qu'un ouvrage enlève, ravit, trans-
porte." There is not much for the reasonable judgment to

do in such a case. "Le style sublime veut toujours de grands mots: mais le sublime se peut trouver dans une seule pensée, dans une seule figure, dans un seul tour de paroles. Une chose peut être dans le style sublime et n'être pourtant pas sublime, c'est-à-dire, n'avoir rien d'extraordinaire ni de surprenant. Par exemple: *Le souverain arbitre de la nature d'une seule parole forma la lumière*: voilà qui est dans le style sublime; cela n'est pas néanmoins sublime, parce qu'il n'y a rien là de fort merveilleux, et qu'on ne pût aisément trouver. Mais, *Dieu dit: Que la lumière se fasse, et la lumière se fit*: ce tour extraordinaire d'expression, qui marque si bien l'obéissance de la créature aux ordres du Créateur est véritablement sublime, et a quelque chose de divin. Il faut donc entendre par sublime dans Longin, l'extraordinaire, le surprenant, et comme je l'ai traduit, le merveilleux dans le discours."[18]

The example is, of course, out of Longinus. That there was some controversy over its authenticity is beside the point, as is the question of Boileau's interpretation of Longinus, for it is Boileau's conception of literature which interests us. There is again the connection of Biblical style to the sublime and the divine, recalling Balzac. But there is also in this same preface a remark about Longinus' own style which makes the familiar allusion to *honnêteté*: "Le caractère d'honnête homme y paraît partout et les sentiments ont je ne sais quoi qui marque non seulement un esprit sublime, mais une âme fort élevée au-dessus du commun."[19]

The extraordinary, the mysterious, the inexplicable; these are the "values" with which Boileau was dealing. They are not intellectual values. They reside in the artist and in the work of art and render them superior, but they are spiritual values. They are sensed by the superior critic.

But they are also instinctively recognized by many who lay no claim to special skill in judgment. Boileau knew, as his friends Racine and Molière knew, that in the enormously complicated business of artistic creation the apprehender not acting as a reasoning critic plays a part which is not measurable and which is consequently often forgotten by the narrow professional critic who depends on rules. In the eleventh *Réflexion sur Longin* this participation was taken into account in the discussion of Racine's always controversial "récit de Théramène."* La Motte had criticized the line where, having brought the Neptune-ordered monster to the shore,

Le flot qui l'apporta recule épouvanté . . .

La Motte had thought this too bold. Boileau defended its very audacity and said, "Aussi a-t-on remarqué que toutes les fois qu'on joue la tragédie de *Phèdre*, bien loin qu'on paraisse choqué de ce vers . . . on y fait une espèce d'acclamation; marque incontestable qu'il y a là du vrai sublime," and he quoted Longinus: "Car lorsqu'en un grand nombre de personnes différentes de profession et d'âge, et qui n'ont aucun rapport ni d'humeurs ni d'inclinations, tout le monde vient à être frappé également de quelque endroit d'un discours, ce jugement et cette approbation uniforme de tant d'esprits si discordants d'ailleurs est une preuve certaine et indubitable qu'il y a là du merveilleux et du grand."[20]

The translation of Longinus is Boileau's own. His conclusion was, "Lorsqu'un endroit d'un discours frappe tout le monde, il ne faut pas chercher des raisons ou plutôt de vaines subtilités, pour s'empêcher d'en être frappé, mais faire si bien que nous trouvions nous-mêmes les raisons pourquoi il nous frappe."[21]

Standards of criticism are then in Boileau's view at once more simple and more complex than any set of rules could make them. Whatever they might be, there was somewhere a recognition of instinctive appreciation which left the whole problem finally open and questionable. Boileau was, like Molière and Racine, encouraging the audience not to suspect its reactions but to justify them.

* See the analysis of this passage from *Phèdre* made by Leo Spitzer in his *Linguistics and Literary History*, Princeton University Press, 1948.

This was not however to say that reason played no part in the process. He tried to clarify the mystery and, as I have said, to give at least a partial explanation in the preface to the 1701 edition of his works. In this preface perhaps is the final statement of the moderate Classic position. He began by thanking the public for its kindness to him, and then said, "Je ne saurais attribuer un si heureux succès qu'au soin que j'ai pris de me conformer toujours à ses sentiments, et d'attraper, autant qu'il m'a été possible, son goût en toutes choses. C'est effective-ment à quoi il me semble que les écrivains ne sauraient trop s'étudier. Un ouvrage a beau être approuvé d'un petit nombre de connaisseurs: s'il n'est plein d'un certain agrément et d'un certain sel propre à piquer le goût géné-ral des hommes, il ne passera jamais pour un bon ouvrage, et il faudra à la fin que les connaisseurs eux-mêmes avou-ent qu'ils se sont trompés en lui donnant leur approbation. Que si on me demande ce que c'est que cet agrément et ce sel, je répondrai que c'est un je ne sais quoi, qu'on peut beaucoup mieux sentir que dire. A mon avis néan-moins il consiste principalement à ne jamais présenter au lecteur que des pensées et des expressions justes. L'esprit de l'homme est naturellement plein d'un nombre infini d'idées confuses du vrai, que souvent il n'entrevoit qu'à demi; et rien ne lui est plus agréable que lorsqu'on lui offre quelqu'une de ces idées bien eclaircie et mise dans un beau jour."[22] These *pensées* are not new, but newly said, and illumined. After some examples of good and bad *pensées*, Boileau concluded, "Puis donc qu'une pen-sée n'est belle qu'en ce qu'elle est vraie, et que l'effet in-faillible du vrai, quand il est bien énoncé, c'est de frapper les hommes, il s'ensuit que ce qui ne frappe point les hommes n'est ni beau ni vrai, ou qu'il est mal énoncé, et que par conséquent un ouvrage qui n'est point goûté du public est un très-méchant ouvrage." A temporary suc-cess or failure is possible of course, but a good piece is like a stick of wood held under water: the minute it is let go it will rise to the surface. "Je pourrais dire un nom-bre infini de pareilles choses sur ce sujet, et ce serait la matière d'un gros livre; mais en voilà assez ce me semble, pour marquer au public ma reconnaissance et la haute idée que j'ai de son goût et de ses jugements."[23]

Now there is very little said in these passages about anything resembling a fixed or communicable code of judgment. The beautiful, or the sublime, or the *je ne sais quoi* are felt, recognized by those whose taste enables them to do so. They reside in the true, the simple, and the natural. But what are the rules for achieving them or perceiving them finally? They are ultimately mysterious. There are a great many precepts in all of Boileau's work. But, though he judged vigorously and sharply, he never, so far as I can tell, judged according to any set of formal rules, and never supposed that criticism should be so conducted. As La Bruyère said of him in his speech of acceptance to the Academy "on y remarque une critique sûre, judicieuse, et innocente, s'il est permis du moins de dire de ce qui est mauvais qu'il est mauvais."[24] His very positiveness and influence came from the fact that he judged in the light of the sublime, but from the heart.

LA BRUYÈRE

La Bruyère's approach to the sublime, though in the long run no more penetrating than Boileau's, was more subtle. He seems to sum up much of the Seventeenth Century. He looks back to the Ancients, but through La Rochefoucauld, Pascal, and Boileau, whose voices are echoed in his maxims, his portraits, and his *pensées* about man and his doings. He looks forward to the time, now close at hand, as we shall see, when the unity of the century was to be destroyed in favor of a less real but more immediately apparent oneness. Of all the major Classic figures, it is he who asks the most questions. He had for instance La Rochefoucauld's and Pascal's consciousness of the complexity of personality. But he was puzzled and troubled by it, more explicitly than La Rochefoucauld, if more superficially than Pascal. And he applied his awareness of it to specific individuals, "d'après nature" as he said.[1] So when he spoke of the "lourd" La Fontaine and the "ennuyeux" Corneille and the fantastic Santeul (who became three persons), this lack of correspondence between their personalities and their writings was *incompréhensible*, a *prodige*.[2]

There is in other words the sound of a new emotional note in La Bruyère's observations. "Qu'il est difficile d'être content de quelqu'un."[3] There is a suggestion of personal experience in many of them. "Il y a des lieux que l'on admire, il y en a d'autres qui touchent et où l'on aimerait à vivre. Il me semble que l'on dépend des lieux pour l'esprit, l'humeur, la passion, le goût, et les sentiments."[4] There is a tentativeness about them. "On ouvre un livre de dévotion, et il touche; on en ouvre un autre qui est galant, et il fait son impression. Oserai-je dire que le coeur seul concilie les choses contraires, et admet les incompatibles?"[5]

The above passages are all from *Du Coeur*. In *De Quelques usages* there is a passage which, though it is on a different level of observation, expresses very well this feeling of groping, of tentativeness, of being surrounded by a web of mysterious forces. "Que penser de la magie et du sortilège? La théorie en est obscure, les principes vagues, incertains, et qui approchent du visionnaire; mais il y des faits embarrassants, affirmés par des hommes graves qui les ont vus ou qui les ont appris de personnes qui leur ressemblent. Les admettre tous ou les nier tous paraît un égal inconvénient, et j'ose dire qu'en cela, comme dans toutes les choses extraordinaires et qui sortent des communes règles, il y a un parti à trouver entre les âmes crédules et les esprits forts."[6] The truth lies somewhere between Sganarelle and Dom Juan.

This questioning tone however does not mean that La Bruyère had no opinions or was timid about them. The publication of the *Caractères*, though at first anonymous, was itself an act of boldness. Its author, while distinctly wishing to avoid any accusation of real dogmatism, nevertheless intended the book to have a direct moral significance and a sharp satirical bite. There is a militant

Christianity about it, and it reflects a definite sociological conscience. Besides this, we know that La Bruyère was a firm anti-Modern. Aside from the indications of this in the *Caractères*, his acceptance speech at the Academy, bold in style to begin with because it eschewed all the consecrated formulae, praised only living "Ancients," among them Boileau, La Fontaine, Racine and Bossuet.

There is however some connection between the tentativeness of the *Caractères* and the general air of discontent which pervades it. La Bruyère found the world in which he lived a shifting, shadowy one, an old one, and a weary one, too tired to cling to those standards which he regarded as valid, but which perhaps he himself did not see too clearly. And so he too seems affected by that same weariness, as though unable to draw sufficient strength from his convictions. The empty weight of time sat heavy on him. "Chaque heure en soi, comme à notre égard, est unique; est-elle écoulée une fois, elle a péri entièrement, les millions de siècles ne la ramèneront pas: les jours, les mois, les années, s'enfoncent et se perdent sans retour dans l'abîme des temps; le temps même sera détruit: ce n'est qu'un point dans les espaces immenses de l'éternité, et il sera effacé. Il y a de légères et frivoles circonstances du temps qui ne sont point stables, qui passent et que j'appelle des modes, la grandeur, la faveur, les richesses, la puissance, l'autorité, l'indépendance, le plaisir, les joies, la superfluité. Que deviendront ces modes, quand le temps même aura disparu? La vertu seule, si peu à la mode, va au delà des temps." (*De la Mode*).[7] But, "Qui a vécu un seul jour a vécu un siècle: même soleil, même terre, même monde, mêmes sensations, rien ne ressemble mieux à aujourd'hui que demain." (*Des Esprits forts*)[8] Hence the famous statement which begins the *Caractères*, "Tout est dit, et l'on vient trop tard depuis plus de sept milles ans qu'il y a des hommes, et qui pensent."[9] Yet the last remark in the opening section (*Des Ouvrages de l'esprit*), with its tone of protest, belies the philosophical acceptance of the first: "HORACE ou DESPREAUX l'a dit avant vous.—Je le crois sur votre parole; mais je l'ai dit comme mien. Ne puis-je pas penser après eux une chose vraie, et que d'autres penseront après moi"?[10]

This sort of ambivalence runs all through the *Caractères*. La Bruyère was always disturbed, I believe, by the question of the real relationship between permanence and change. "Deux choses toutes contraires nous préviennent également, l'habitude et la nouveauté." (*Des Jugements*)[11] He believed that there were standards. He knew that his Christianity gave him an anchor. But he did not know where to fix the line from this anchor. He did not know how far into the world of human affairs a conception of permanence and rightness might be carried. His remark about perfection is often quoted as typical of his critical position, "Il y a dans l'art un point de perfection comme de bonté ou de maturité dans la nature: celui qui le sent et qui l'aime a le goût parfait, celui qui ne le sent pas et qui aime en deçà ou au delà a le goût défectueux. Il y a donc un bon et un mauvais goût, et l'on dispute des goûts avec fondement."[12]

Perfection exists then, and as he says later on, it must be sought for by the writer beyond even the taste of his own times.[13] But if it is only felt, as he suggests, how is it attained? The reason, nature, to be sure. La Bruyère accepts these, along with the imitation of the Ancients, even to the point of fearing the imagination, "Il ne faut pas qu'il y ait trop d'imagination dans nos conversations ni dans nos écrits; elle ne produit souvent que des idées vaines et puériles, qui ne servent point à perfectionner le goût et à nous rendre meilleurs: nos pensées doivent être prises dans le bon sens et la droite raison, et doivent être un effet de notre jugement." (*De la Société et de la conversation*)[14]

But where is this point of perfection? One can fall short of it; one can go beyond it. Is it then in some mean area? La Bruyère was reluctant to put it that way, for he had a keen distaste for mediocrity. "Il y a de certaines choses dont la médiocrité est insupportable: la poésie, la musique, la peinture, le discours public."[15] And, "Un esprit médiocre croit écrire divinement; un bon esprit croit écrire raisonnablement." (*Des Ouvrages de l'esprit*)[16] The implication of the second of these remarks is that somehow the writer who hopes to write "raisonnablement" is actually the one who has the best chance of writing "divinement."

But there exists somewhere a distinction between what is ordinarily thought of as a reasonable soul and the really superior soul: "L'esprit de modération et une certaine sagesse dans la conduite laissent les hommes dans l'obscurité; il leur faut de grandes vertus pour être connus et admirés, ou peut-être de grands vices." (*Des Jugements*)[17] However the great soul, though obviously not the average soul, ought not to be confused with the merely eccentric soul. And yet it seems that eccentricity can, if properly controlled, lead to something good. The reason for this will emerge in this remark: "Le commun des hommes est si enclin au dérèglement et à la bagatelle, et le monde est si plein d'exemples ou pernicieux ou ridicules, que je croirais assez que l'esprit de singularité, s'il pouvait avoir des bornes et ne pas aller trop loin, approcherait fort de la droite raison et d'une conduite régulière." (*Des Jugements*)[18]

But it is hard to see much difference between the "esprit de singularité" and the genius. They are certainly not mutually exclusive. And the genius is the one who is able and willing to risk violating the common conception of right reason and regularity. "Il y a des artisans ou des habiles dont l'esprit est aussi vaste que l'art et la science qu'ils professent; ils lui rendent avec avantage, par le génie et par l'invention, ce qu'ils tiennent d'elle et de ses principes; ils sortent de l'art pour l'ennoblir, s'écartent des règles si elles ne les conduisent pas au grand et au sublime; ils marchent seuls et sans compagnie, mais ils vont fort haut et pénètrent fort loin, toujours sûrs et confirmés par le succès des avantages que l'on tire quelquefois de l'irrégularité. Les esprits justes, doux, modérés, non-seulement ne les atteignent pas, ne les admirent pas, mais ils ne les comprennent point, et voudraient encore moins les imiter; ils demeurent tranquilles dans l'étendue de leur sphère, vont jusques à un certain point qui fait les bornes de leur capacité et de leurs lumières; ils ne vont pas plus loin, parce qu'ils ne voient rien au delà; ils ne peuvent au plus qu'être les premiers d'une seconde classe, et exceller dans le médiocre." (*Des Ouvrages de l'esprit*)[19]

Perfection then is not to be found in moderation, nor is it to be found in "justesse," or rather, those whom these qualities principally characterize will never attain it. It inhabits a region beyond right reason and regularity, though it does not necessarily exclude them. I am assuming here that perfection and sublimity were one and the same for La Bruyère. But I am not sure that this assumption is always possible. I think he sometimes wondered himself if they were. I think of his remark about the *Cid*: "Quelle prodigieuse distance entre un bel ouvrage et un ouvrage parfait et régulier! Je ne sais s'il en est encore trouvé de ce dernier genre. Il est peut-être moins difficile aux rares génies de rencontrer le grand et le sublime, que d'éviter toutes sortes de fautes."[20] The *Cid* had many faults, but the public approved of it unanimously, regardless of variations in their standards or backgrounds. And this was as we remember an infallible sign of sublimity.

La Bruyère felt the insufficiency of criticism in the face of such mysteries. He was aware that the process of apprehending a work of art included an experience not altogether identifiable with the conscious application of clear-cut criteria. "Le plaisir de la critique nous ôte celui d'être vivement touché de très-belles choses."[21] As for the efficacy of criticism as generally practiced, "Il n'y a point d'ouvrage si accompli qui ne fondît tout entier au milieu de la critique, si son auteur voulait en croire tous les censeurs qui ôtent chacun l'endroit qui leur plaît le moins."[22] He did not see therefore why any author should not agree with the critics who praise his work when that work is praised and blamed for the same reasons by those who pass for experts. Too many people, he thought, were unwilling or unable to understand how really complicated a work of literature can be. "Les sots lisent un livre et ne l'entendent point; les esprits médiocres croient l'entendre parfaitement; les grands esprits ne l'entendent quelquefois pas tout entier; ils trouvent obscur ce qui est obscur, comme ils trouvent clair ce qui est clair. . . ."[23] The standards upon which everyone might agree beforehand do not always give the expected answers. The *Sentiments de l'Académie* took these difficulties into account, and that is why La Bruyère said, "l'une des meilleures critiques qui ait été faite sur aucun sujet est celle du *Cid.*"[24]

There was one simple criterion for judging which had already been given by Longinus-Boileau, and which La Bruyère repeated: "Quand une lecture vous élève l'esprit, et qu'elle vous inspire des sentiments nobles et courageux, ne cherchez pas une autre règle pour juger l'ouvrage; il est bon, et fait de main d'ouvrier."[25]

Yet, if the sublime was recognizable in one's own reaction to it, as it were, still La Bruyère could not keep from wondering where it came from, how it was attained, and what it was. It was probably his interest in eloquence and particularly in pulpit eloquence which led him to the problem. In the section *De la Chaire* there is a passage which is especially interesting because it bases his feeling for the delicacy of the secret on the sense of limitation which I mentioned earlier: the fact that all has been said and that the truth is known. "L'éloquence de la chaire, en ce qui y entre d'humain et du talent de l'orateur, est cachée, connue de peu de personnes et d'une difficile exécution: quel art en ce genre pour plaire en persuadant! Il faut marcher par des chemins battus, dire ce qui a été dit, et ce que l'on prévoit que vous allez dire. Les matières sont grandes, mais usées et triviales; les principes sûrs, mais dont les auditeurs pénètrent les conclusions d'une seule vue. Il y entre des sujets qui sont sublimes; mais qui peut traiter le sublime?" The preacher's subject matter is not only old, it is limited. If it is moving, perhaps the one who preaches can take no credit for having made it so. He has not the advantages of the lawyer whose themes are always new, strange, and full of conjecture. Moreover he must be careful lest he be accused of not preaching the gospel. The irony of it is that "il n'a besoin que d'une noble simplicité, mais il faut l'atteindre, talent rare, et qui passe les forces du commun des hommes: ce qu'ils ont de génie, d'imagination, d'érudition et de mémoire, ne leur sert souvent qu'à s'en éloigner."[26]

So, in the section *Des Ouvrages de l'esprit* his mind, questioning as always, turns about these hidden arts of eloquence and the mystery of the sublime. Eloquence, he says in good Ciceronian fashion is a "don de l'âme." Where logic convinces, eloquence captures the heart. It is to the sublime what the whole is to its part. But, "Qu'est-ce que le sublime? Il ne paraît pas qu'on l'ait défini." La Bruyère wishes, evidently, to supply what Boileau had failed to provide in the introduction to his translation of Longinus. What is its source? he asks. What is its relation to figures of speech? Is it found only in the *grand sujet*? Or are the naturalness and the delicacy which seem to determine the excellence of smaller genres the way these genres have of being sublime? It is through the figure of speech that La Bruyère works back into his general position.

Synonym, he says, is for the *esprit médiocre*; it is the mediocre mind's way of trying to illuminate the truth; antithesis attracts the young by its éclat; the *esprits justes* who like precision, run to metaphor and comparison; the *esprits vifs*, full of fire and a vast imagination, go too far "hors des règles et de la justesse" and overwork the hyperbole. But the sublime "ne peint que la vérité, mais en un sujet noble; il la peint toute entière, dans sa cause et dans son effet; il est l'expression ou l'image la plus digne de cette vérité."[27]

The point of the sublime is the point of grand rightness. It is perfection, but of an order beyond the perfection of regularity and of ordinary rightness. Enthusiasm, "justesse," imagination, all would seem to contribute to it, but it needs more than these, and without that addition those otherwise desirable qualities fail to attain it. Genius itself is not always enough. "Pour le sublime, il n'y a, même entre les grands génies, que les plus élevés qui en soient capables."

The authority of genius, the limitations of criticism, the indefinability of the sublime: these forces, so bothersome to the maintenance of a well-ordered literary universe, mystified La Bruyère. "Qu'est-ce que le sublime? Où entre le sublime?" he asked.[28]

Is it the decline of Classicism that is reflected in all the remarks which I have too generously quoted? Only perhaps in the questioning and almost discouraged tone. Is this questioning a premonition of Eighteenth Century scepticism? Only possibly in an earnest effort to avoid dogmatism, for La Bruyère is consciously doing so: "C'est la profonde ignorance qui inspire le ton dogmatique; celui qui ne sait rien croit enseigner aux autres ce qu'il vient d'apprendre lui-même; celui qui sait beaucoup pense à peine que ce qu'il dit puisse être ignoré, et parle plus indifféremment."[29]

As for the thoughts, La Bruyère was merely repeating rather conservatively what had been said before him all through the century. To be sure, he knew it.

4. "DOUCEUR ET CLARTÉ": FÉNELON

No one could more fittingly close this procession of Seventeenth Century figures than François de Salignac de la Mothe-Fénelon, Archbishop of Cambrai. This aristocratic churchman died in 1715, in the last year of that piece of the Eighteenth Century which still belongs officially, if decliningly, to the Age of Louis XIV. Boileau, it is true, inhabited this period, and fruitfully too. But he really belonged to the generation of 1660, whereas Fénelon's literary activity dates from around 1680, so far as we are concerned with it, and is weighted at the very end of his career by the *Lettre sur les Occupations de l'Académie*, written in 1714 but published only after his death, in 1716. Like Boileau he had his say in the last phase of the Quarrel of the Ancients and Moderns and contributed thus to that alignment of opposed critical standards which balances so nicely with the Quarrel of the *Cid*.

The *Lettre* was not Fénelon's only effort at stating literary principles. There are some *Dialogues sur l'Eloquence*, written in 1681-1686, but not published until 1718. (Their authenticity was questioned by Gibert in the *Jugements des Savants*, but this assertion seems to have carried no weight.)[1] There are also: the discourse made on the occasion of his entrance into the Academy in 1693; the *Mémoire sur les Occupations de l'Académie*, composed in answer to a request from the Academy in 1713, afterwards expanded into the *Lettre*; the brief correspondence with La Motte written in 1713 and 1714; and finally there is a critique of a contemporary poet, addressed to an unknown, and undated. These other writings, while they are overshadowed by the *Lettre*, are still not without interest.

Fénelon's role in the history of criticism, is thus not a large one. But it has come to be seen as a notable one. Nisard compared the *Lettre* to Horace's *Ars Poetica*, or rather he compared the Roman's work to Fénelon's. Since Nisard's day he has been regarded not only as a superior theorist of letters but as an advanced one. "Avec la *Lettre à l'Académie*, la relativité du goût devient secrètement le principe de la critique," said Lanson.[2] "Esprit moins tourné vers le passé que vers l'avenir,"[3] said A. Cherel, who saw him as a sort of pre-pre-romantic (if I may be permitted this one use of the term) in his cult of "le naturel."[4] And A. Schinz found his opinions foreshadowing very distinctly those of Rousseau and forming a program of literary reorganization based on ideas which "l'éloignent du classicisme et l'approchent du rationalisme du XVIIIe siècle et du romantisme du XIXe."[5]

Now it was felt that this progressivism had to be pointed out, because what is most evident in Fénelon after his piety, is his hellenism or more precisely his atticism.[6] His heart is with the Greeks; and with the Church Fathers. He is, then, a *Janus bifrons* in the doorway of the

Modern Age. Perhaps, but what did he see when he looked back? Did his gaze arch over the centuries directly back to the Greeks? Or did he see them through his own disappearing epoch?

The answer to this question might first be sought in his opinion of that epoch. The reception speech to the Academy offers one. It was naturally destined to flatter the new confreres, since they must be considered the fashioners and guardians of the public taste, but it is sufficiently in harmony with Fénelon's general point of view to indicate at least an ideal—what he hoped the century might have accomplished. He had of course to praise his predecessor Pellisson, the historian of the Academy. He had thus a graceful opportunity to praise also the achievements of that body. As usual, no mention of the living, "dont je blesserais la modestie par mes louanges."[7] But Malherbe, Racan, Vaugelas, Corneille, and Voiture were mentioned as having played a part in an "heureux renouvellement des lettres."[8] This progress in literature he described in enough detail to make one think he meant it fairly seriously. "Depuis que les hommes savants et judicieux ont remonté aux véritables règles, on n'abuse plus, comme on le faisait autrefois, de l'esprit et de la parole; on a pris un genre d'écrire plus simple, plus naturel, plus court, plus nerveux, plus précis."[9] What follows this statement reveals a conception of literature which is in the most correct tradition of French Classicism. Thought, solid and conclusive, must guide the choice of words; erudition must show itself only if useful; even skill must be hid, because perfection in art means imitating nature so naturally that copy and model are indistinguishable. "Ainsi on ne donne plus le nom d'esprit à une imagination éblouissante; on le réserve pour un génie réglé et correct qui tourne tout en sentiment, qui suit pas à pas la nature toujours simple et gracieuse, qui ramène toutes les pensées aux principes de la raison, et qui ne trouve beau que ce qui est véritable." The "style fleuri" then can never rise above the mediocre; true sublimity is in simplicity, and one must write as the Raphaels, the Carracci, and the Poussins have painted, not with dazzling brush-play, but "d'après nature." The ideal is one of function-alism: no useless ornamentation, but only the ornament of necessary structure and proportion.[10]

With all of this insistence on simplicity there is one unconsciously ironic touch in the *Discours* which I can-not refrain from mentioning. It is the manner in which Fénelon himself described Pellisson's style as revealed in the History of the Academy: "Il y montra son caractère, qui était la facilité, l'invention, l'élégance, l'insinuation, la justesse, le tour ingénieux. Il osait heureusement, pour parler comme Horace. Ses mains faisaient naître les fleurs de tous côtés; tout ce qu'il touchait était embelli. Des plus viles herbes des champs, il savait faire des couronnes pour les héros; et la règle si nécessaire aux autres de ne toucher jamais que ce qu'on peut orner ne semblait pas faite pour lui. Son style noble et léger ressemblait à la démarche des divinités fabuleuses, qui coulaient dans les airs sans poser le pied sur la terre. Il racontait (vous le savez mieux que moi, messieurs,) avec un tel choix de circonstances, avec une si agréable variété, avec, etc."[11] In Fénelon's own words Pellisson's style, breath of an earlier day (forty years before, to be exact) could not quite have measured up to the standard set down in the *Discours*. But then, how functional was Fénelon's de-scription of it?

In any case the standard represented the opposite of Gothic architecture, as Fénelon liked to say. This antith-esis appears also in the *Dialogues sur l'Eloquence*, and helps, along with other similarities, to support their au-thenticity, although they show a face of things different from the one so optimistically shown to the Academy. They were an attack on "l'affectation du bel esprit dans les sermons."[12] They were thus carrying on a long tradi-tion. If they were composed some ten years before the *Discours*, I still cannot believe that this would account for the different tone. I know of no great revolution in the kingdom of eloquence that would cause Fénelon to change his judgment, and anyhow the attack was to be continued years later in the *Lettre*. False eloquence was a long time a-dying, if die it ever did. Its birth accompanied the fall of the Roman Empire, thought Fénelon, and this corruption lasted "jusqu'à nous."[13]

The dialogues are full of Cicero, Longinus, and the Plato of the *Gorgias* and the *Republic*. Boileau, incidentally, is warmly recommended as "un homme qui connaît bien non-seulement le fond de la poésie, mais encore le but solide auquel la philosophie, supérieure à tous les arts, doit conduire le poète."[14] In the fashion of Plato, Fénelon's approach is thoroughly utilitarian. After all he was aiming at the pulpit. But the emphasis is always on attractiveness, on hidden order as opposed to division, which is "une invention très moderne qui nous vient de la scolastique,"[15] and against Aristotelianism. If he wanted to combat the display of skill, the *jeu d'esprit*, he wanted also to encourage the imaginative, the moving, and even the poetic. The orator, says the rubric at the head of the second dialogue, must "prouver, peindre et toucher."[16] "Que diriez vous d'un homme qui prouverait la vérité d'une manière exacte, sèche, nue; qui mettrait ses arguments en bonne forme, ou qui se servirait de la méthode des géomètres dans ses discours publics, sans y ajouter rien de vif et de figuré? serait-ce un orateur?"[17] The answer of course is no.

I said that Fénelon wished to encourage the poetic. "Vous me feriez croire qu'il n'y a point d'éloquence sans poésie" says one of the persons of the dialogue to the principal interlocutor, who answers, "Vous pouvez le croire hardiment." For it is not to be thought that poetry consists in versification. Many people make verses without poetry and just as many make poetry without verses. "Laissons donc là la versification. Pour tout le reste, la poésie n'est autre chose qu'une fiction vive qui peint la nature." Now man, says this principal interlocutor (who is of course Fénelon), has never since the Fall been able to think without his senses. Hence "la poésie . . . est comme l'âme de l'éloquence."[18] The curious turn thus given to the question presents another way in which, in the minds of the period, poetry and grace are related. But Fénelon makes it clear that he is not confusing the poet and the orator, for the former has an "enthousiasme" which raises the vivacity and the boldness of his expression.

This last distinction recalls Cicero, for whom poets were "next of kin" to orators. Cicero himself, Fénelon believed, was not free from a certain number of florid passages in his earlier speeches, but they were admittedly effective. However in the later orations this reproach could not be made, "C'est là qu'il est véritablement éloquent; tout y est négligé comme il dit lui-même dans *l'Orateur* qu'on le doit être lorsqu'il s'agit d'être véhément: c'est un homme qui cherche simplement dans la seule nature tout ce qui est capable de saisir, d'animer et d'entraîner les hommes."[19]

Fénelon's predilection for the Ancients in these matters of eloquence is obvious though not at all surprising or even worthy of any special comment, unless one wishes to underscore his preference for Longinus and Plato over Aristotle and thereby see a trend in the similarity to Boileau and La Bruyère. But even the Chevalier de Méré had already shown this leaning, and the standard of taste implied by the principles expounded in Fénelon's dialogues was common to the century.

Another pillar of right eloquence erected in the dialogues however is Judaeo-Christian rather than Classical. Fénelon thought that the Bible surpassed even Homer "pour peindre naïvement les choses"[20] though he considered its eloquence to be of the same order as that of the best Greeks. And one versed in Classical Antiquity would not be surprised at this, for "ce sont presque les mêmes coutumes, les mêmes narrations, les mêmes images des grandes choses, les mêmes mouvements."[21] But Homer never reached the sublimity of the Songs of Moses, and no Greek or Latin ever attained the heights of the Psalms. Isaiah, now tender as an eclogue, now soaring high, Jeremiah touching, Nahum vivid and Daniel awe-inspiring, all outstrip "les plus sublimes originaux de l'antiquité."[22]

Fénelon is speaking of the Bible as literature, but he does not forget that it is no ordinary literature. "Il y a autant de différence entre les poètes profanes et les prophètes, qu'il y en a entre le véritable enthousiasme et le faux. Les uns, véritablement inspirés, expriment sensiblement quelque chose de divin; les autres, s'efforçant de s'élever au-dessus d'eux-mêmes, laissent toujours voir en eux la faiblesse humaine."[23]

Inevitably, recalling Balzac, Pascal, and Méré, the conversation comes to the simple eloquence of Jesus. Once more, "Cette simplicité de style est tout-à-fait du goût antique." But Fénelon is anxious to avoid confusing simplicity with the bareness of the unimaginative, so that "quoique simple et familier, il est sublime et figuré en bien des endroits. Il serait aisé de montrer en détail, les livres à la main, que nous n'avons point de prédicateur en notre siècle qui ait été aussi figuré dans ses sermons les plus préparés, que Jésus-Christ l'a été dans ses prédications populaires."[24]

The case of the Apostles is understandably different. Weighed down with revealed truth, they faltered, and words failed them. But again, "Toute cette irrégularité de style marque, dans Saint Paul et dans les autres Apôtres, que l'esprit de Dieu entraînait le leur: mais, nonobstant tous ces petits désordres pour la diction, tout y est noble, vif et touchant."[25]

The practical point is that the preacher can borrow this eloquence. When he does so, however, he should take care *not* to use only the passages generally considered beautiful, for "ces passages, tout beaux qu'ils sont, ne peuvent seuls faire sentir toute leur beauté, quand on ne connaît point la suite; car tout est suivi dans l'Ecriture, et cette suite est ce qu'il y a de plus grand et de plus merveilleux."[26]

We are on familiar ground in all of this, and we realize it even more when we continue to follow Fénelon's thought to its conclusion. For it is not really a question of passages to be quoted. It is a question of explaining principles of doctrine, and in so doing of catching the spirit, the style, and the figured presentation in order to inculcate not only the knowledge of, but the taste for the Scriptures. "Il n'en faudrait pas davantage pour être éloquent: car ce serait imiter le plus parfait modèle de l'éloquence."[27] Jesus the model of the *honnête homme*; the Scriptures the model of eloquence.

The two ideals that Fénelon cherished, with the one surpassing the other, always remained in his mind I think, though in the *Lettre* one is not nearly so conscious of the Church tradition as of the Classical. (It emerges nonetheless in the remarks on pulpit eloquence and in the defense of the Fathers, both of which themes he had treated extensively in the dialogues.) But in the *Lettre* their effect is felt otherwise, it seems to me. For example, the short section IX is an answer to a possible objection to the various projects which he has suggested to the Academy. The objection would be that no author having completed one of the projects would wish to submit it to the Academy for examination, since there would be every likelihood of disagreement as to its merits, leading to its probable rejection. Fénelon's answer was that the work would not be thus submitted and that the Academy would not accept or reject it, but would act as an advisory body to discuss the author's doubts (it is assumed he would have them) and to offer him individual and perhaps contrary advice, which he might use as he saw fit. The discussions arising from these deliberations would be published in a journal containing short dissertations "qui perfectionneraient le goût et la critique." Furthermore, "Cette occupation rendrait MM. les académiciens assidus aux assemblées. L'éclat et le fruit en seraient grands dans toute l'Europe."[28]

What strikes one in this answer is a combination of confidence in the prestige and effectiveness of the Academy with an understanding of its advisory rather than legislative function. Such a combination is, I think, characteristic of Fénelon's views on literature in general as displayed in the *Lettre*. I am certain that the religious faith which was peculiarly his gave him a means of appraising all things human and lifted him above the violent attachments which ended by splitting the century apart. He had a sublime by which to judge the sublime. He knew an eloquence more real than eloquence.

It was perhaps this detachment which enabled him to expand a required memorandum into a monument of criticism. The *Mémoire* is more practical, more modern in tone, and more dogmatic than the *Lettre*. He was more concerned with setting up standards for French literature to grow by. And these standards would be based on the best French practice as well as on the precepts of the Ancients. The geographical determinism is there however. "Chaque langue a son génie, son éloquence, sa poésie, et, si j'ose parler ainsi, ses talents particuliers. Les Italiens ni les Espagnols ne feront jamais peut-être de bonnes tragédies ni de bonnes épigrammes, ni les Français de bons poèmes épiques ni de bons sonnets."[29] But the *Mémoire* ends with a call for more discipline in the Academy.

In the *Lettre* the various projects seem to be merely points of departure for an essay on literary excellence where Fénelon's admiration of the Ancients dominates entirely. The projects were: the Dictionary of course, a Grammar, the enrichment of the language, a Rhetoric and a Poetic (projected from the first days of the Academy), and treatises on tragedy, comedy, and history. And the letter concludes with the section on the Ancients and Moderns. I shall not go into great detail in discussing the letter, but I shall try to disengage from the text (without distortion, I hope) some of Fénelon's observations which bear directly on my theme, and which can be supported by remarks from his correspondence with La Motte, and illustrated by his judgment of a contemporary poet.

First, a remark on the poverty of the French language, revealing Fénelon's supposed modernism. In the third section he said, "Notre langue manque d'un grand nombre de mots et de phrases: il me semble même qu'on l'a gênée et appauvrie, depuis environ cent ans, en vou-

lant la purifier. Il est vrai qu'elle était encore un peu in-
forme et trop *verbeuse*. Mais le vieux langage se fait
regretter, quand nous le retrouvons dans Marot, dans
Amyot, dans le cardinal d'Ossat, dans les ouvrages les
plus enjoués, et dans les plus sérieux. Il avait je ne sais
quoi de court, de naïf, de hardi, de vif, et de passionné."[30]

There is nothing in this remark which does not make
one think of Boileau, of La Fontaine, and even of Chapelain.

The section on the rhetoric covers much the same
ground as the dialogues on eloquence, though the tone is
less positive. The purpose was less specific, and Fénelon
is some thirty years older and wiser. He is still fighting
ostentatious pulpit eloquence and apologizing for the
shortcomings of Patristic oratory. But it is now more a
question of *bienséance*. "J'avoue que le genre fleuri a ses
grâces; mais elles sont déplacées dans les discours où il
ne s'agit point d'un jeu d'esprit plein de délicatesse, et
où les grandes passions doivent parler. Le genre fleuri
n'atteint jamais au sublime. . . . Il y a une bienséance à
garder pour les paroles comme pour les habits. Une veuve
désolée ne porte point de deuil avec beaucoup de broderie, de frisure et de rubans."[31] The "reine de village"
has seen sad times.

The section on the poetic is still praising the poetry of
the Bible, adding the book of Job now to the literary
masterpieces therein, and making the distinction between
poetry and versification.[32] His complaint about the strict-
ness of French verse conventions and the monotony of
the Alexandrine are supposed to mark him as advanced
in his thinking. Ironically though, in a letter to La Motte
the monotony is put forward as a reason for doubting the
ability of French to translate the *Iliad*, as La Motte was
attempting to do. Fénelon encouraged him nonetheless,
but in a later letter, having read La Motte's completed
translation, he still politely asserted that Alexandrines
were always "ou languissant ou raboteux."[33] But we have
seen Chapelain and Rapin making the same complaint,
and Boileau, at least on his own account, felt the tyranny

of rhyme. Ronsard, says Fénelon, certainly went too far, but he was right in trying.[34] His excess however threw the French into the opposite extreme, and Malherbe, though his best lines are "clairs et faciles comme la prose la plus simple, et . . . nombreux comme s'il n'avait songé qu'à la seule harmonie" wrote a great many bad verses.[35]

Again, this judgment is in every way consistent with the general opinion of the century.

If the modern emphasis on correctness excludes suspense, surprise, variety, and any grandeur of cadence, the fault is not entirely on the side of the rules. Writers must know how to avoid excess. But the old human weaknesses prevail: "On ne se contente pas de la simple raison, des grâces naïves, du sentiment le plus vif, qui font la perfection réelle; on va un peu au delà du but par amour propre. On ne sait pas être sobre dans la recherche du beau: on ignore l'art de s'arrêter tout court en deçà des ornements ambitieux. Le mieux, auquel on aspire, fait qu'on gâte le bien, dit un proverbe italien."[36]

Amour propre and lack of *mesure*: how often these moral defects are used to explain bad taste and obscurity. And what is more: the greater the power, the greater the danger, as Fénelon sees it. "Les poètes qui ont le plus d'essor, de génie, d'étendue de pensées et de fécondité, sont ceux qui doivent le plus craindre cet écueil de l'excès d'esprit. C'est, dira-t-on, un beau défaut, c'est un défaut rare, c'est un défaut merveilleux. J'en conviens; mais c'est un vrai défaut, et l'un des plus difficiles à corriger."[37] The problem has not changed throughout the century, because it is a basic and eternal problem.

A kind of paradox is involved here, for Fénelon wants passion too, but simply, easily stated. Catullus, despite his "obscénités," is a model of "simplicité passionnée" in the *Odi et amo* for instance, whose lines Fénelon describes as "négligées, où le coeur saisi parle seul dans une espèce de désespoir!"[38]

Bel esprit kills this kind of passion. It is too intellectual, too self-conscious. There must be forgetfulness of self in the sublime. "Je veux un sublime si familier, si doux et si simple, que chacun soit d'abord tenté de croire qu'il l'aurait trouvé sans peine, quoique peu d'hommes soient capables de le trouver . . . Je veux un homme qui me fasse oublier qu'il est auteur."[39]

Sometimes it is not easy to feel precisely what Fénelon means by *doux*. It is of course linked with simplicity and naturalness as is passion. It is hard not to connect it with softness, but I doubt if he meant it that way. I think it meant for him harmony and ease: the gentleness of aesthetic security, which goes to the heart. "Le beau qui n'est que beau, c'est à dire brillant, n'est beau qu'à demi: il faut qu'il exprime les passions pour les inspirer; il faut qu'il s'empare du coeur pour le tourner vers le but légitime d'un poème."[40]

Much of what Fénelon says in the section on the poetic is taken from Horace, and Virgil is his constant example. Indeed the section is a string of quotations from these two poets. Fénelon's Hellenism is seen naturally more clearly in the part on rhetoric and in his love for Homer. His opinion here was so sure, that he had no difficulty in acknowledging the shortcomings of the Ancients as found in the *Iliad* or in Greek drama. The basis of much of the criticism derived from the change which society has undergone as a result of Christianity. This is of course good, but on the other hand said Fénelon, Homer ought not to be blamed for having lived in a period where religion was "extravagante et monstrueuse." He did not invent that religion, but "il l'a trouvée; il n'a pu la changer, il l'a ornée; il a caché dans son ouvrage un grand art, il a mis un ordre qui excite sans cesse la curiosité du lecteur; il a peint avec naïveté, grâce, force, majesté, passion: que veut-on de plus?"[41]

But Fénelon is not, as La Bruyère seemed to be, discouraged about either the future or the destiny of the past. He wrote to La Motte about the Quarrel of the Ancients and Moderns, "Cette guerre civile du Parnasse ne m'alarme point. L'émulation peut produire d'heureux efforts. . . ."[42] His faith in good literature was such that all the usual criticism of detail could not shake it. Rather his faith in the critic was shaken. It was *à propos* of this type of Homeric criticism that he said, "Le censeur médiocre ne goûte point le sublime, il n'en est point saisi: il s'occupe bien plutôt d'un mot déplacé, ou d'une expression négligée; il ne voit qu'à demi la beauté du plan général, l'ordre et la force qui règnent partout. J'aimerais autant le voir occupé d'orthographe, des points interrogants, et de virgules."[43]

With this familiar conception of *honnête* versus pedantic criticism as a background we may watch Fénelon's reaction to the work of a contemporary poet. In an undated communication addressed to an unidentified recipient he criticizes the work of an unknown poet. I am sorry about this general anonymity, but at least we believe it to be Fénelon's criticism, and the Lebel edition thinks the poet might have been Jean-Baptiste Rousseau. Fénelon wrote of him, "Ses vers sont pleins, ce me semble, d'une poésie noble et hardie; il pense hautement, il peint bien et avec force; il met du sentiment dans ses peintures, choses qu'on ne trouve guère en plusieurs poètes de notre nation. Mais je vous avoue que, selon mon faible jugement, il pourrait avoir plus de douceur et de clarté.* Je voudrais un je ne sais quoi, qui est une facilité à laquelle il est très difficile d'atteindre." He then goes on to admit that the combination he desires is made difficult by the restrictions put upon the language and upon versification: that maybe he is being too hard on the poet; that he really is forced to praise him almost everywhere, and that what he wants is perhaps simply impossible in French.[44]

So in spite of all his boldness, his high thoughts and his vigorous yet feeling images, this poet left Fénelon unsatisfied, and the embarrassed but honest prelate was forced to fall back upon a "je ne sais quoi." I am not suggesting he could not have done better. In the conclusion of the letter he complained that the waters he was taking at the time disturbed his head and his hand, but not his heart. I believe it. My point is that he knew what poetry

---

* Cf. Swift's and Matthew Arnold's "sweetness and light."

was and that he did not find it here, though he could not tell precisely why.

The case was somewhat the same for the whole position of the supporters of Ancients. They had in the long run very few concrete arguments at their disposal. They had to agree that many of the objections raised by the Moderns were justified, and they were forced to rely, as had indeed the good critics of the Seventeenth Century, upon a *sense* of rightness, of exaltation, and of satisfaction. They knew what they wanted: simplicity, naturalness, control—and something besides. Paradoxically their insistence upon some of the qualities which they were able to name, such as the ones I have mentioned, could easily contribute to that intellectuality and dry mediocrity which they were trying to fight. They had a wealth of examples to fortify their judgments, but what if the examples were assailed? That of course is precisely what was happening.

But Fénelon, as we have seen, was not much bothered by the attack. He liked the Ancients. Whether he liked them because of their virtues or the virtues because of them made little difference. In any case, he did not see the causes of beauty as finally external. Climate could produce certain peculiarities, and a form of society facilitate various kinds of superiority,[45] but nowhere does Fénelon suggest that the Ancients are inevitably superior to the French.

Of course it is very hard not to think that for him they *were* superior. But that was a matter of personal opinion. In one of the letters to La Motte he said something which helps to provide a key to his critical position and also to his position in the history of letters. He wrote, "Je ne blâme le goût d'aucun homme, et je consens qu'on blâme le mien. Si la politesse et la discrétion, nécessaires pour le repos de la société, demandent que les hommes se tolèrent mutuellement dans la variété d'opinions où ils se trouvent par les choses les plus importantes à la vie humaine, à plus forte raison doivent-ils se tolérer sans peine dans la variété d'opinions sur ce qui importe très peu à la sûreté du genre humain."[46]

But just as Fénelon's spirit of tolerance had its limits when it came to le P. Quesnel and the Jansenists, (whose progress he feared even in his death-bed letter[47]) so his lack of dogmatism did not paralyze his sense of the real demands of literature nor lead him to say, as it might have, that any poetry was good so long as you liked it.

However his first importance to this study lies in this fact: that his love of the simple and the natural (where literature was concerned), his disapproval of the restrictions placed on French poetry, his wish to see the language enriched, and his desire for the attractiveness of an indefinable quality which produces excellent poetry do not seem in any way to indicate the beginning of a breakdown of Classic standards. Rather they follow along lines which we have seen were well established. If they represent "la relativité du goût," then the whole century was infected with it. It would not be far from the truth to say that the nature of real Classicism was such that, because it was living, it contained within itself this relativity, which constituted the germ of its transformation and of its decay.

VI: The Complex of Classicism

I T IS now time to state the generalizations toward which which the preceding chapters of this study have been leading us.

The critics and artists of the French Seventeenth Century knew that literature is not made according to specifications, that artists are human beings and that human beings are complex to the point of being enigmatic. They were therefore as much empiricists as they were dogmatists, and from Balzac on they attempted to maintain as far as they could an urbane liberality even as they applied their critical standards. Some of course were able to do this more than others, but generally speaking, as they argued for simplicity and for naturalness and ease, they were combatting a dogmatic Scholasticism and a dry professionalism as much as they were reacting against Renaissance mannerism. For they appreciated the inexplicable in art and the *élan* of the artist. They feared the effect of certain restrictions as much as they agreed on certain principles. They knew the force of hidden beauty and secret charm; they knew the mystery of the sublime. They knew also the reality of instinctive emotional judgments.

There was even considerable doubt as to the possibility of any kind of agreement on standards because of the complex nature of the aesthetic reaction and the part played by the heart therein. Some, because they had no positions as professional men of letters, could afford to recognize this fact more easily than others. But everyone understood the problem.

The independence of art was at stake, and naturally no one felt this more keenly than the artists themselves. Each of the four great writers of the century fought in his own way for this independence. They all reflect that concern in their works as well as in their critical statements. None of them reflects any assumption of finality, aesthetically, philosophically or ethically speaking, unless it is in the pleasure given by their works. All of them re-

2 3 5

main vitally and basically inconclusive not to say contradictory.

They were of course sensitive men, these critics and artists, and they were all afraid that if a formal, intellectualized and, as it were, materialized expression of standards were rigidly applied to special cases (and every work of art is a special case) literature might be destroyed. So no one wished to close the system.

Thus ease, grace, "le bon air," *urbanité, honnêteté*, and the instinctive sense of rightness were set against those forces which work too ardently for the establishment of obvious order and convention, whether they were represented by the *pédant* or by the *précieux*. The professional scholar and the *bel esprit* are favorite targets for the real critic and for the real artist.

And so all those terms which express the indefinable: *agrément inexplicable, grâces secrètes, finesse*, the "je ne sais quoi," and the like, take on a positive value. They are the symbols of intimate individuality which protect the admittedly superior intuition of the critic and the artist from the killing finality of applied reason. It is significant that the laconicism of Jesus' style and the simple power of the Bible were models of eloquence from Balzac to Fénelon. There was safety in that divinity, and the Seventeenth Century was striving in literature as elsewhere to maintain the link between human and divine. But just so, it knew that the artistic experience involves an interoperation of artist, work of art, and public which is so complicated as to be finally mysterious. It is impossible to understand Seventeenth Century French Classicism without understanding this.

But what I have said so far represents only one side of the complex. For no sane critic or historian is going to say that the distinguishing characteristic of the century is its antirationalism or its individualism. There is too much evidence of the contrary. Besides, the very men whom we have been studying believed in the existence of order in some sense or other. They accepted such general standards as unity, symmetry, clarity, simplicity, the mean, adherence to truth and to nature and so on. They were able to reconcile secrecy and mystery with clarity and sense, even if it was sometimes at the expense of strict logic.

So it would be as wrong to call the century antirational as it would be to call it predominantly authoritarian or doctrinaire. But it would also be wrong to say that the truth lies somewhere in between. The truth, I think, lies simply in the fact that the century was both, moreover that it was positively and characteristically both, and not merely as all centuries are both.

Now Henri Peyre warned against overstressing the rationalism of the century and preferred to speak of its "intellectualism,"[1] its desire to understand. This is certainly correct, and the material of this study bears witness to the fact. Yet the same material indicates also that there existed as well a significant willingness to relinquish understanding. I take leave here to repeat Ariste's remark in the conclusion of the Bouhours dialogue which I quoted earlier: "Je suis bien aise que vous preniez enfin le bon parti et que vous vous contentiez d'admirer ce que d'abord vous vouliez comprendre."

So another way of suggesting the nature of Classicism would be to say that this willingness in an ambience of intellectualism was one of its principal characteristics. This, it seems to me, is not hard to believe of a century as acutely religious as was the Seventeenth.

But of course one must go further. What, as far as literature is concerned, was the source of such a willingness? It can only be, as the opening paragraphs of this chapter suggested, that with all its formalism, with all its yearning for stability and order and agreement on things, the century remained as profoundly reluctant as any other century to deny vitality. But then, things being what they were, a highly paradoxical situation resulted, for vitality and form are normally antagonistic, vitality being in the order of nature and form being in the order of reason. And the insistence on one ought logically to imply the denial of the other. But such a denial one way or the other would lead to extreme naturalism or to extreme idealism, and this was precisely what the century wished to avoid. So it willed *not* to understand, and this included necessarily the acceptance of the illogical position in which it thus found itself.

So the paradox was accepted. But the acceptance was made easier for this intellectual century by one important condition, namely the belief in the validity of affective rather than intellectual awareness. This kind of awareness amounted to knowledge and involved the possession of a secret. Not everyone possessed the secret, but few seemed to doubt that the secret existed.

It was not a frivolous or a defeatist belief, for it was based on, or at least it had a justification in a broader and deeper belief, which was the certainty that there exists a reality transcending *but not excluding* those antagonistic orders of reason and nature, of form and vitality, of the intellect and of the senses. In terms of literature I suppose this reality can be called the order of poetry. Pascal called it the order of the heart. In this order the conflicting demands of form and of vitality are conciliated, and the inevitable struggle which occurs when one attempts to apply general standards to a highly individual process is resolved. But the opposition remains, and the resulting tensions remain. The conciliation of opposites does not mean their elimination. It is the condition of the *oxymoron.**

The Italian poet Marino made use of an analogous paradox to describe his impression of France in the year 1615. In a letter[2] written from Paris where he had newly arrived, he said, "Circa il paese, che debbo io dirvi? Vi dirò ch'egli è un mondo. Un mondo dico non tanto per la grandezza, per la gente e per la varietá, quanto per ch'egli è mirabile per le sue stravaganze. Le stravaganze fanno bello il mondo, percioché, essendo composto di contrari, questa contrarietá constituisce una lega che lo mantiene. Né piú né meno la Francia è tutta piena di ripugnanze e di sproporzioni, le quali formano una discordia concorde che la conserva. Costumi bizzarri, furie

* Cf. Leo Spitzer, *op.cit.*, pp. 122-23.

THE COMPLEX OF CLASSICISM

terribili, mutazioni continue, guerre civili perpetue, dis-
ordini senza regola, estremi senza mezzo, scompigli, gar-
bugli, disconcerti e confusioni; cose insomma, che la
doverebbono distruggere, per miracolo la tengono in
piedi. Un mondo veramente, anzi un mondaccio piú
stravagante del mondo istesso."*

Marino's letter exaggerates consciously to the point of
burlesque, and was itself the kind of manneristic play
which Baroque naturalism tried to overcome. Though by
1660 things had certainly quieted down, still, fundamentally the situation described remained much the same.
The Baroque reaction was carried out partly in the terms
of that very mannerism it was opposing.†

If the description of the Seventeenth Century French
Classic position which I have given is acceptable we are
faced with another paradox. The attitude which allowed,
for example, the substantive "je ne sais quoi," was itself,
though quite consciously adopted, instinctive rather than

---

* "Concerning the country, what should I tell you? I will tell
you that it is a world. I say a world not so much because of its
size, its population, or its variety, but because it is marvellous in
its excesses. Excesses embellish the world, since, being composed
of contrasts this conflict constitutes a bond which keeps it together. No more and no less France is full of oppositions and inconsistencies which form a *concordia discors* that preserves her.
Bizarre customs, terrible rages, continual upsets, perpetual civil
wars, disorder without rule, extremes without means, disturbance
and agitation, disharmony and confusion, things in sum, which
ought to destroy her, miraculously hold her up. A world truly,
rather a frightful world, more extravagant than the world itself."
I have not modernized the Italian text.

† Dr. Erwin Panofsky of the Institute for Advanced Study, in
a lecture on the Baroque in Italian painting and sculpture. In 1656,
Samuel Sorbière (the translator of More and Hobbes), in a discourse on the theme of Paris as "la plus belle et la plus charmante
de toutes les villes barbares," while admiring the order and symmetry of Dutch and Italian cities, admitted their monotony and
said: "Il n'en est pas de même à Paris. Le désordre, la confusion
et la témérité des mouvements changent à toute heure la face de
cette monstrueuse Ville. On n'y voit jamais deux fois la même
chose; la scène y change à tout moment; et de la bizarrerie de
ces Spectacles différents on tire le même plaisir que l'on reçoit ailleurs de la symétrie et de la juste proportion." In this same discourse he quoted the very passage from Marino which I have
given above, and made the same restrictions. The discourse may
be found in Marolles, *op.cit.*, pp. 338ff.

planned. By this I mean that the need for such a wholeness of outlook as the one which the century developed
was not met by the purely rational acceptance of the
paradox. Rather the century, or at least those writers
whom we have consulted, acted and thought in terms of
the paradox from a variety of more homely and immediate motives: from experience with the public, from a
desire to be not pedantic, from the artist's sense of self-
sufficiency, or from sheer common sense in the face of
practical problems. The attitude in short was, as I have
said elsewhere, empirical and pragmatic. In another century, as in our own perhaps, the need to live with such a
paradox might be widely recognized, but the ability to
act in fulfillment of that need might still be sadly lacking.*

What I have tried to describe in the foregoing paragraphs is, I expect, true classic balance. It was an equilibrium which found its means of maintenance in a much
deeper and far more vital set of forces than those attending the careful counterweighing of effects which charac-
terizes for instance the pseudo-classic "juste milieu." And
this was because it faced squarely and willingly that en-
gulfing and limitless depth of a total reality, and with it,
as a necessary and welcome part of it, the endlessly de-
structive vitality of the forces of nature. Without this, no
Racine, no Molière.

Now this sort of equilibrium, I need scarcely say, was
extremely difficult to maintain. No wonder then at the
fact of the Quarrel of the Ancients and Moderns. The
Quarrel represented the very human tendency to abandon
a total outlook in favor of a logicalistic, or perhaps we
should say a totalitarian solution. In this case it was for

* Cf. Mr. T. S. Eliot's remark in *Notes towards the Definition of
Culture*, N.Y., 1949, p. 18, ". . . culture is the one thing that we
cannot deliberately aim at. It is the product of a variety of more
or less harmonious activities, each pursued for its own sake: the
artist must concentrate upon his canvas, the poet upon his type-
writer, the civil servant upon the just settlement of particular problems as they present themselves upon his desk, each according to
the situation in which he finds himself."

a rationalistic monism much more dogmatic than anything to be found in the pages from which I have
quoted.* It is exemplified in Terrasson[3] and finally in
Batteux[4] on the one hand and in Du Bos[5] on the other,
the first two upholding the strict application of reasonable
standards, and the last denying the possibility of any
kind of criterion except the one of individual emotional
reactions. The Seventeenth Century was tempted by both
of these—Méré practically falls into complete impression-
ism—but its secret was that it never allowed such devel-
opments to assume anything like a definitive form.

Indeed, for all its talk about the rules, the century
seems completely lacking in the kind of self-consciousness with respect to its artistic mission which we have
come to expect from our artists. It did not feel the necessity of choosing. This sort of assurance which the artist
no longer feels can be seen in the fact that the questions
which inspired the Sixteenth Century and plagued the
Nineteenth seem to have taken up relatively little of
people's time. There was some question of the poet's
usefulness to the state, and undoubtedly the government
encouraged an official literature, while the writers played
the game. But the position of the artist in society and his
responsibilities to society as a whole, and society's to him,
seem to have been perfectly well understood. The notion
that great poetry is uplifting and can even be directly
instructive was certainly accepted, but there was no feeling that the poet himself should be a great moral leader
and visionary, or a deep thinker and representative of
the mass will. His task was to create objects to delight
or to awe. His critical statements had to do with the examination of his work and occasionally with the defense
of it against the *pédants*, or the *doctes*, or the *dévots* or
the *beaux esprits*. As I said in connection with Corneille,

* Cf. R. Naves, *Le Goût de Voltaire*, Paris, Garnier, n.d. pp. 1-
128, where the author presents an analysis of the Quarrel which is
a necessary and illuminating supplement to the classic works of
Rigault and Gillot, and which makes clear in great detail the dis-
integration of the Seventeenth Century Classic point of view. See
also Lombard, *op. cit.*

you will find no ringing challenges like the *Deffense et illustration* or the preface to *Cromwell*. There were no over-publicized "battles" like that of *Hernani*, and there were no such clusters of schools and movements, of insurgences and reactions as file across the Nineteenth Century, to the dismay of the conscientious historian and to the delight of the lazy one. There were *querelles*, like that of the *Cid*, or those attending the productions of Racine's plays, but they were never made to involve supposedly profound principles of history, politics, sociology and so on. To be sure, in the Quarrel of the Ancients and Moderns deep implications were apparent, but as it was going on it remained essentially a literary conflict. And even here, as in the other arguments, the artist, if he joined in at all, made no assumption of omniscience, took up no sacred trust, allowed himself no such absurdities as tempted the Hugo of the prefaces or the Balzac of the *Avant-propos*. He mostly appealed to the public and said, "If you liked my work forget about the rest." His consciousness of genius was tempered with craftsmanship, and his sense of independence was most often restrained.

The critic on his side may have felt the obligation to protect literature from an increasing corruption of taste, or, if he was a Modern, to improve upon the imperfections of the past in the light of a newly developed sense of order, decorum, and confidence. But from Balzac to Fénelon the real issue was the same: the relaxed if mysterious sense of rightness which is the secret of the real *amateur*, the lover, versus the brilliant, up-to-date irreverence of the progressive intellectual.

If the atmosphere was as I have supposed, it is understandable that much of what had for centuries characterized opposing types of literature was blended together at the same time as the whole national tradition was being joined to that of antiquity. Out of this came a specially French brand of Baroque. It had its own peculiar tensions and its own way of seeking to relax them. In this literature the formal aspect of the Graeco-Roman tradition figured more noticeably if not more vigorously than in the literature of England or of Spain, but it is very significant that this strong learned tendency did not kill the popular elements, whether they were carried over from the Middle Ages as in the comedy of Molière or whether they were borrowed from Italy or Spain as in Corneille and the burlesque. So the romantic, the *précieux*, the burlesque, the natural and simple, the heroic and the sublime all found their way into the main stream.* And without any of these, French Seventeenth Century Classicism is incomprehensible. Thus the intensity of the highly formal Racine, the directness of the exquisite artist La Fontaine, or the fundamental realism of the conventional Mme de La Fayette (who, by the way, devoured with impatience the successive volumes of the *Clélie*†), and the sense of the gratuitously funny in the moralistic Molière.

However this literature was at the same time animated by a desire for aesthetic purity, and individual works do not therefore possess the richness and the generality of expression that is found in other literatures. Density seemed more important than variety of tone, so that the blending of which I have spoken results in an effect upon separate categories rather than in a mixture of those categories, though it seemed for a time as though this mixture might occur. This is another way in which the literature of the period retained its vitality.** Its purity was accompanied by a pragmatism which kept it within the spirit of the times, so that the general public was never forgotten. This is perhaps a further contradiction, but it

* See P. Bénichou, *Morales du Grand Siècle*, Paris, Gallimard, 1948, for a detailed discussion of the century as an assault by a new alliance of naturalism with absolutism upon traditional notions of chivalric heroism and *courtoisie*.

† See *Lettres de Mme de La Fayette et de Gilles Ménage*, ed. H. Ashton, University Press of Liverpool, London, 1924, pp. 34ff. Her high opinion of Mlle de Scudéry, expressed in one of these letters, is mentioned by Baldensperger, *op. cit.*, p. 5.

** Cf. Thierry Maulnier (Jacques Talagrand), *Introduction à la poésie française*, Paris, Gallimard, 1939. Also his *Racine*, Paris, Gallimard, 1939, which is the most stimulating study of Racine to date. Also Jean Giraudoux, *Littérature*, Grasset, 1941 (printed in Canada), essay on Racine.

has something to do with the fact that Seventeenth Century Classicism is no mere movement and that it is so hard to fix its chronological and ideological limits other than arbitrarily. Certainly I find it unsatisfactory to limit it as is frequently done to the years 1660-1680. And I find it equally unsatisfactory to attempt to distinguish between Classic and Baroque, as is also frequently done.

Even so, in the history of French literature, it does seem possible to set off against this Seventeenth Century Classicism two other attitudes. First, there appears to be another sort of classicism, more characteristic of the Eighteenth Century, which is indeed reasonable and which is for the moment contented because it seems to have resolved the paradox. But it is an imitative and lifeless classicism because with its idealism it solved, or thought it solved, only the *intellectual* problem, and this solution was possible precisely only by denying the vital and so the *artistic* problem. Secondly there is Romanticism, which tried to reassert for the protection of the individual the dualism lost at the end of the Seventeenth Century. But it was unhappy because it never succeeded in controlling either the naturalism or the idealism which made up that dualism. For the interdependence of these two attitudes had been made possible only by their mutual faith in the order of the heart. Having lost that faith they each developed an independent strength which put them beyond the power of anyone to join them together again. Nature could not be a substitute for God.

Both Eighteenth Century Classicism and its true enemy Romanticism, then, were crippled by their "inability . . . to understand the paradox of the form-creating and form-destroying capacity of human spirituality."[6] Seventeenth Century Classicism was neither contented nor unhappy because it knew that it had to exist in tension, as a paradox. Ironically the interposition of later classicism and the Romanticism which opposed it was responsible for much modern misunderstanding of Seventeenth Century Classicism, for the Nineteenth Century saw all classicism as principally devoted to the rules and as very little else.

Later generations inherited that view, and naturally sought to justify it historically.

The basically and predominantly dualistic literature of the Seventeenth Century in its best and most real expression refused to fall into the errors of its posterity. Because of this it is a literature bred much more on irrationality, contradiction, and paradox than the conventional descriptions of it would lead one to suppose. Its position in history undoubtedly favored it. It hung precariously between the humanism of the Sixteenth Century and the naturalism of the Eighteenth. It was flanked on one side by an upsurge of religious sentiment, and on the other by a growing libertinism. But it found an anchor in the certainty of the indefinable and the rationally incomprehensible, and in so doing it enabled itself to express the infinite complexity of man's nature as few other literatures have done. It did this not only in an analytical sense, but also in an historical sense, for besides reflecting its essentially rationalistic Graeco-Roman inheritance it was also a literature of modern Christianity, and as such it produced Blaise Pascal, the core and glory of its spirit, whose remark, "Deux excès: exclure la raison, n'admettre que la raison," might well serve as its device.[7]

Bibliography

BABBITT, I. *The New Laokoon*, Houghton Mifflin, 1910.

BALDENSPERGER, F. "Pour une 'revaluation' littéraire du XVIIe siècle classique," *Revue d'histoire littéraire*, 1937.

BALZAC, G. DE. *Oeuvres*, 2 vols., ed. Conrart, 1665.

———. *Oeuvres*, ed. L. Moreau, Paris, Jacques Lecoffre et Cie, 1854.

———. *Lettres Choisies*, Paris, Augustin Courbé, 1647.

———. *Les Premières Lettres de Guez de Balzac, 1618-1627*, ed. H. Bibas et K.-T. Butler, Paris, E. Droz, 1933-1934.

BARBIER D'AUCOUR, J. *Sentiments de Cléante*, Paris, Le Monnier (1672), Fourth edition, 1776.

BATTEUX, C. *Les Beaux-arts réduits à un même principe*, Paris, Durand ed. 1747.

BÉNICHOU, P. *Morales du Grand Siècle*, Paris, Gallimard, 1948.

BÖHM, J. *Die Dramatischen Theorien Pierre Corneilles*, Berlin, Mayer and Müller, 1901.

BOILEAU, N. *Oeuvres*, ed. Gidel, Paris, Garnier, 1870.

———. *Oeuvres*, ed. Boudhors, Paris, Belles Lettres, 1934-1943.

———. *Les Héros de roman*, ed. T. F. Crane, Boston, Ginn and Co., The Athenaeum Press, 1902.

BOUCHARD, M. "Un précurseur de La Bruyère (Rapin)," *Revue d'histoire littéraire*, 1931.

BOUDHORS, CH.-H. "Divers propos du Chevalier de Méré en 1674-1675," *Revue d'histoire littéraire*, 1922-1925.

BOUHOURS, D. *Entretiens d'Ariste et d'Eugène*, Paris, Mabre-Cramoisy, 1671.

———. *Entretiens d'Ariste et d'Eugène*, ed. R. Radouant, Paris, Bossard, 1920.

———. *La Manière de bien penser dans les ouvrages d'esprit*, Paris, Florentin Delaulne, 1715.

BOULVE, L. *De l'hellénisme chez Fénelon*, Paris, ed. A. Fontemoing, 1897.

BOURGOIN, A. *Les Maîtres de la critique au XVIIe siècle*, Paris, 1889.

BRASILLACH, R. *Pierre Corneille*, Paris, Arthème Fayard, 1938.

BRAY, R. *La Formation de la doctrine classique*, Paris, Droz, 1931. (2nd ed.).

———. *La Tragédie cornélienne devant la critique classique*, Paris, Hachette, 1927.

———. "La Dissertation sur la 'Joconde,' est-elle de Boileau?," *Revue d'histoire littéraire*, 1931.

———. *Boileau, l'homme et l'oeuvre*, Paris, Boivin, 1942.

———. *La préciosité et les précieux, de Thibaut de Champagne à Jean Giraudoux*, Paris, Michel, 1948.

BREMOND, H. *Histoire littéraire du sentiment religieux en France*, Paris, Bloud et Gay, 1920-1933.

BRISSON, P. *Les Deux visages de Racine*, Paris, Gallimard, 1944.

BRUNETIÈRE, F. *L'Evolution des genres dans l'histoire de la littérature*, vol. I, *L'Evolution de la critique depuis la renaissance jusqu'à nos jours*, Paris, Hachette, 1898.

BUSSON, H. *La Religion des classiques*, Paris, Presses Universitaires de France, 1948.

CENTENO, A. Introduction to *The Intent of the Artist*, Princeton University Press, 1941.

CHAMAILLARD, E. *Le Chevalier de Méré*, Niort, 1921.

CHAPELAIN, J. *Lettres*, ed. Tamizey de Larroque, 2 vols., Imprimerie nationale, 1880-1883.

———. *Opuscules critiques*, ed. Hunter, Paris, E. Droz, 1936.

CHEREL, A. "L'Idée du 'naturel' et le sentiment de la nature chez Fénelon," *Revue d'histoire littéraire*, 1911.

CHICOTEAU, M. *Studies in the Ephectic Attitude*, no. 3, "Les attributs de l'éphectisme grec et leur survivance dans une cosmologie racinienne," Cardiff, Priory Press, 1943.

CHINARD, G. *En lisant Pascal*, Genève, E. Droz, 1948.

CLARAC, P. *La Fontaine; l'homme et l'oeuvre*, Paris, Boivin, 1947.

CLARK, A. F. B. *Jean Racine*, Harvard University Press, 1939.

COLLAS, G. *Jean Chapelain*, Paris, Perrin, 1911.

CORNEILLE, P. *Oeuvres*, ed. Marty-Laveaux, Paris, 1862.

CRÉTIN, R. *Les Images dans l'oeuvre de Corneille*, Paris, Champion, 1927.

——. *Lexique comparé des métaphores dans le théâtre de Corneille et de Racine*, Paris, Champion, 1927.

CROCE, B. *Estetica*, Bari, Laterza, 1912 (translated by Douglas Ainslee, Macmillan, London, 1922).

——. *Ariosto, Shakespear e Corneille*, Bari, Laterza, 1912.

DONCIEUX, G. *Un Jésuite homme de lettres au dix-septième siècle: le père Bouhours*, Paris, Hachette, 1886.

DORCHAIN, A. *Pierre Corneille*, Paris, Garnier, 1918.

DU BOS, J. B. *Réflexions critiques sur la poésie et sur la peinture*, Paris, Jean Mariette, 1719.

EGGER, E. *L'Hellénisme en France*, Paris, Didier, 1869.

ELIOT, T. S. *Notes towards the Definition of Culture*, New York, Harcourt Brace, 1949.

FÉNELON, F. *Oeuvres*, Paris, Lebel, 1824.

FIDAO-JUSTINIANI, J. *L'Esprit classique et la préciosité au XVIIe siècle*, Paris, Picard, 1914.

GAIFFE, F. *L'Envers du grand siècle*, Paris, Michel, 1924.

GASTÉ, A. *La Querelle du Cid*, Paris, Welter, 1898.

GIBERT, B. *Jugements des savants sur les auteurs qui ont traité de la Rhétorique*, 3 vols. 1712-1719.

GILLOT, H. *La Querelle des anciens et des modernes en France*, Paris, Champion, 1914.

GIRAUDOUX, J. *Les Cinq tentations de La Fontaine*, Paris, Grasset, 1938.

——. *Littérature*, Grasset, 1941 (printed in Canada).

GOHIN, F. *L'Art de La Fontaine dans ses fables*, Paris, Garnier, 1929.

——. *La Fontaine, études et recherches*, Paris, Garnier, 1937.

GOMBERVILLE, M. LE R. DE. *Polexandre*, Paris, Augustin Courbé, 1638.

GOURNAY, M. DE. *L'Ombre de la Damoiselle de Gournay*, Paris, 1626.

GUILLAUMIE, G. *J-L. Guez de Balzac et la poésie française*, Paris, Picard, 1927.

HERVIER, M. *Les Ecrivains français jugés par leurs contemporains*, Paris, Mellottée, n.d.

JACOUBET, H. "A propos de *Je ne sais quoi*," *Revue d'histoire littéraire*, 1928.

Journal of Aesthetic and Art Criticism, December 1946 (vol. V, no. 2) issue devoted to the question of the Baroque. See especially article by R. Wellek, "The Concept of the Baroque in Literary Scholarship," and bibliography.

LA BRUYÈRE, J. DE. *Oeuvres*, ed. Servois, Paris, Hachette, 1878.

LA FAYETTE, MME DE, ET GILLES MÉNAGE. *Lettres*, ed. H. Ashton, University Press of Liverpool, London, 1924.

LA FONTAINE, J. DE. *Oeuvres*, ed. Régnier, Paris, 1883.

————. *Contes et Nouvelles*, ed. Clarac, Paris, Belles Lettres, 1934.

————. *Oeuvres diverses*, ed. Clarac, Paris, Bibliothèque de la Pléiade, 1942.

LANCASTER, H. C. *French Dramatic Literature in the Seventeenth Century*, The Johns Hopkins Press, Baltimore, 1929-1942.

LANSON, G. *Corneille*, Paris, Hachette, 1898.

————. *Histoire de la littérature française*, Paris, Hachette, 1912.

LA ROCHEFOUCAULD, F. DE. *Oeuvres*, ed. M. D. L. Gilbert, Paris, Hachette, 1868.

LEGOUIS, P. "Corneille and Dryden as dramatic critics," *Seventeenth Century Studies*, presented to Sir Herbert Grierson, Oxford, 1938.

LEMAÎTRE, J. *Corneille et la poétique d'Aristote*, Paris, 1888.

————. *Fénelon*, Paris, Fayard, 1910.

————. *Jean Racine*, Paris, Calmann-Lévy, 1908.

LIVET, C-L. *Précieux et précieuses*, Paris, ed. H. Welter, 1895.

LOMBARD, A. *La Querelle des anciens et des modernes, l'Abbé du Bos*, Neuchâtel, 1908.

MAGENDIE, M. *La politesse mondaine et la théorie de l'honnêteté en France de 1600-1660*, Alcan, 1925.

MAIRET, J. DE. *Silvanire*, ed. R. Otto, Bamberg, Buchner, 1890.

MALHERBE, F. *Oeuvres Complètes*, ed. M. L. Lalanne, Paris, Hachette, 1862-1869.

MARINO, G. *Epistolario*, ed. Borzelli and Nicolini, Bari, Laterza, 1911.

MAULNIER, T. (J. TALAGRAND). *Introduction à la poésie française*, Paris, Gallimard, 1939.

———. *Racine*, Paris, Gallimard, 1939.

MÉLÉSE, P. *Le théâtre et le public à Paris sous Louis XIV, 1659-1715*, Paris, E. Droz, 1934.

MENÉNDEZ Y PELAYO, M. *Historia de las Ideas Estéticas en España*, Madrid, 1940.

MÉRÉ, A. GOMBAUD, CHEVALIER DE. *Oeuvres*, ed. CH.-H. Boudhors, "Les textes français," Paris, 3 vols., 1930.

MOLIÈRE, J-B. P. *Oeuvres*, ed. Despois et Mesnard, Paris, Hachette, 1873-1900.

MONGRÉDIEN, G. *La vie littéraire au xvii⁰ Siècle*, Paris, Tallandiér, 1947.

MONK, S. H. "Grace beyond the Reach of Art," *Journal of the History of Ideas*, April, 1944.

MORNET, D. *Histoire de la littérature française classique (1660-1700)*, Paris, Colin, 1940.

NAVES, R. *Le Goût de Voltaire*, Paris, Garnier, n.d.

NIEBUHR, R. *The Nature and Destiny of Man*, New York, Scribner, 2 vols., 1941.

OGIER, F. *Apologie pour Monsieur de Balzac*, Paris, Pierre Rocolet, 1628.

PASCAL, B. *Oeuvres*, ed. Brunschvicg, Paris, Hachette, 1921.

———. *Pensées, Edition paléographique*, Z. Tourneur, Paris, Vrin, printed 1942.

———. *Pensées*, ed. Z. Tourneur, Cluny, Paris, printed 1938.

BIBLIOGRAPHY

PATTERSON, W. F. *Three Centuries of French Poetic Theory*, (*1328-1630*), University of Michigan Press, Ann Arbor, 2 vols., 1935.

PELLISSON ET OLIVET. *Histoire de l'Académie*, ed. Livet, Paris, Didier, 1858.

PEYRE, H. *Le Classicisme français*, Editions de la Maison française, New York, 1942, a revision of *Qu'est-ce-que le classicisme?*, Paris, 1933.

PINTARD, R. *Le Libertinage érudit dans la première moitié du XVIIe siècle*, Paris, Boivin, 1943.

PRAZ, M. *Studies in Seventeenth Century Imagery*, London, The Warburg Institute, 1939.

RACINE, J. *Oeuvres*, ed. P. Mesnard, Paris, Hachette, 1885-1890.

RAPIN, R. *Oeuvres*, ed. P. Gosse, The Hague, 1725.

REESE, H. R. *La Mesnardière's 'Poétique' (1639): Sources and Dramatic Theories*, The Johns Hopkins Press, Baltimore, 1937.

REYNOLD, G. DE. *Le XVIIe siècle, le classique et le baroque*, Editions de l'Arbre, Montreal, 1944.

RIGAL, E. *Molière*, Paris, Hachette, 1908.

RIGAULT, H. *Histoire de la querelle des anciens et des modernes*, Paris, Hachette, 1859.

ROCHE, L. *La Vie de Jean de La Fontaine*, Paris, Plon, 1913.

SAINTSBURY, G. *A History of Criticism and Literary Taste in Europe from the Earliest Texts to the Present Day* (vol. 2), Edinburgh and London, W. Blackwood and Sons, 1900-1904.

SAULNIER, V. L. *La Littérature française du siècle classique*, Paris, Presses Universitaires de France, 1943.

SCHINZ, A. "Fénelon, critique littéraire, précurseur," *Revue de Cours et conférences*, 1925-1926, vol. I.

SCUDÉRY, M. DE. *De la poésie française*, ed. G. Michaut, Paris, Sansot, 1907.

SEARLES, C. "L'Académie française et le *Cid*," *Revue d'histoire littéraire*, 1914.

SÉVIGNÉ, M. DE. *Lettres*, ed. Monmerqué, Paris, Hachette, 1862-1868.

SPINGARN, J. *Critical Essays of the Seventeenth Century*, 3 vols., Oxford, 1908.

————. *Literary Criticism in the Renaissance*, New York, 1924.

SPITZER, L. *Linguistics and Literary History*, Princeton University Press, 1948.

TALLEMANT DES RÉAUX, G. *Historiettes*, ed. Monmerqué et Paris, Paris, Techener, 1854-1860.

TERRASSON, J. *Dissertation critique sur l'Iliade*, Paris, Fournier, 1715.

————. *La Philosophie applicable à tous les objets de l'esprit et de la raison*, Paris, Prault, 1754.

TILLEY, A. *Molière*, Cambridge University Press, 1936.

TOURNEUR, Z. *"Beauté poétique." Histoire d'une pensée de Blaise Pascal et ses annexes*, Paris, Vrin, 1933.

————. *Une vie avec Blaise Pascal*, Paris, Vrin, 1943.

TURNELL, M. *The Classical Moment*, New Directions, 1948.

VEDEL, V. *Deux classiques français* (Corneille, Molière), Paris, Champion, 1935.

VIAL, F., et DENISE, L. *Idées et doctrines littéraires*, 3 vols., Paris, Delagrave, 1937.

VIGUIÉ, P. *Le Chevalier de Méré*, Paris, Sansot (Liberre), 1922.

VOSSLER, K. *Jean Racine*, Munich, Max Hueber, 1926.

————. *La Fontaine und sein Fabelwerk*, Heidelberg, Carl Winter, 1919.

WILMOTTE, M. *Études critiques sur la tradition littéraire en France*, Paris, Champion, 1909.

WRIGHT, C. H. C. *French Classicism*, Harvard University Press, 1920.

Notes

II. THE NEW LIBERALISM

BALZAC

1. *Lettres choisies du Sieur de Balzac*, 2 vols. Paris, Courbé, 1647, I, 394ff.
2. *Ibid.*, pp. 399-400.
3. *Ibid.*, p. 406.
4. *Oeuvres*, ed. Moreau, 2 vols. Paris, 1854, I, 234-35.
5. *Ibid.*, p. 235.
6. *Ibid.*, p. 262.
7. *Lettres choisies, ed. cit.* I, 379.
8. *Ibid.*, II, 86-87.
9. *Oe. ed cit.* I, 277-78.
10. *Ibid.*, pp. 278-280.
11. *Ibid.*, p. 283.
12. *Lettres choisies*, II, 587.
13. *Ibid.*, I, 356.
14. *Oe.*, I, 295.
15. *Ibid.*
16. *Ibid.*, p. 299.
17. *Ibid.*, p. 300.
18. *Ibid.*
19. *Ibid.*, p. 303.
20. *Ibid.*, p. 304.
21. *Ibid.*, p. 305.
22. *Ibid.*, II, 190.
23. *Lettres choisies*, I, 345-46.
24. *Oe.*, II, 11-13.
25. *Ibid.*
26. *Ibid.*, p. 53.
27. *Ibid.*, pp. 54-56.
28. *Ibid.*, p. 56.
29. *Ibid.*, p. 35.
30. *Ibid.*, pp. 35-37.
31. *Lettres choisies*, I, 580-81.
32. *Oe.*, II, 57.
33. *Ibid.*, I, 330.
34. *Premières lettres*, 1618-1627, ed. H. Bibas and K. T. Butler, S.T.F.M., Paris, Droz, 2 vols. I, 155, n. 2.
35. *Oe.*, II, 457.
36. *Ibid.*, pp. 457-58.
37. *Ibid.*, p. 458.
38. *Premières lettres, ed. cit.* I, 147-48.
39. *Oe.*, II, p. 463.
40. *Ibid.*, p. 366.
41. *Ibid.*, p. 328.
42. *Lettres choisies*, II, 606.
43. *Oe.*, II, 496.
44. *Ibid.*, p. 469.
45. *Lettres choisies*, I, 511.
46. *Correspondance*, ed. Tannery, Paris, 1899, II, 349.
47. *Historiettes*, ed. P. Paris, IV, 96-97.
48. See above, p. 9, note, and Balzac, *Oeuvres*, ed. 1665, II, 169.
49. *Oe.*, II, 317.
50. *Ibid.*, p. 72.
51. *Ibid.*, p. 103.
52. *Ibid.*, p. 47.
53. *Ibid.*, p. 51.
54. *Ibid.*, p. 26.
55. *Ibid.*, p. 23.
56. *Ibid.*, pp. 130-31.
57. *Ibid.*, p. 191.
58. *Ibid.*, p. 74.
59. *Ibid.*, p. 96.
60. *Ibid.*, pp. 99-100.
61. *Ibid.*, p. 386.
62. *Ibid.*, p. 437.
63. *Ibid.*, p. 43.

CHAPELAIN

1. *Lettres*, ed. Tamizey de Larroque, 2 vols., Paris 1880-1883, letter to Huet 1662 II, 217, no. 124.
2. To Balzac 1638 *ibid.*, I, 238, no. 163.
3. *Lettres, ed. cit.*, I, 1639, 430-31, no. 287.
4. *Ibid.*, 1639, no. 349.
5. *Op. cit.*

6. *Lettres*, 1639, I, 511-12, no. 344.
7. *Ibid.*, 1640, pp. 586-87, no. 382.
8. *Ibid.*, 1640, pp. 697-98, no. 441.
9. *Ibid.*, p. 698 n.
10. To Huet 1662 *ibid.*, II, 215.
11. *Ibid.*, I, 156, no. 109.
12. *Ibid.*, p. 164, no. 115.
13. *Ibid.*, p. 159, no. 111.
14. *Opuscules critiques*, ed. A. C. Hunter, Paris, Droz, 1936 (S.T.F.M.), p. 169.
15. *Ibid.*, p. 195.
16. *Lettres*, I, 194, no. 137.
17. *Ibid.*, 1639, I, 420-21, no. 281.
18. *Ibid.*, 1639, p. 493, no. 333.
19. *Ibid.*, 1639, p. 367, no. 250.
20. *Opuscules critiques, ed. cit.*, p. 197.
21. *Lettres*, I, 18, no. 8.
22. *Ibid.*, p. 636, no. 406.
23. *Ibid.*, II, 210 n.
24. *Ibid.*, I, 631-33, no. 404.
25. *Ibid.*
26. *Ibid.*, p. 636, no. 406.
27. Bray, *Formation*, p. 107.
28. *Opuscules critiques*, p. 259.
29. *Lettres*, II, 823 n.
30. *Ibid.*, 1632, I, 18, no. 8.
31. *Ibid.*, II, 317-18, no. 180.
32. *Ibid.*, pp. 835-36, no. 586.
33. *Ibid.*, pp. 275-76, no. 155.
34. *Ibid.*, I, 207, no. 146.
35. *Ibid.*, II, 80, no. 43.
36. *Ibid.*, p. 521, no. 312.

CORNEILLE

1. Corneille, P., *Oeuvres*, ed. Marty-Laveaux, VI, 363.
2. *Oe.*, III, 277.
3. *Oe.*, V, 146-47.
4. *Oe.*, I, 94.
5. *Oe.*, I, 138.

6. *Oe.*, I, 20.
7. *Oe.*, VI, 571.
8. *Oe.*, III, 474.
9. *Oe.*, II, 430.
10. *Oe.*, V, 501.
11. *Oe.*, V, 154.
12. *Oe.*, I, 261.
13. *Oe.*, I, 263.
14. *Oe.*, I, 264.
15. *Oe.*, VIII, 20.
16. *Oe.*, IV, 24.
17. *Oe.*, IV, 130.
18. *Oe.*, IV, 279.
19. *Oe.*, III, 381.
20. *Oe.*, V, 298.
21. *Oe.*, V, 308.
22. *Oe.*, X, 490-91.
23. *Oe.*, X, 491-92.
24. *Oe.*, III, 382.
25. *Oe.*, V, 311.
26. *Oe.*, VIII, 5.
27. *Oe.*, IV, 11.
28. *Oe.*, V, 501-502.
29. *Oe.*, V, 504.
30. *Oe.*, VII, 104.
31. *Oe.*, VIII, 20.
32. *Oe.*, IX, 6.
33. *Oe.*, III, 471.
34. *Lettre à Lord * * * Vigny, Théâtre*, ed. Baldensperger, Paris, Conard, 1926, I, xii-xiv.
35. *Oe.*, I, 18.
36. *Oe.*, I, 70.
37. *Oe.*, III, 77.
38. *Oe.*, III, 258.
39. *Oe.*, III, 369.
40. *Oe.*, X, 138.
41. *Oe.*, VI, 122.
42. *Oe.*, II, 332-33.
43. *Oe.*, I, 32.
44. *Oe.*, III, 503.
45. *Oe.*, X, 407-409.
46. *Oe.*, IV, 420-21.
47. *Oe.*, II, 116.
48. *Oe.*, V, 147-48.
49. *Oe.*, I, 122.
50. *Oe.*, I, 262-63.
51. *Oe.*, VII, 5.
52. *Oe.*, II, 119-20.

53. *Oe.*, ɪ, 3.
54. *Oe.*, ɪ, 50-51.
55. *Oe.*, ɪ, 66.
56. *Oe.*, ɪ, 63.
57. *Oe.*, vɪɪɪ, 8.
58. *Oe.*, vɪɪɪ, 9.

59. *Oe.*, vɪɪɪ, 376.
60. *Oe.*, vɪɪɪ, 336.
61. *Oe.*, ɪx, 5.
62. *Oe.*, ɪx, 335.
63. *Oe.*, ɪx, 233.

III. THE AMATEUR SPIRIT

MÉRÉ

1. Balzac, *Oeuvres* ed. Moreau, 490 n.
2. *RHL* 1922, p. 95.
3. *Ibid.*, 1922, p. 94.
4. Editions Fernand Roches, Paris.
5. The editions I use is of 1689, with the *achevé* of 1681.
6. *RHL* 1922, p. 216.
7. *Ibid.*, 1923, p. 526.
8. *Oe.*, ɪɪ, 40.
9. *Oe.*, ɪ, 96.
10. *Oe.*, ɪɪ, 109.
11. For instance, *RHL* 1925, p. 452.
12. *Ibid.*, 1922, p. 92.
13. *Lettres, ed. cit.*, ɪ, 110ff.
14. *Oe.*, ɪ, 30.
15. *De l'Esprit, Oe.*, ɪɪ, 79.
16. *Ibid.*
17. *Ibid.*, p. 70.
18. *Lettres*, ɪɪ, 704.
19. *Oe.*, ɪɪ, 49.
20. Letter cxLɪx, A Monsieur * * * *Lettres*, ɪɪ, 544-45; cf. also Letter cxɪ, A Monsieur de Luns, *ibid.*, p. 371.
21. *Oe.*, ɪɪ, 78.
22. *Ibid.*
23. *Lettres*, ɪ, 21-22.
24. *Ibid.*, p. 23.
25. *Ibid.*, pp. 23-24.
26. *Ibid.*, p. 13.
27. Letter cxLɪv, A Madame la Duchesse de Lesdiguières. *Lettres*, ɪɪ, 528-30.
28. *Quatrième Conversation, Oe.*, ɪ, 60.

29. *Cinquième Conversation, Oe.*, ɪ, 72.
30. Letter cxxx, A Monsieur * * * *Lettres*, ɪɪ, 489-90.
31. *Discours des Agrémens, Oe.*, ɪɪ, 17; cf. also Letter cLxxvɪɪɪ, A Madame la Maréchale de * * * *Lettres*, ɪɪ, 620ff.
32. Letter cLxxvɪɪɪ *op. cit.*
33. *Oe.*, ɪɪ, 39.
34. *Oe.*, ɪɪ, 19ff.
35. See below, p. 107.
36. *Op. cit.*, p. 22.
37. *RHL* 1922, p. 217.
38. Letter x, *Lettres*, ɪ, 73ff.
39. *Ibid.*, p. 75.
40. *Ibid.*, pp. 77-78.
41. Cf. also Letter cxxɪ, *Lettres*, ɪɪ, 457ff.
42. Letter xɪv, A Monsieur de * * *, *ibid.*, ɪ, 94-95.
43. *Première Conversation, Oe.*, ɪ, 9-10.
44. Letter Lvɪ, A Balzac, *Lettres*, ɪ, 267ff.
45. Letter Lxvɪɪɪ, *ibid.*, ɪ, 305.
46. *Oe.*, ɪɪ, 12.
47. Cf. however above, p. 86.
48. Letter cLvɪɪɪ, *Lettres*, ɪɪ, 568.
49. *Discours des Agrémens, Oe.*, ɪɪ, 15 and 37.
50. Letter cxLvɪɪ, A Monsieur * * *, *Lettres*, ɪɪ, 538-39.
51. *Oe.*, ɪɪ, p. 128.
52. *Oe.*, ɪ, 55.
53. *Discours de l'Esprit, Oe.*, ɪɪ, 91-92.
54. *Ibid.*, p. 92.
55. *Discours des Agrémens, Oe.*, ɪɪ, 35.

56. *Discours de l'Esprit, Oe.*, II, 93.
57. *Ibid.*
58. *Discours des Agrémens, ibid.*, p. 48.
59. Letter xxII, *Lettres*, I, 138-39.
60. Letter IV, I, 33.
61. Letter xxII, *Lettres*, I, 133.
62. *Ibid.*, p. 134.
63. Cf. *Propos.*
64. *Lettres, op. cit.*, pp. 140-41.
65. Letter x, *Lettres*, I, 73-74.
66. Letter CLXXXI, *Lettres*, II, 634-35.
67. *Oe.*, II, 28.

LA ROCHEFOUCAULD

1. G. E. F., M. D. L. Gilbert, Paris, Hachette 1868.
2. *Oe.*, I, 343.
3. No. 435.
4. No. 297.
5. *Oe.*, I, 310.
6. No. 488.
7. No. 135.
8. No. 41.
9. No. 265.
10. No. 569.
11. *Oe.*, I, 325ff.
12. *Ibid.*, p. 328.
13. *Réflexion* x, *op. cit.*, pp. 304-305.
14. *Réflexion* xvi, *op. cit.*, p. 326.
15. No. 106.
16. *Réflexion* I, *op. cit.*, p. 279.
17. No. 52.
18. No. 613.
19. No. 102.
20. No. 625.
21. No. 626.
22. *Oe.*, I, 286-87.
23. *Réflexion* xiii, *op. cit.*, p. 314.
24. *Oe.*, I, p. 141.
25. *Réflexion* x, *op. cit.*, p. 306.
26. *Op. cit.*, p. 313.
27. *Ibid.*, p. 330.
28. No. 282.

29. *Réflexion* I, *op. cit.*, p. 281.
30. *Ibid.*
31. *Oe.*, I, 330-31.
32. *Op. cit.*, 305-306.
33. *Ibid.*
34. *Op. cit.*, 306-7.
35. No. 67.
36. La Rochefoucauld, *op. cit.*, I, 259, note 2.

PASCAL

1. *Oeuvres*, G. E. F., ed. Brunschvicg, Paris, Hachette, 1921, xii, p. 30, no. 18.
2. *Oe.*, xiii, 50, no. 134.
3. *Ibid.*, p. 75, no. 151.
4. *Oe.*, xii, 48, no. 39.
5. *Ibid.*, p. 47, no. 38.
6. *Une vie avec Blaise Pascal*, Paris, Vrin, 1943.
7. *Oe.*, xiii, 10, no. 82.
8. *Ibid.*, p. 231, no. 309.
9. *Ibid.*, p. 34, no. 105.
10. *Oe.*, xii, 42, no. 33.
11. *Oe.*, xiii, 248, no. 329.
12. *Ibid.*, p. 292, no. 383.
13. *Ibid.*, p. 199, no. 274.
14. *Ibid.*, pp. 34-35, no. 106.
15. *Ibid.*, pp. 290-91, no. 381.
16. *Oe.*, xii, 70, no. 71.
17. *Ibid.*, p. 69, no. 69.
18. *Oe.*, xiii, 288-89, no. 378.
19. *Oe.*, xii, 69-70, no. 70.
20. *Oe.*, xiii, 41, no. 114.
21. *Ibid.*, p. 11, no. 82.
22. *Oe.*, xii, 41, no. 32.
23. *Ibid.*
24. *Ibid.*, pp. 42-43, no. 33.
25. *Oe.*, xiii, 309, no. 408.
26. *Oe.*, xii, 41, no. 32.
27. *Ibid.*, pp. 26-27, no. 14; *ibid.*, p. 66, no. 64.
28. *Oe.*, xiii, 51, no. 135.
29. *Oe.*, xii, 37-38, no. 28.
30. *Oe.*, xiv, 235, no. 797.
31. *Oe.*, xii, 38, no. 29.
32. *Ibid.*, p. 37, no. 27.
33. *Ibid.*, p. 50, no. 41.
34. *Ibid.*, p. 34, no. 23.
35. *Ibid.*, p. 33, no. 22.

36. *Ibid.*, p. 54, no. 49.
37. *Ibid.*, pp. 53-54, no. 48.
38. *Ibid.*, p. 55, no. 50.
39. *Ibid.*, p. 36, no. 25.
40. *Oe.*, xiv, 121-22, no. 684.
41. *Oe.*, xiii, 38, no. 111.
42. *Ibid.*, p. 258, no. 339 bis.
43. *Oe.*, xii, 50, no. 41.
44. *Ibid.*, pp. 39-40, no. 30.
45. *Oe.*, xiii, 123, no. 196.
46. *Ibid.*, p. 117, no. 194 bis (12); *ibid.*, p. 118, no. 194 bis (16); *ibid.*, p. 116 no. 194 bis (8).
47. *Ibid.*, p. 251, no. 332.
48. *Ibid.*, pp. 251-52, no. 332.
49. *Ibid.*, pp. 371-72, no. 460.
50. *Oe.*, xiv, 231, no. 793.
51. *Oe.*, xii, 15, no. 2.
52. *Oe.*, xiii, 205-206, no. 283.
53. *Oe.*, xii, 17-18, no. 4.
54. *Oe.*, xiv, 233, no. 793.
55. *Ibid.*, p. 230, no. 793.
56. *Oe.*, ix, 241-42.
57. *Ibid.*, p. 246.
58. *Ibid.*, p. 247.
59. *Ibid.*, p. 253.
60. *Ibid.*, pp. 269-70.
61. *Ibid.*, p. 215ff.
62. *Ibid.*, pp. 216-17.
63. *Oe.*, xii, 61-62, no. 61.
64. *Oe.*, ix, 271.
65. *Ibid.*, p. 275.
66. *Ibid.*, p. 276.
67. *Oe.*, xii, 11-12, no. 1.
68. *Ibid.*, pp. 12-13, no. 1.
69. See above, note 52.
70. *Oe.*, xii, 17, no. 3.
71. See above, note 52.
72. *Oe.*, xiii, 284, no. 373.
73. See above, note 28.
74. *Oe.*, xiii, 302, no. 395.
75. *Ibid.*, p. 173, no. 233.
76. *Ibid.*, p. 39, no. 112.

IV. THE SECRET OF THE PRACTITIONERS

LA FONTAINE

1. La Fontaine, J. de, *Oeuvres*, ed. Régnier, ix, 474.
2. *Ibid.*, pp. 227-28.
3. *Ibid.*, p. 232.
4. *Ibid.*, Letter, v, pp. 258ff.
5. *Oe.*, vii, 7.
6. *Oe.*, vii, 164ff.
7. *Oe.*, viii, 262ff.
8. *Oe.*, viii, 268.
9. *Oe.*, i, 14-15.
10. *Oe.*, i, 363.
11. *Oe.*, iii, 233.
12. *Oe.*, i, 281-82.
13. *Oe.*, i, 19.
14. *Oe.*, i, 398.
15. *Oe.*, iv, 4 and 146.
16. *Oe.*, i, 362.
17. *Oe.*, ii, 77.
18. *Oe.*, iii, 84.
19. *Oe.*, iv, 150.
20. *Oe.*, ii, 459.
21. *Oe.*, ix, 186.
22. *Oe.*, viii, 233.
23. *Oe.*, i, 414-15.
24. *Oe.*, vii, 9.
25. *Oe.*, viii, 22.
26. *Oe.*, viii, 239.
27. *Oe.*, viii, 20-21.
28. *Oe.*, viii, 244.
29. *Oe.*, iv, 147.
30. *Oe.*, viii, 181ff.
31. Nouvelle édition, Amsterdam, 1727, p. 149.
32. La Fontaine, *Oeuvres ed. cit.*, vi, 233.
33. *Correspondance complète de Madame, Duchesse d'Orléans, née Princesse Palatine*, trans. and ed. Brunet, Paris, Champion, 1891, letter of 14 Apr. 1719.
34. *Oe.*, i, 19.
35. *Oe.*, ii, 154.
36. *Oe.*, ii, 367.
37. *Oe.*, iv, 23.
38. Boileau, *Oeuvres*, ed. Gidel, iii, 157.
39. *Oe.*, ix, 360.
40. Mornet, *Histoire de la Lit-*

térature Classique, Paris, 1940, p. 275.
41. *Oe.*, ii, 354.
42. *Op. cit.*, pp. 156-58.

MOLIÈRE

1. *La Critique de L'Ecole des femmes*, sc. v, line 57ff.
2. *Ibid.*, sc. vi, line 333ff.
3. *Les Femmes savantes*, iv, iii, 1331ff.
4. *La Critique*, sc. vi, line 244ff.
5. Molière, *Oeuvres*, ed. Despois and Mesnard, G. E. F., Paris, Hachette, 1873-1900, iii, 158.
6. *Ibid.*, pp. 28-29.
7. *Oe.*, v, 294.
8. *Oe.*, ii, 47.
9. *Ibid.*, 50.
10. *La Critique*, sc. vi, line 270ff.
11. *Oe.*, ii, 50.
12. *Oe.*, iii, 29.
13. *La Critique*, sc. vi, line 360ff.
14. *Oe.*, ii, 50-51.
15. Rigal, E., *Molière*, Paris, 1908, i, 237.
16. *Le Tartuffe*, i, v, 331ff.
17. *Le Misanthrope*, i, i, 145ff.
18. *Ibid.*, line 173ff.
19. *Ibid.* As quoted by Philinte, iv, ii.
20. *La Critique*, sc. vi, line 415ff.
21. *Ibid.*, line 485ff.
22. *Le Misanthrope*, iv, i, 1163ff.

RACINE

1. Racine, *Oeuvres*, ed. Paul Mesnard, G. E. F., Paris, Hachette 1885-1890, i, 529.
2. *Ibid.*, ii, 37-38.
3. *Ibid.*, pp. 42-43.
4. *Ibid.*, p. 147.
5. *Ibid.*, pp. 148-49.
6. *Ibid.*, p. 254.
7. *Ibid.*, pp. 254-57.
8. *Ibid.*, p. 258.
9. *Ibid.*, p. 378.
10. *Ibid.*, iii, 147.
11. Rapin, *Réflexions sur l'éloquence, Oeuvres*, the Hague, 1725, ii, 58.
12. ii, ii, line 117.
13. *Phèdre*, iv, vi, 1241ff.
14. *Ibid.*, v, vii, 1641ff.
15. *Ibid.*, v, vi, 1498ff.
16. *Ibid.*, v, vii, 1644ff.
17. *Oe.*, iii, 299.
18. *Ibid.*

V. THE SECRET OF THE CRITICS

LE P. RAPIN

1. *History of Literary Criticism*, Edinburgh, 1900-1904, ii, 310-14.
2. *Oeuvres*, the Hague, ed. Pierre Gosse, 1725, ii, 171.
3. *Ibid.*, p. 172.
4. *Ibid.*, pp. 178-79.
5. *Ibid.*, p. 186.
6. *Ibid.*, pp. 192-93.
7. *Oe.*, i, 42.
8. *Oe.*, ii, 69-70.
9. *Ibid.*, *Préface*, last page, unnumbered.
10. *Ibid.*, p. 22.
11. *Ibid.*, p. 99.
12. *Ibid.*, p. 106.
13. *Ibid.*, pp. 127-28.
14. *Ibid.*, p. 130.
15. *Ibid.*, pp. 132-33.
16. *Ibid.*, pp. 135-36.
17. *Ibid.*, p. 485.
18. *Ibid.*, p. 490.
19. *Ibid.*, pp. 490-91.
20. *Ibid.*, p. 491.
21. *Ibid.*, p. 492.
22. *Ibid.*, pp. 493-94.
23. *Ibid.*, p. 495.
24. *Ibid.*, p. 496.

LE P. BOUHOURS

1. Pellisson, *Histoire de l'Académie,* ed. 1672, p. 101.
2. *Pensées,* ed. Brunschvicg no. 162.
3. La Rochefoucauld, *Oeuvres, ed. cit.,* I, 12.
4. pp. 264-65. See bibliography of present work for full titles of all works mentioned in this chapter.
5. p. 271.
6. p. 328.
7. pp. xciv-ci.
8. p. 200, note 1.
9. p. 63.
10. ed. 1909, p. 407.
11. Vol. xxxv, no. 1, pp. 73ff.
12. pp. 165-66.
13. *Ibid.,* p. 12.
14. Mairet, J. de, *Silvanire,* ed. Richard Otto, Bamberg, 1890.
15. *Op. cit.,* pp. 250-51.
16. Ed. 1715, I, 98.
17. Ed. 1671, p. 23.
18. *Ibid.,* p. 29.
19. *Ibid.,* p. 320.
20. *Ibid.*
21. Bouhours, *Entretiens,* ed. Radouant, p. 19.
22. I, v; Bouhours, *op. cit.,* p. 196.
23. Bouhours *op. cit.,* p. 197.
24. *Ibid.,* pp. 198-200.
25. *Ibid.,* p. 204.
26. *Ibid.,* p. 205.
27. *Ibid.,* p. 206.
28. *Ibid.,* pp. 206-7.
29. *Ibid.,* p. 209.
30. *Ibid.,* p. 210.
31. Cf. Badouant in Bouhours, *op. cit.,* p. 28, and Doncieux, *op. cit.,* pp. 51ff.
32. Bouhours, *op. cit.,* pp. 211-12.
33. pp. 119ff.

BOILEAU

1. Boileau, *Oeuvres,* ed. Gidel, Paris, Garnier, 1870, II, 252.

2. *Ibid.,* p. 247.
3. *Oe.,* IV, 314.
4. *Ibid.,* pp. 318-19.
5. *Oe.,* I, 25.
6. *Ibid.,* pp. 11-12.
7. *Ibid.,* p. 4.
8. *Ibid.,* p. 74.
9. *Oe.,* II, 282.
10. *Ibid.,* p. 387.
11. *Ibid.,* p. 295.
12. *Ibid.,* p. 316.
13. *Oe.,* III, 15.
14. *Ibid.,* p. 25.
15. *Ibid.,* p. 16, note 1.
16. *Ibid.,* pp. 5-6.
17. *Ibid.,* p. 6.
18. *Ibid.,* p. 442.
19. *Ibid.,* p. 439.
20. *Ibid.,* p. 425.
21. *Ibid.,* p. 428.
22. *Oe.,* I, 18-19.
23. *Ibid.,* pp. 20-21.
24. La Bruyère. *Oeuvres.* G. E. F. ed. Servois. Paris, Hachette, 1878, II, 461.

LA BRUYÈRE

1. *Oe.,* I, 105.
2. *Oe.,* II, pp. 101-103, no. 56.
3. *Oe.,* I, 210, no. 65.
4. *Ibid.,* p. 214, no. 82.
5. *Ibid.,* p. 213, no. 73.
6. *Oe.,* II, 201-2, no. 70.
7. *Ibid.,* pp. 161-62, no. 31.
8. *Ibid.,* p. 249, no. 32.
9. *Oe.,* I, 113, no. 1.
10. *Ibid.,* p. 150, no. 69.
11. *Oe.,* II, 74, no. 4.
12. *Oe.,* I, 116, no. 10.
13. *Ibid.,* p. 150, no. 67.
14. *Ibid.,* p. 223, no. 17.
15. *Ibid.,* p. 114, no. 7.
16. *Ibid.,* p. 119, no. 18.
17. *Oe.,* II, 123, no. 112.
18. *Ibid.,* p. 76, no. 10.
19. *Oe.,* I, 147-48, no. 61.
20. *Ibid.,* p. 125, no. 30.
21. *Ibid.,* p. 119, no. 20.
22. *Ibid.,* p. 123, no. 26.
23. *Ibid.,* p. 127, no. 35.

24. *Ibid.*, p. 125, no. 30.
25. *Ibid.*, pp. 125-26, no. 31.
26. *Oe.*, ii, 230-32, no. 26.
27. *Oe.*, i, 143-45, no. 55.
28. *Ibid.*
29. *Ibid.*, p. 243, no. 76.

FÉNELON

1. Gibert, *Jugements des savants sur les auteurs qui ont traité de la Rhétorique* 1712-1719, 3 vols.; cf. Lanson bibl. nos. 6317-6625.
2. Lanson, *Hist. de la litt. fr.*, 1912, p. 614.
3. *Fénelon au XVIIIe siècle*, Hachette, 1917; quoted by A. Schinz, "Fénelon, critique littéraire, précurseur." *Rev. des Cours et Conf.* 1925-26, i, 587-601.
4. "L'idée du 'naturel' et le sentiment de la nature chez Fénelon," *Rev. d'Hist. Litt.* 1911, pp. 810ff.
5. *Op. cit.*, p. 590.
6. Cf. L. Boulve, *De l'Hellénisme chez Fénelon*, Paris, 1897.
7. Fénelon, *Oeuvres*, Paris, J. A. Lebel, 1824, xxi, 127.
8. *Ibid.*
9. *Ibid.*, p. 128.
10. *Ibid.*, pp. 128-29.
11. *Ibid.*, pp. 125-26.
12. *Ibid.*, p. 3.
13. *Ibid.*, p. 114.
14. *Ibid.*, p. 21.
15. *Ibid.*, p. 69.
16. *Ibid.*, p. 42.
17. *Ibid.*, p. 43.
18. *Ibid.*, pp. 48-49.
19. *Ibid.*, p. 46.
20. *Ibid.*, p. 78.
21. *Ibid.*, p. 92.
22. *Ibid.*, pp. 92-93.
23. *Ibid.*, p. 93.
24. *Ibid.*, p. 94.
25. *Ibid.*, p. 95.
26. *Ibid.*, p. 96.
27. *Ibid.*, pp. 166ff.
28. *Ibid.*, pp. 182ff.
29. *Ibid.*, pp. 237-38.
30. *Ibid.*, p. 153.
31. *Ibid.*, p. 159.
32. *Ibid.*, p. 175.
33. *Ibid.*, p. 185.
34. *Ibid.*, Letter v, p. 269.
35. *Ibid.*, p. 191.
36. *Ibid.*, *Jugement de Fénelon sur un Poète de son Temps*, pp. 286-87.
37. *Ibid.*, p. 193.
38. *Ibid.*
39. *Ibid.*, p. 210.
40. *Ibid.*, pp. 194-95.
41. *Ibid.*, p. 211.
42. *Ibid.*, p. 259.
43. *Ibid.*, Letter v, p. 269.
44. *Ibid.*, pp. 250-51.
45. *Ibid.*, pp. 286-87.
46. *Ibid.*, Letter viii. p. 277.
47. *Ibid.*, pp. 278-79.

VI. THE COMPLEX OF CLASSICISM

1. *Op.cit.*, p. 68, and Chap. iv.
2. Giambattista Marino, *Epistolario*, Bari, Laterza, 1911, ed. Borzelli and Nicolini, i, 197 (to Don Lorenzo Scoto, from Paris).
3. *Dissertation critique sur l'Iliade*, 1715, and *La philosophie applicable à tous les objets de l'esprit et de la raison*, 1754.
4. *Les Beaux-arts réduits à un même principe*, 1748.
5. *Réflexions critiques sur la poésie et sur la peinture*, 1719.
6. R. Niebuhr, *The Nature and Destiny of Man*, Scribner, 1941, 2 vols., i, 37.
7. *Pensées, ed. cit.*, no. 253, ii, 186.

Index